ODETTA

ODETTA

A LIFE IN MUSIC AND PROTEST

IAN ZACK

BEACON PRESS
BOSTON

BEACON PRESS
Boston, Massachusetts
www.beacon.org

Beacon Press books
are published under the auspices of
the Unitarian Universalist Association of Congregations.

23 22 21 20   8 7 6 5 4 3 2 1

This book is printed on acid-free paper that meets the uncoated
paper ANSI/NISO specifications for permanence as revised in 1992.

Text design and composition by Kim Arney

Library of Congress Cataloging-in-Publication Data

Names: Zack, Ian, author.
Title: Odetta : a life in music and protest / Ian Zack.
Description: Boston : Beacon Press, 2020. | Includes bibliographical
references and index.
Identifiers: LCCN 2019056298 (print) | LCCN 2019056299 (ebook) |
ISBN 9780807035320 (hardcover) | ISBN 9780807035337 (ebook)
Subjects: LCSH: Odetta, 1930–2008. | African American women
singers—Biography. | Women singers—United States—Biography. | Folk
singers—United States.. | Civil rights movements—United
States—History—20th century.
Classification: LCC ML420.O34 Z3 2020 (print) | LCC ML420.O34 (ebook) |
DDC 782.42162/130092 [B]—dc23
LC record available at https://lccn.loc.gov/2019056298
LC ebook record available at https://lccn.loc.gov/2019056299

To fighters for freedom, then and now

He would not Africanize America, for America has too much to teach the world and Africa. He would not bleach his Negro soul in a flood of white Americanism, for he knows that Negro blood has a message for the world. He simply wishes to make it possible for a man to be both a Negro and an American, without being cursed and spit upon by his fellows, without having the doors of Opportunity closed roughly in his face.

—W. E. B. DU BOIS

Perhaps, in the end, where your anger comes from is less important than what you do with it.

—HARRY BELAFONTE

CONTENTS

AUTHOR'S NOTE

Odetta is based on hundreds of hours of interviews I conducted over a period of four years with more than seventy-five people, including friends, loved ones, fellow musicians, and music promoters; information I culled from thousands of newspaper clippings, scores of archival interviews, legal documents, and Odetta's personal papers, which are currently housed at the New York Public Library's Schomburg Center for Research in Black Culture; and a heartfelt listening to the music that gushed like wildfire from her troubled soul. Odetta gave hundreds of interviews over the course of her half-century career in show business, but she had difficulty remembering names and dates, and she didn't keep detailed diaries that we know of. Where no shred of paper spelled out her itinerary or her feelings about a given topic, I relied on the testimony of those who knew her and the revelation of her art to tell her story. I hope the reader finds, as I did, much to admire in her lifelong search for freedom.

A VOICE LIKE THUNDER

In the fall of 1952, at a party outside Los Angeles, Odetta made the walls come down, or so it seemed. Pete Seeger witnessed it and so did Woody Guthrie. They had gathered with a group of young musicians at a home in Topanga Canyon to sing folk songs in a round-robin affair known as a hootenanny.

As everyone took their turns one by one, Seeger couldn't help but notice the young black woman, tall and heavy set, with short, kinky hair—not straightened, as was the accepted style then for African American women—sitting alone, observing the others with a warm smile but keeping her distance. With encouragement, she finally agreed to sing, and the room stilled as she rose with her guitar, gathering herself. Head back, eyes closed, she belted out "Take This Hammer," the chain gang song first made famous by Lead Belly. Her voice, so impossibly huge that it seemed to rumble from the heavens, nearly felled the others in the room.

"We had to hunt to find her, very shy, sitting in the farthest corner," Seeger remembered. "But when she was persuaded to sing, power, power, intensity and power!"[1]

Her friends knew the then-unknown singer as Odetta Felious, but she'd soon drop her surname, tackle her stage fright, and bill herself simply as Odetta.

It was a tense political moment for the nation. Amid the witch hunts, which targeted artists of all stripes, Seeger and members of his hit group the Weavers had recently been outed as Communists. The rest of the folk music movement, harassed by the FBI, the House Un-American Activities Committee, and other Red-baiters, was running scared, lying low, or hiding underground.

But if McCarthyism was at its height then, two other currents were quietly gathering force: a rising youth culture and the civil rights movement. Odetta would help spur both on, letting loose her thunderous singing in concert halls across the nation. With her opera-trained voice, she would help ignite the folk revival that swept America in the late 1950s and early 1960s, singing ballads and prison songs with a passion and intensity that thrilled audiences and attracted a host of followers, from Harry Belafonte, Joan Baez, and Bob Dylan to Roger McGuinn, Janis Joplin, and Carly Simon. Odetta's impact, especially on a good chunk of the female singers who came of age then, was vast.

"It always starts with one thing that kind of points you in that direction, one person becomes the arrow," Simon recalled, looking back on her own career. "I mean I didn't know I wanted to sing until I heard Odetta."[2]

No less important, Odetta's rise coincided with the flowering of the civil rights era, and her songs about freedom and the plight of prisoners and the downtrodden helped inspire activists and the general public alike, providing lessons in black history that weren't being taught in schools. Odetta's artistry, her regal bearing, and her brave decision to stop straightening her kinky hair were a potent expression of black pride just at the moment when middle-class America was beginning to warm to the idea that the nation could no longer deny the fruits of full citizenship to African Americans.

Born in Birmingham, Alabama, during the height of Jim Crow, Odetta wasn't the first black folk singer to channel intense anger into great art. But she found a more receptive audience than, say, Lead Belly, who had often "shouted with violence" when he sang, in the words of the jazz and blues scholar Frederick Ramsey. Like Lead Belly, a paroled murder convict from Louisiana whose real name was Huddie Ledbetter, Odetta poured her darkest emotions into her music, and that partly accounts for her immense power. But if he had aroused fear in white America after his discovery in the 1930s—*Time* magazine once described his "coal-black face gleaming fiercely and his horny hands scratching his twelve-string guitar"—the soft-spoken and dignified Odetta conjured hope. Her soaring vocals and preternatural ability to inhabit the characters she sang about left her predominantly white audiences spellbound and a little more open to the notion that someone could be both wonderfully American and proudly black at the same time.[3]

Odetta, in fact, gave them cause to celebrate blackness. "She is more than an eloquent Negro voice," one reviewer would note in the 1960s. "She is the eloquent voice of the Negro."[4] As blacks demanded freedom at Southern lunch counters, at voter registrar offices, and on frontline protest marches before seething sheriffs' deputies, many Northern whites were looking to embrace the nation's better angels. The young woman with the trailblazing Afro, who sang about prisoners and chain gangs and talked about the black history not being taught to schoolchildren, helped rouse a political consciousness among a searching and surging youth generation.

For a brief but seminal period, Odetta was a star, selling out concerts in the US and around the world, appearing on TV and in films. Our cultural memory can be short-lived, but at the height of her fame, Odetta's singing and magnetic stage presence exerted such a force over her acolytes that sometimes their knees went weak, they fainted in front of her, or they tried to steal her food in the hope that it contained some kind of magic elixir.

Her freedom songs echoed not only in clubs and college auditoriums but during the March on Washington, the Selma to Montgomery march, and countless other protests and rallies for civil rights and the many other righteous causes Odetta supported, from early childhood education to nuclear disarmament. The Rev. Martin Luther King Jr. understood the crucial role that music, and Odetta's in particular, could play in pushing the cause of freedom. "Odetta was by far one of his favorites," King's friend and collaborator Harry Belafonte remembered decades later. "He was a great lover of art and culture. He understood its power."[5]

And yet, despite her epoch-making voice, Odetta never achieved a sustained mass appeal like Belafonte or Dylan or Baez, all artists who bore her imprint. And a public that once considered her musical royalty was quick to forget her seminal contributions, even as her influence extended quietly to new generations of musicians, from Jewel and Tracy Chapman to Miley Cyrus and Rhiannon Giddens.

With her status diminished, Odetta struggled, professionally and personally. Real recognition of her cultural importance came to her late in life, when she was honored by a president and made a career-rejuvenating shift to blues—defying folk fans who had earlier dismissed her as a blues singer.

It was a fitting coda in a way. If the blues is essentially about for-lorn love, Odetta never stopped wrestling her childhood feelings of worthlessness stemming largely from society's rejection of her race as undeserving of its love. During her long career, one question always hovered in the background, even when Odetta was captivating audi-ences around the globe. It was there that day in Los Angeles when she hid from Seeger and the others, a question she began asking as a frightened child suddenly banished to a segregated train car: Am I not worthy?

CHAPTER ONE

FROM BIRMINGHAM TO LOS ANGELES

The black girl, large for someone in grade school, was playing in her great aunt's backyard in Birmingham, Alabama, when the man walked up, clothed in grimy overalls, his face and hands dirty from the steel mill. She'd never seen him before, and he'd never laid eyes on her. "Is that big girl my daughter?" Ruben Holmes wondered aloud.[1] He probably meant "big" in the way a relative might compliment a young child who appears more grown up than imagined in the mind's eye. Odetta, already insecure about her size, felt her heart sink. But before she could learn for certain who the man was, Aunt Lee, a husky woman with salt-and-pepper hair, hurried outside and stood between them like a bulwark. She told Holmes to go away and never come back, warning her grandniece that he was the boogie man. It was Odetta's only childhood encounter with her biological father.

During the height of her fame, Odetta would never discuss the matter. When quizzed about her early life, she had a way of quickly skirting the subject of Ruben Holmes. He died before Odetta was born, according to the publicity materials issued by her manager, Albert Grossman, and interviewers didn't press her for details. Perhaps reporters were wary, during an era of civil rights upheaval, of nosing into the struggles of a black family from the Deep South. Whatever the reason, the tidbit of familial data that Odetta offered her inquisitors constituted a little white lie, a bit of biographical subterfuge that papered over a more complicated and painful story—which began with a forced marriage.

A gorgeous, sunlit spring day greeted Birmingham on April 9, 1930, with temperatures easing into the mid-seventies. That was the setting when Ruben Holmes wedded Odetta's mother, Flora Sanders. It's safe to assume, however, that Flora wasn't the image of a glowing bride. A tiny young woman of eighteen, she'd been promised to the older man by her father. Though relatively little is known about Holmes, he comes briefly into fuzzy focus with the help of census and marriage records. He was thirty. He had a sixth-grade education. He'd recently lost his wife and had a young son and namesake. Beyond those more certain details, he was more than likely a sturdy and muscled man, as befitting someone who toiled long hours in the boiling heat forging steel. In adulthood, Odetta would learn one other tantalizing detail: Holmes had once sung and played the guitar.

The Rev. G. H. Word stood in the pulpit that day, probably in a small black Baptist church, with family gathered to witness the union, including Flora's mom, born Lizzie Randle, and her dad, Jim Sanders. Sanders worked with Holmes at the steel plant, and he knew that Ruben Jr., age two, needed a mother, so he hadn't hesitated to offer his own little girl. "Marry Flora," he'd told Holmes.[2]

That Sanders would marry away the youngest of his three children is unthinkable today, but it was fairly common at the time, especially for families like those who lived in Ensley, a poor Birmingham enclave that had sprouted, mushroomlike, in the shadows of the city's world-famous steel mills west of downtown. Before it became a crucible in the civil rights movement, Birmingham was renowned as the South's steel capital, its towering smokestacks a symbol of the nation's burgeoning industrial might in the early years of the twentieth century. As Southerners tried to convert a stunted agrarian economy built on slave labor into something more modern and sustainable, Birmingham emerged as a beacon of the "New South"—the "Magic City" in the words of a giant electric sign that greeted passenger trains at Birmingham Terminal Station.

Today, little remains of the once-thriving web of steel-related industries that employed tens of thousands in and around Birmingham other than the decrepit graffiti-laden shells of some of the old mills, their floors subsumed by weeds and moss, and a skeleton or two of the stacks that once stood proud like some futuristic urban skyline.

But back then, the city's promise of steel jobs—and upward mobility—probably is what brought Jim Sanders's family from Virginia and Lizzie Randle's clan from Kentucky, as census records show. (Ruben Holmes's kin were Alabama bred.)

When the Depression came, however, the nation's manufacturing and housing sectors sputtered. Suddenly, Birmingham's single-minded reliance on steel became an albatross. "The mills are down/The hundred stacks are shorn of their drifting fume," the Alabama poet John Beecher—a great, great, great nephew of Harriet Beecher Stowe—wrote about Ensley.

Despite his lack of education, Ruben Holmes had seniority at the Ensley steelworks, and Jim Sanders considered him "a very good risk," someone who at least stood a chance of weathering the economic storm. For Jim and Lizzie, marrying off their daughter had the added advantage of having one less mouth to feed.[3]

Still, that doesn't mitigate the shock of going from naive teenager to dutiful wife overnight without so much as a courtship. On the marriage certificate, Flora's age was nudged up a couple of years, to twenty, no doubt to make the union seem slightly more respectable. "So they got married," Odetta would later recount. "My mother knew nothing about anything. . . . She thought if a boy's elbow touched your elbow, you get pregnant. That's how out of it she was. And I can't begin to imagine the terror of her on their wedding night."[4]

Flora was soon with child. It was clear that she didn't want the baby, and who could blame her? Ruben kept the door locked during the day when he trudged off to the steel mill, so pregnant Flora, who had Ruben Jr. to care for and the cooking and cleaning to do, couldn't escape. This was not the recipe for a loving relationship. Finally, with the help of another aunt named Tea, Flora managed to flee the shackles of forced matrimony. Safely out of Ruben's reach, Tea prepared a home-brewed concoction that was supposed to abort Flora's pregnancy, but it failed to do the job, though it made her sick. "Lord, girl, I'm glad your momma didn't get rid of you!" Aunt Tea would tell Odetta years later—after Odetta became famous.[5]

Flora went to live with her uncle Bud, an Ensley grade-school principal. At his home on December 31, 1930, Odetta Holmes came into the world, an unwanted child. She was a big girl compared to her "little maw" and "the ugliest BLACK baby ever born," Flora said. Again, given the circumstances, who could blame her? [6]

Though she didn't know her father until much later in life, Odetta, like most poor blacks from the South, was nurtured by a large extended family. There was a network of aunts, uncles, and cousins in Ensley, along with her grandparents, Papa Jim and Mama Lizzie, who must have seen fit to forgive Flora for running out on Ruben. Odetta was close to her grandmother, but at some point Papa Jim went away, perhaps after losing his job at the mill as so many other men in Ensley would, leaving Odetta without a grandfather.

She had strong women in her life, though, including Aunt Lee, who had sought to protect her from her father. Lee had light skin and was forever powdering her face to lighten it even more, telling the girls that she was white and they were black—one of the first times Odetta would have heard that blackness was something inferior that needed correcting.

Her ill-fated marriage behind her, Flora soon met a more compatible mate, Zadock Felious, another Ensley steelworker, originally from Opelika in eastern Alabama near the Georgia border. In September 1933, she bore him a daughter, Jimmie Lee—Odetta's half-sister and lifelong confidante. They didn't marry until nine months later, on June 28, 1934. Flora was twenty-two, and the groom, twenty-seven. On the marriage certificate, she listed her status as single, an effort most likely to expunge the bitter past.

To Odetta, Zadock became "Daddy." Remembered as kind and gentle by his family, he "was the closest to . . . an angel I've ever been around, just a splendid man," Odetta recalled. Zadock would later adopt Odetta, and she took the name Felious. From the start, however, his extended family made it clear that they preferred Jimmie Lee, a true-blooded Felious granddaughter. "If you weren't a Felious," Odetta once said, "you barely made it on the human charts." [7]

By the time Odetta was six, Zadock, who had worked in the coal mines as well as the steel mills, had developed black lung disease and was at risk for tuberculosis. The city had the second-highest death rate from TB in the nation (behind Denver), and doctors suggested a drier climate might do some good. Zadock and Flora decided to uproot their young family and move to Los Angeles.

Health considerations aside, they had plenty of other reasons for taking flight. As the Depression sucked the life out of the economy, President Franklin D. Roosevelt's administration declared Birmingham, so dependent on steel production, as "the worst hit city in the nation." Many thousands of jobs disappeared and families became destitute. The district's congressman, George Huddleston, summed up the city's dire situation to a Senate subcommittee: "Any thought that there has been no starvation, that no man has starved, and no man will starve, is the rankest nonsense. Men are actually starving by the thousands today."[8]

Even in the best of times, Birmingham's Negroes knew they were second-class citizens with few rights and little power in the grip of Jim Crow. And it was more than clear that anyone daring to challenge the status quo was going to be dealt with harshly. Just a few months before Odetta's birth, twenty-five hundred members of the Ku Klux Klan had staged a rally in Birmingham, dressed "in full regalia of sheets and pillowcases," a black newspaper reported, to protest the planned visit of a black congressman from Chicago. A few years later, during the infamous Scottsboro Boys case, when nine black youths were condemned to die in the electric chair for the alleged rape of some white Alabama girls, the Klan sent a notice to newspapers, warning of the "Communists" trying to defend the boys, who were almost certainly innocent: "Alabama is a good place for good Negroes, but it is a bad place for bad Negroes who believe in SOCIAL EQUALITY. THE KU KLUX KLAN IS WATCHING YOU—TAKE HEED." Only a toddler, Odetta was probably spared the particulars of these kinds of threats, but she later remembered the colored drinking fountains, colored toilets, and colored balcony at the movie theater—early slaps at her dignity that dug deep.[9]

She couldn't have felt any more sanguine about the two-tiered municipal bus system. Odetta's longtime friend, the poet Sonia Sanchez (née Wilsonia Driver), who was born in Ensley in 1934, remembered going with her aunt Pauline to work on the bus as a young girl and being ordered to move to the back and then to get off when more whites got on needing seats. Her aunt became one of the many unheralded Rosa Parkses in the long struggle for equality. "The bus driver told her to get off and she said . . . I'm not gonna get off the bus," Sanchez recalled. "And the bus driver stopped and walked towards her, you know, like he was gonna put her off. And she spit in his face. We were arrested. . . . And by that night, Pauline was sent out of town by the family."[10]

For the Feliouses, California promised to be much more welcoming. Indeed, to the nation at large, it allured as a kind of dreamland in waiting, a place of adventure and wish fulfillment, where the "Eureka" on the state seal evoked the possibility of riches and sudden transformation, whether as a result of finding gold flakes sifted from a nineteenth-century river mill or, later, by dint of a different kind of discovery—by a Hollywood producer.

The city of Los Angeles, founded in the late 1700s by Spanish, black, biracial, and American Indian settlers, boasted romantic Spanish architecture, purple mountains, wide-open spaces, and a soul-tickling climate. "To many a newcomer, Los Angeles is a modern Promised Land," proclaimed a guidebook compiled by the Federal Writers' Project in the 1930s. "There is a heady fragrance in the air, and a spaciousness of sky and land and sea that give him a new sense of freedom."[11]

To Southern blacks, the city had long been portrayed as racially tolerant and a land of opportunity, and perhaps it was, if you were grading on a curve. "Los Angeles was wonderful," the black educator W. E. B. Du Bois declared after an early twentieth-century visit. "The air was scented with orange blossoms and the beautiful homes lay low crouching on the earth as though they loved its scents and flowers. Nowhere in the United States is the Negro so well and beautifully housed." Du Bois, however, also noted that "the color line is there and sharply drawn." In reality, blacks did face discrimination in hotels, restaurants, and other accommodations, and white neighborhoods would later get sanction from the California Supreme Court to legally exclude blacks.[12]

By the end of 1936, Zadock Felious and his younger brother Otto set off for Los Angeles in a Model T Ford, finding jobs as janitors and getting a place to live before sending for the Felious clan. On March 28, 1937, Easter morning, Flora, six-year-old Odetta, and three-year-old Jimmie Lee boarded a train in Birmingham for a cross-country trek that would likely have taken them first to New

Orleans, to connect with the Southern Pacific railroad to the West Coast on one of the favored routes of the Great Migration. (Mama Lizzie, who for better or worse considered Birmingham her home, stayed behind and never left.)

The girls wore starched dresses. Flora packed food enough for an army, knowing that for a black family, getting served en route would be difficult and dangerous. Along the way, she woke the girls to point out bunnies hopping through the fields. However, any notion that the trip would be a fun adventure for the Felious daughters ended when a conductor came through at one of the stations and told them that all Negroes had to move to a segregated "Jim Crow" car. Flora didn't raise a fuss, leaving Odetta scared and confused. "I cannot tell you the depth of how that affected me," she recalled. That little girl silently pondered a question that wrenched her gut and ate at her soul: "Is there something wrong with me?" It was the first of what she would later call her "wounds," and it was so devastating that for most of her life riding trains made her sick to her stomach.[13]

Zadock had rented the smaller side of a tiny stucco duplex home at 1244 North Virgil Avenue in East Hollywood, where he, Flora, Jimmie Lee, Odetta, and Otto would live for the better part of a decade amid the grumble and screech of the streetcars ambling by their front door. The apartment had room for a stove, icebox, and beds, but no table, so the family ate standing up, laughing at the absurdity of it. Zadock had found work as a drugstore janitor, and Flora would earn what she could cleaning houses.

They had plenty of company, including some of the extended family. In the slightly larger duplex apartment lived Zadock's other younger brother, Chester, and his wife and daughter. Another brother, Austin, and sisters Emma and Ella would also live nearby. The neighborhood was ethnically very mixed, including other black families from Alabama and elsewhere in the South and immigrants from Japan, Puerto Rico, Mexico, the Philippines, and Eastern Europe, mainly Russia.

Los Angeles in the 1930s, in fact, was a city of newcomers, including migrants from the Midwest and points east, who'd escaped failed farms and factories during the Depression looking for jobs in the tire, aircraft, automobile, garment, and movie industries. In Odetta's working-class neighborhood, it was easy enough to make out two rungs of economic opportunity: the blacks worked as janitors, maids, laborers, elevator operators, and Pullman porters, while the whites and Japanese became teachers, carpenters, salesmen, tailors, and gardeners.

Some of what the Feliouses heard about Los Angeles seemed true at first. Racial violence was minimal compared with other big cities, even in the North. And unlike northern urban centers, LA was a sprawling metropolis with plenty of room to spare, so blacks who arrived during the first wave of the Great Migration before World War II didn't have to stuff themselves into dense ghettos as they would in places like Chicago or New York. Many blacks lived in mixed-race neighborhoods, which helped keep feelings of isolation somewhat at bay and, for a time, masked racial tensions.

"Everybody co-existed with each other," Odetta recalled. "And if somebody was sick and my mother had only said hello to them [once], she would immediately go over to their house, find out what they needed—if there's washing or the cleaning or the shopping or whatever. And when we got up to age, we would be sent to do those chores. It was community."[14]

Odetta attended Lockwood grammar school with the other neighborhood kids. Once Edgar Bergen and Charlie McCarthy came through to entertain the pupils, and Odetta enjoyed it, unaware that a puppet show would play an important role in her future. It was in grade school, however, that she first got a taste, she said, of the warped way in which the lives of African Americans were portrayed in the popular culture. In class, she learned about the serfs in Europe and the unfairness of the feudal system. "And then we got to the place in the history book where they said that we, slaves, were happy and singing all the time," Odetta said. "I was at the age then when if it was in the book it was true. And I felt disgraced, shamed."[15] That was wound number two, she often said.

It was an example of the kind of racism that often gets overlooked in the history of the African American struggle. By escaping the South, Odetta never witnessed a lynching or had her life threatened for trying to register to vote, but her emotional scars from the distorted view of her people's history—or even simply the omission of any history of achievement—was palpable. Civil rights groups and black educators such as Carter G. Woodson were already well aware of the toll that a white-centric historical narrative was taking, not only on the psyches of black children but also on the racial views of impressionable white kids. In 1939, the NAACP published a pamphlet entitled *Anti-Negro Propaganda in School Textbooks*, in which it argued that blacks weren't portrayed as having a respectable past. "These American authors would have us believe that there was nothing wrong with slavery, that it was not only economically necessary, but was enjoyed by the slaves themselves," the pamphlet said. It continued, "Prejudiced authors have set themselves up as authorities in spreading the vicious propaganda that Negro American citizens have contributed nothing to the great movements of labor, suffrage, industrialization, invention, health, education and legislation in our land."[16]

One of the more widely used textbooks in American grammar schools in that period, and very possibly the one Odetta's class read at Lockwood, was *American History* by Gertrude Van Duyn Southworth and John Van Duyn Southworth, a mother and son from Syracuse, New York. The book promised "the complete history of our country, from the discovery of America to the present day."[17]

In discussing the antebellum period, the book noted that "plantation life in the South was very pleasant. The master of the house spent his time in overseeing the labor of the slaves, in hunting, in taking long rides through the country on his fine, thoroughbred horses, or in entertaining at his home." It went on:

> The slaves, too, usually led a happy life. Although they were educated only in the work they had to do, almost never traveled beyond the home plantation, and seldom developed into anything but mere working machines, they were usually treated humanely and often with great consideration. They had good food and warm clothing. When their daily work was done they were allowed to go to their cabins, which were built in a group not far from the plantation house of their master. There they could sing, and dance, and enjoy themselves in other ways.[18]

The book's treatment of Reconstruction is equally cringe-worthy, though it was pretty mainstream at the time, a reflection of how far the South's "Lost Cause" ideology of the war and its aftermath had seeped into the national consciousness; it discussed how "the ignorant Negro vote" was manipulated by Northern carpetbaggers and Southern scalawags to bear "unpleasant fruit" in the South. It described how Southern white men, facing "oppression," fought back unsuccessfully with their minority voting rights and in the "far more practical" rise of the Ku Klux Klan, which targeted "Negroes who were abusing their power." As far as the book was concerned, Negroes had done nothing since Reconstruction to warrant inclusion in later chapters.[19]

Part of the problem was that, decades before the advent of black studies departments in colleges, unbiased research that textbook writers could draw upon wasn't in wide circulation and many libraries simply didn't bother to include it in their collections, although scholars like Woodson, W. E. B. Du Bois, and James Weldon Johnson were trying to document the real history and accomplishments of African Americans. It would be through her study of folk music that Odetta would get what she would call her true education "about a history that was not projected in the schools"—one she would later deliver to her audiences.[20]

Given the lack of positive reinforcement about their race, it's not surprising that most American blacks in the late 1930s and early 1940s calculated that it was best to try to blend in to win acceptance from whites, to prove they deserved the freedoms and opportunities they sought. Flora ran a strict household and thought the road to success was paved with refined tastes. Like the vast majority of Negro women and girls, she straightened their naturally kinky hair with hot combs (and, later, chemical straighteners) to more closely mimic Caucasian hair. Flora made sure Odetta learned precise and proper diction. On Saturdays, they cleaned house together. But when the Metropolitan Opera came on KECA on the AM dial, Flora, Jimmie Lee, and Odetta stopped everything and perched in front of the console radio, ears to the speakers. When it was over, they resumed their washing, ironing, and dusting. "I was into classical music," Odetta said, "and I had swallowed this whole pill that society had given us: that if it was classical and from Europe it was legitimate."[21]

Her stepfather favored less lofty music, much to Odetta's chagrin. Zadock took the girls to the Paramount Theater, where the colored swing bands performed: Duke Ellington, Count Basie, Jimmie

Lunceford, Nat King Cole's trio. On Saturday nights Zadock tuned to KFI for the Grand Ole Opry in Nashville. "I listened to the Grand Ole Opry with my eyebrows raised," Odetta recalled with a laugh. "I mean, really, I was supposedly sophisticated and all that arrogant stuff." Yet Zadock's eclectic tastes rubbed off, even if she didn't know it at the time. [22]

Despite the drier climate in Los Angeles, Zadock's lung condition worsened, and within a few years, he wound up at a sanitarium. He spent most of his days there, coming home for a week at a time to see his family. When a census worker showed up in 1940, Zadock had been unable to work for at least a year. His brother Chester had earned $950 the previous year as a janitor, while Otto, still living with Zadock's family and presumably chipping in, had his own janitorial business. Flora took on more domestic work, visited Zadock daily, and accepted welfare assistance to help pay for his care. The extended family was always ready to help with rent or money to put food on the table.

But the Feliouses lived day to day. To afford a movie ticket, the girls had to trade in Coca-Cola bottles and save the deposits. Even a Christmas gift was something Odetta's mother couldn't afford to give them. "Maybe it would have been better if I'd have gotten one skate for Christmas and the other for my birthday but I didn't," Odetta remembered. "And I didn't notice how much it bothered me until I grew up."[23]

Flora did, however, scrape together some quarters so that Odetta could have music lessons. At age eleven, Odetta began taking piano along with a neighborhood friend, a black girl named Janie Craddock. One day as they waited for their teacher to arrive, the girls were singing scales. "The teacher walked up, I guess, when I was hitting something like a C above a high C and it was really just a screech but she was very impressed," Odetta said.[24] She told Flora, who found a voice teacher for her daughter. But after a few lessons during which Odetta trilled like a soprano, the teacher said her body was still developing and she should wait until she turned thirteen to resume her studies.

After the United States entered World War II, the sense of community Odetta had felt in her neighborhood was shattered. On February 20, 1942, President Roosevelt issued executive order 9066 to evacuate more than a hundred thousand Japanese civilians from "combat zones" near the West Coast, including more than sixty thousand in California. With the attack on Pearl Harbor a few months earlier, hysteria about a land invasion by Japan had reached a crescendo, as did concerns that Japanese living near the Pacific would assist the invaders with acts of sabotage. "Don't kid yourselves and don't let someone tell you there are good Japs," California congressman A. J. Elliott told the House of Representatives. "Perhaps one out of 1,000."[25]

Most of the affected were American citizens who took pains to affirm their allegiance to the United States. They relinquished their freedoms with stoicism, holding fire sales to liquidate their businesses, abandoning their homes and farms, and packing up a few belongings by the time the buses and trains arrived for the mass evacuations barely a month later. Some white real estate agents took advantage of the panic by buying homes at cut-rate prices after warning the Japanese that the future was unpredictable.

Odetta began hearing at school that people were destroying dishes and other goods with "made in Japan" labels. Then her neighbors, including an elderly Japanese couple on the block, prepared to leave. "All of a sudden, we're seeing that our neighbors and friends are putting their refrigerators out to sell, their beds out to sell, and they're getting rid of as much as possible, so they could be ready when the buses came to take them to the concentration camp. . . . I knew through that how dastardly those representing the government [could be] and how low they could sink. They did not arrest Italians, and they did not arrest Germans."[26]

Around this time, Odetta had begun attending the progressive Mt. Hollywood Church on New Hampshire Avenue in Los Feliz, where she would sing in the choir. The charismatic minister, Allan Hunter, served as a counterweight to the prevailing winds of segregation that were by then blowing through Los Angeles. Mt. Hollywood was one of the earliest churches in the city to integrate, in the 1930s, and Hunter preached a universal love in words and deeds. "Reverend Allen [sic] . . . had his Sunday school teachers take us as kids to other churches, to mosques, and to synagogues," Odetta recalled.[27]

After Roosevelt issued the order for the internment camps, Hunter had seen to it that church members sprang into action, taking care of

Japanese-owned homes and a nearby Japanese church, Hollywood Independent, until the war's end. The folk singer Frank Hamilton, who attended Mt. Hollywood Church later on, said that Hunter had a profound impact on Odetta and her political views. "Odetta was undoubtedly impressed by his humanity and peaceful way," he recalled. "There was a consistent pattern of the goals of natural Christianity— turning the other cheek—and its antiwar implications."[28]

Racial lines in Los Angeles had begun to harden as the black population multiplied. More and more restaurants started denying service to Negroes, and segregation became common in everything from bowling alleys to dance halls to pet cemeteries. Even public swimming pools were off-limits, except during the one day a week when blacks could swim by themselves, after which the pools were drained and refilled for whites. The Ku Klux Klan resurfaced and marched by city hall. "Everywhere there were borders, as dangerous to breach as if they were electrified," a historian of the era noted. Odetta corroborated the account. "They didn't have any signs, but my sister and I knew where we shouldn't go," she said.[29]

To make matters worse, the Feliouses lived just a few miles from Hollywood, where few blacks were employed, other than in menial jobs, and where the studios depicted Negroes as shiftless ne'er-do-wells, bug-eyed coons, obsequious Uncle Toms, and faithful mammies. If Hattie McDaniel, one of the most successful black stars of the 1930s and 1940s, had managed to win recognition for her acting talents and comedic timing, she'd had little choice but to accept the stereotypical roles as maids and servants that came her way if she wanted a career in the movies. (Her character in *Gone with the Wind*, which brought her the first-ever Oscar for an African American, was notably called "Mammy.")

That such a warped view of black Americans was being perpetuated by studios so close to home only seemed to magnify the impact on young Odetta, who long recalled the anger and hurt she felt as a child at the lack of any honorable roles for people of her race. Add to it Hollywood's fixation on superficial beauty, which was hard for any girl to measure up to. "The mode of beauty was not my color, not my shape, not my people," she said. "For a long time," she added on another occasion, "Negro kids were growing up in this country, feeling . . . that they were only seen in the movies and on TV in derogatory roles. But a pride is necessary. . . . No one can dub you a valid human being. You have to *feel* you are a valid human being."[30]

At the age of thirteen, Odetta was still searching for that validity, unable to escape the feeling of being an outsider. As a young Negro, she had concluded that "society's foot is on your throat, [and] every which way you turn you can't get from under that foot."[31] She kept her anger well hidden, but her lack of pride and sense of worthlessness were evident. On her first day of seventh grade at Thomas Starr King Junior High School, she met Jo Mapes (born Joanne Shanas), a white foster kid from Chicago who shared her sense of alienation and, like Odetta, watched as the other students all made their way inside the imposing concrete edifice. It didn't take long for the two outcasts to spot one another.

"She was large for her age, much too big for her age, very aware of it," Mapes recalled. "We were the only two left on the grounds and I walked over to her because she was alone on one side, I was alone on the other side of the yard, and everyone else had gone in. . . . She is clutching her notebook and her schoolbook, whatever she had, she is clutching them against her large body, her head is bowed over, and she's not looking at anyplace but looking down at her feet, which are toes inward."[32]

Mapes figured it was her only chance to make a friend that day. "I'm new too and I'm Jewish," she told Odetta. As Mapes later recalled, "I was pimply, fat, shy, and white. She was pimply, fat, shy, and black. We hit it off immediately."[33]

Mapes was the child of a schizophrenic, unwed Jewish mother, and she'd gone through a series of foster homes in Chicago, suffered abuse as a toddler, and eventually reconnected with her mother and ended up in Los Angeles by age thirteen, living at what she described as a "crumb bum" transient hotel above a liquor store overlooking Sunset Boulevard.[34]

King Junior High was less than a mile from both the girls' homes, in Los Feliz. Although it was only a short walk in geographic terms from East Hollywood, it was a great socioeconomic leap from the run-down streets, vacant lots, auto repair garages, and currency exchanges that Mapes saw out her window, and from the no-frills, tightly grouped homes on North Virgil Avenue where the Feliouses still lived, a few doors down from their original apartment. In Los Feliz, there were nice white Spanish-style houses with picket fences, green lawns, flower gardens, driveways, dogs, and two-parent families.

The school was largely white. Mapes sardonically remembered her female classmates as the "Hollywood Golden girls in their soft pastel colors of short sleeve cashmere or angora sweaters and matching bobby sox." In the cafeteria, Jo, Odetta, and another girl, Ondine, who lived in the hotel with Jo, sat apart from the in-crowd, not far from the tough Latino kids, the other outliers in the building. Their dreams kept them from succumbing to their present reality. "'Detta was going to find a way to be proud, to be looked at as proud," Mapes recalled. "We both felt that way."[35]

With Odetta having begun voice lessons again and Jo aspiring to a career as a singing actress like Jane Powell, the girls joined the glee club at school, where the teacher, Miss Taves, had false teeth that rattled when she talked. The girls sang songs from Gilbert and Sullivan and from the operetta *The Student Prince.* Jo, however, was soon booted from the squad for pretending she could read music.

Odetta was apparently a no-show for the glee club yearbook photo in seventh grade, something she often did, probably out of shame for the way she stood out. The photo that year captured a group of forty-six girls, all white except for two named Chung, dressed in dark skirts and white blouses with jaunty neck bows. Despite whatever misgivings Odetta had, at some point the school informed Flora that "Odetta needed a better opportunity in training, better than the school could provide her," Mapes recalled. "So obviously they had discovered that they had a serious singer on their floor."[36] And Mapes's memory of their outcast status notwithstanding, Odetta also seems to have made a good impression on homeroom 106, which elected her vice president in the fall of 1944.

After school, the girls retreated to the Feliouses' apartment. Odetta, Jo, and Jimmie Lee spent many afternoons jitterbugging to records. One day, Jimmie Lee brought home a stack of used 78s, and they popped one on the record player and heard, instead of dance music, the sound of a loud guitar going blangety-blang and an old black singer. "Yek, pooh, phooey!" they said, and yanked the needle off. It was their first taste of Lead Belly.[37]

Flora, slim and dainty and usually attired in a housecoat or simple dress, kept busy in the kitchen. She snuck extra food to Jo to take home for dinner. Although Mapes remembered Flora as "lovely, giving, smiling," Flora had a complicated relationship with her own daughter, who hadn't been a child conceived in love. The folk singer Lynn Gold Chaiken, who knew Odetta much later, recalled Odetta saying that when she was a little girl, Flora had told her, "You were a mistake" or "I wasn't supposed to have you"—a declaration that could only have added to Odetta's sense of alienation.[38]

By late 1944, Odetta's stepfather was in bad shape. Doctors had recently diagnosed full-blown tuberculosis, and Zadock Felious was admitted to Los Angeles County General Hospital. A month later, on January 4, 1945, he died at the age of thirty-seven. For Odetta, it was another big blow; the only real father she'd ever known was gone. It wasn't something she discussed, however, even with her closest friends. She would usually keep her deepest thoughts and feelings to herself. "I knew that something was going on with 'Detta and her family," Mapes recalled. "It was obvious. I'd been through the same thing, but we never talked about it."[39]

It's impossible, of course, to know how much of the anger Odetta felt growing up arose from family dynamics and how much stemmed from her lowly status in society, the denial of her race's history, the cartoonish portrayals of black Americans in Hollywood, and an education system that seemed oblivious to her self-worth. But there's no doubting how angry she was. Looking back many decades later, Odetta said that, as a teenager, "I was furious and I was angry and I hated . . . everything, everybody, including myself."[40]

CHAPTER TWO

STRAIGHTENED MY BACK, KINKED MY HAIR

One of the unlikelier Hollywood in-spots during the 1940s was a puppet show on La Cienega Boulevard called the Turnabout Theatre. It was the creation of Harry Burnett, Forman Brown, and Richard "Roddy" Brandon, who'd started the Yale Puppeteers at Yale Drama School in the 1920s and later settled in Los Angeles. Burnett and Brown—gay cousins who'd once briefly been lovers—and their friend Brandon (who became Brown's lifelong romantic partner) dreamed up an innovative brand of musical theater, with Burnett, who looked like a lankier version of Chico Marx, acting as master puppeteer, the more dapper Brown composing the music and serving as emcee, and Brandon handling the business side of things, as well as helping pull the strings. The first half of the show featured some of Burnett's hundreds of singing marionettes, including caricatures of celebrities from Franklin Roosevelt and Groucho Marx to Bette Davis and Alfred Hitchcock. After an intermission, there was vaudeville-style entertainment, with a cast headed by Elsa Lanchester, a big-eyed British character actress best known at the time for her film portrayal as the Bride of Frankenstein.

The Turnabout took its name from the surplus Red Car trolley seats installed between the two stages perched at opposite ends of the theater. After intermission, audience members swung over the backs of the reversible seats to face the other way, so the last row for the puppet show became the first row for musical theater: turnabout was fair play. With its topical humor and gossipy vibe, the Turnabout, just a stone's throw from the Sunset Strip and the tony mansions of Beverly Hills, attracted a glamorous crowd, with Charlie Chaplin, Jane Russell, Greta Garbo, and a host of others among the glitterati turning up to take in the latest send-up of Hollywood or Washington, DC—and to see themselves as marionettes.

Flora Felious, now a single parent (she would never remarry), had gotten a part-time job as a custodian for the Turnabout by 1946, supplementing her domestic work. On Saturdays, she took Odetta and Jimmie Lee with her to the theater, and they helped her with the cleaning before heading together to the farmers market to do the week's shopping. That is, sometimes they helped with the cleaning. "Harry was always playing operatic records, so Odetta would sit and listen and moon over the records instead of doing the dusting as her mother wanted her to," Forman Brown recalled. "But we found she had a lovely voice." Flora had been trying to earn enough to afford Odetta's voice lessons, but she couldn't keep up with the payments. Desperate, she hatched a plan: could she bring Odetta in to sing for the Puppeteers, a tryout of sorts? "I got up there, and at that point I was a coloratura soprano, very high voice, and I screeched out a few notes and they heard something evidently that led them to believe that maybe it would be good to give me voice lessons," Odetta remembered.[1]

Burnett agreed to sponsor her, and Odetta found her first serious voice teacher, Janet Spencer. A contralto originally from Boston, Spencer had toured the US and Europe as a concert and oratorio singer in the early 1900s and made some of the first records for the Victor Talking Machine Company's famous Red Seal label. When her concert career ended, she retired to Hollywood, where she took on singing pupils. Odetta began a study of German lieder and other art songs.

When it came time for ninth grade, Odetta and Jo got separated. Odetta lived closest to predominantly white Marshall High School, but she was bused to Belmont High in nearby Westlake, a school with a large proportion of Asian, black, and Hispanic students. Officially,

Los Angeles had a no-segregation policy for education, but in practice, gerrymandered school districts and other sleights of hand concentrated blacks and other minorities together. "All of us went to the same school, until we got to high school," Odetta recalled. "But [blacks] were sent to Belmont High School and we had to take a bus there. And that's not hard for an innocent kid to read."[2]

As she began high school, the Cold War that would play a big role in Odetta's early political awakening had escalated, and the search for subversives filtered all the way down to Belmont. The atmosphere in Los Angeles, as in many American cities, became oppressive and thick with suspicion—and not just for closet Communists. Robert Carl Cohen, who was a year ahead of Odetta at Belmont High, remembered taking a current issues class at a time when a state legislative committee was investigating the views of local educators. "One day the teacher . . . said we're focusing too much on politics," Cohen recalled. "So when my turn came I started reading the baseball scores. At which point the woman instructor broke into tears and ran out of the classroom. . . . They were scared shitless that they were going to be called before the Un-American Activities Committee. And they didn't want students speaking about things like the Berlin airlift and stuff like that."[3]

In high school, Odetta kept a low profile. In her four years at Belmont, she showed up for only one yearbook photo—the group glee club portrait during her sophomore year. But for the first time, she began attracting attention for her singing. Aside from joining the glee club, she became the soloist in the school's Madrigal Singers.

She rebelled against segregation by joining the South Hollywood Civic Chorus, an interracial community group that gathered Monday nights in an elementary school auditorium. With the city's race relations at an ebb, the group was considered innovative enough in 1949 to merit a profile in the *Los Angeles Times*: "Here you find voices of butchers, bakers, and candlestick makers—all singing in harmony. . . . Voices may range from the baritone of 78-year-old James Atkinson . . . a retired schoolteacher, to the soprano of Miss Odette [sic] Felious, 18."[4]

Other than for her musical pursuits, Odetta remained shy and reclusive in her social life, unable to shake her outcast status. She still occasionally saw Jo, who tried to push her into uncharted waters. "I was a stuck-in-the-mud, follow-the-rules kind of kid," Odetta recalled. "Jo was adventurous. I don't even think I've begun to figure out how that woman, that personality, helped release me."[5]

Once, on a lark, they visited Club Laurel in Studio City, one of the first lesbian nightclubs in the area. They slicked their hair back, put on jeans and leather jackets, trying to look tough and butch. "You've never seen a sorrier set of dykes than Odetta and me," Mapes remembered. "Odetta couldn't bring her eyes up off the sidewalk, and I felt foolish."[6]

Odetta graduated from Belmont in 1949. A photo snapped after the ceremony shows her standing tall, her straightened hair poking out from under her mortar board, a proud, if subdued, smile on her face as she grips a golden trophy in her large hands. It was a Bank of America Achievement Award for fine arts.

After high school, she worked briefly as a maid in a department store during the day, while attending Los Angeles City College (LACC) at night. With Harry Burnett's sponsorship at an end, however, she found she needed to earn more to pay for her singing lessons, so she soon found work in a button factory, and then as a housemaid, doing the cleaning and taking care of two children, presumably for a white family.

At LACC, she studied European classical music. She was a chorister in productions of Verdi's Requiem and Bach's Mass in B Minor. She joined the Sharps and Flats club, serving as club secretary, and appeared in musicales as a soprano. She performed art songs such as Schumann's "Die Lotosblume" and Rachmaninoff's "In the Silence of the Night," and lyrics by Lord Tennyson. Even with her concert training, she harbored no illusions about an opera career. It was still a few years before her idol Marian Anderson, considered one of the great singers of the century, was invited to perform Aida at the Metropolitan Opera in New York, breaking the color barrier. "So I didn't fool myself there," Odetta said. "I thought, I had a dream of getting a quartet together, learning the repertoire of the oratorios, and then offering ourselves to schools and churches."[7]

Her first real brush with folk music and progressive politics came by happenstance. When producers announced a revival of *Finian's*

Rainbow to be staged at Los Angeles's Greek Theatre in the summer of 1950 and issued an open casting call, Odetta and her friend Janie Craddock both tried out for the musical and passed their auditions, Janie as a dancer and Odetta as a member of the chorus. For the future voice of the civil rights movement, it was the perfect entrée into show business. Yip Harburg, who'd supplied the lyrics to the Tin Pan Alley hit "Brother, Can You Spare a Dime" and "Over the Rainbow" in *The Wizard of Oz*, had conceived the play in a fit of anger over Southern opposition to the cause of black civil rights and as a direct challenge to men like Senator Theodore Bilbo and Representative John Rankin, both of Mississippi, who virulently defended the tenets of white supremacy in Congress. "The only way I could assuage my outrage against their bigotry was to have one of them turn black and live under his own laws and see how he felt about it," Harburg recalled.[8]

The play is set in the mythical Southern state of Missitucky. It revolves around Finian McLonergan and his daughter, Sharon, who arrive from Ireland with a pot of gold. There's a leprechaun, a racist senator (who proclaims, "My whole family's been having trouble with immigrants ever since we came to this country!"), white and black sharecroppers, and a union organizer named Woody, after Woody Guthrie. At the end of act 1, Sharon tells the senator that he should live life as a black man to experience the crippling effects of Jim Crow firsthand, and thanks to the leprechaun, her wish comes true.[9]

The original show ran on Broadway for 725 performances in 1947–1948 and was seen as ahead of its time in how it dealt with race issues: aside from its clear political message, whites were depicted living and working congenially alongside blacks, and the black and white performers danced together and held hands, almost unheard of on the Great White Way at the time.

The summer stock revival opened at the outdoor Greek Theatre in Griffith Park on July 17, 1950, with the original Broadway cast, including stars Ella Logan and Albert Sharpe and the blind country blues harmonica virtuoso Sonny Terry, who reprised their roles. According to one account, Odetta thought *Finian's Rainbow* might launch her into legitimate concert work, albeit not the opera career she craved.

And that's what happened, although not in the way she imagined. Her stage debut behind her, Harry Burnett came calling. With the Turnabout Theatre's success, he and Forman Brown had created a version for children. Turnabout Jr. opened on December 1, 1950, with Odetta in the cast alongside Burnett and Dorothy Neumann, who would go on to a career as character actress in film and on television. The initial monthlong production, which didn't have a puppet show like the adult version, was staged like a circus in a little tent in the parking lot of the farmers market on West Third Street and Fairfax Avenue. Even with Burnett portraying a clown, it was Odetta who won the most raves. "Outstanding singing came from Odetta Felious as 'The Nurse You Never Had,'" the *Los Angeles Times* said. Frank Hamilton recalled that when Odetta started singing for the Turnabout, she was still in a classical mode. "Odetta was singing there very much like Marian Anderson," he said, "kind of like with a contralto voice, singing show tunes and classical tunes."[10]

For her newly realized contralto—the deep, dramatic singing voice that would make an unforgettable imprint on the nation and the world—she had a new voice teacher to thank. Janet Spencer had died by then, and Odetta had begun studying with Paul Reese, a transplanted New Yorker, who helped her find the lower end of her vocal range. Hamilton, who later studied with Reese, said Reese also suggested that Odetta try to take advantage of the brewing excitement in folk music, but Odetta, taught to look down on such lowbrow fare, wasn't quite ready to heed that advice.

The Weavers, who smoothed out the rough edges of folk songs to make them suit the buttoned-down tastes of Americans in that era, were then tearing up the *Billboard* charts with an orchestra-backed, almost chipper version of Lead Belly's mournful ballad "Goodnight, Irene," propelling folk music momentarily into the stratosphere. "The summer of 1950, no American could escape that song unless you plugged up your ears and went out into the wilderness," Pete Seeger recalled.[11]

Throughout the previous decade, folk music had been striving to gain a true foothold in American life. Seeger and Woody Guthrie had led the grassroots push with the Almanac Singers, who had tried, but mostly failed, to fuel a singing union movement and boost the fortunes of progressives in and out of government. Still, leftist groups had provided much needed work for folk singers, including Lead Belly himself, who had died just months before the Weavers rode his song to the big time. The Weavers' success spawned a new surge of interest in folk songs, and in most big cities, groups of young people began picking up guitars and banjos, looking for ballads and blues to sing at hootenannies.

It was in this atmosphere that Odetta was asked, in the summer of 1951, to once again appear in the chorus of *Finian's Rainbow*, as the revival, its original cast still intact, moved up to San Francisco's War Memorial Opera House. It ran in San Francisco for only two weeks, beginning on July 16, before returning to Los Angeles, but as far as Odetta's life was concerned, those fourteen days proved pivotal.

Now twenty, Odetta hadn't been away from home before. "It took about three days before I was crying because I was homesick," she recalled. One night, her old friend Jo Mapes, who got word Odetta was in the show, came to see her. Mapes already had fallen in love with folk music and hopped a Greyhound bus to San Francisco to become a bohemian. She'd dyed her hair black with a silver streak; dressed, she recalled, "like a French whore"; and started singing folk songs. She met her husband Paul Mapes, a merchant seaman, in a bar. He was drunk. They married two weeks later.[12]

Six decades after the fact, Jo Mapes vividly remembered Odetta in *Finian*, resplendent in a spangled gown and wearing one of those ornate and shaky headdresses as she paraded down a stairway. "She was one of the Ziegfeld girls, dressed up like one, who came down the famous Ziegfeld stairway. . . . And there was 'Detta, anything but slim, anything but a dainty beauty."[13]

Some compared San Francisco's North Beach to the Left Bank of Paris in the 1920s and '30s, with its mix of colorful types: artists, writers, poets, folk singers, gritty sailors, and women with long hair and large hoop earrings. One night, Jo and Paul took Odetta to Vesuvio's, a little bar with sawdust on the floor where the poets and musicians hung out reciting verse and singing folk songs. When the bar closed at 2 a.m., a big group headed to the Mapes's garret apartment, where, perched amid sloping beams and candlelight, they sang all night long.

It was there that Odetta, drinking Gallo wine to ward off her homesickness, had an epiphany, hearing tunes like Lead Belly's "Take This Hammer." "I heard songs that touched the core of me," she recalled. "In the songs I heard that night, including prison songs, I found the sadness, the loneliness, the fear that I was feeling at the time. It turned my life around."[14] During her brief stay, Jo and Paul also introduced Odetta to her first lover. She left San Francisco and returned to Los Angeles, her passions stirred.

Back home, Odetta borrowed a guitar from a neighbor, who taught her C, F, and G seventh chords and gave her a capo to easily change keys on the instrument. With some effort, she learned to play "Down in the Valley," but after that she proved to be a quick study. She got hold of some folk music books, such as Carl Sandburg's *American Songbag* and, later, recordings of prison and chain gang songs made by the Library of Congress to build up a repertoire. She also delved into Negro histories to better understand the songs and their lyrics. Folk music was just a hobby at first. To support herself, she got a job as a live-in housekeeper on Hoover Street, near where her mother now lived. Late at night, Odetta would call her friend Janie, barely able to contain her excitement about folk songs. "Listen, listen, Janie!" Odetta would say, and she'd put the phone down and sing her a new tune she'd learned.[15]

Soon Odetta fell in with the folk song crowd in LA, a coterie of young people like her who traded tunes and sang together at parties and hoots. She met Frank Hamilton, still a teenager but already a virtuoso on several instruments, including banjo and guitar. Hamilton taught her some guitar techniques, including a rhythmic double-thumb strum used by Josh White that she would eventually modify into what became known as "the Odetta strum." She became a very adept finger-style guitarist, although she never gave herself the credit she deserved, calling her guitar playing mere "self-defense."[16]

It didn't take long, however, before she began to stand out at hoots, where young musicians tried to display their growing repertoires and instrumental prowess and ability to tap into the murky wellspring of "authenticity" that would become prized during the folk revival. Marcia Berman, who later became known for her albums of children's songs, was about twenty when she heard Odetta sing at a Los

Angeles party around 1952. "Many of the folk songs we were singing were just kind of telling a story and the singer was very objective, you know the singer doesn't put their emotion into the song," Berman recalled. "But of course she was picking up different styles of music and she herself could go deep, I mean she could be very emotional."[17]

That's because, for Odetta, folk music was no abstraction. It was the story of her people and a potent antidote to society's wholly fabricated version of her history, its insistence that there was no respectable place for her in her own country. The music also became an outlet for Odetta's deep-dyed anger, which she shared with a whole generation of young blacks who felt stymied at every turn and, in the words of the writer and social critic James Baldwin, were "taught really to despise themselves from the moment their eyes open to the world."[18] When Odetta sang chain gang songs such as "Take This Hammer" and "Another Man Done Gone" or spirituals like "I've Been 'Buked and I've Been Scorned," she harnessed her rage to produce music that was already beginning to move people in a powerful way. Not that they understood the source of her power, which she later explained in an interview:

> We were living at a time when I couldn't say I hate me and I hate you and I hate. But I'm frustrated. I've been told that I'm worth nothing. I've been told I'm dumb. Hollywood has told me that. School has told me that. White population has, society has told me that. . . . As I sang those songs, nobody knew where the prisoner began and Odetta stopped and vice versa. So I could get my rocks off, being furious.[19]

Odetta, Hamilton, Berman, and a few others formed a group that performed for neighborhood folk song clubs and progressive organizations. Hamilton and Odetta became friends, which didn't come very easily to her, he said. "She was always very defensive. She was very careful in her dealings with people and she wanted to retain an aura of protection around her. There were only certain people that she would allow into her purview, so to speak. And she was very careful that she selected her friends, who would be understanding of her."[20]

It was a good bet that if you sang folk songs with any seriousness in either New York or Los Angeles (and many other cities) in the 1950s, you were going to come into contact with progressive politics, so it's not surprising that some of Odetta's first gigs took place in front of a gamut of left-wing groups, some of them branded pro-Communist. For the performers, who were rarely paid more than a pittance, if anything at all, it was a chance to sing for a captive crowd, maybe even to inspire the union faithful or an activist group and feel the connection between an old lyric and a modern cause.

Today's schoolbook histories often depict the McCarthy era in simplistic terms, as a clash between suspected Communists on one side and overzealous watchdogs intent on safeguarding democracy on the other. But the American political landscape at the time was more complicated than that image suggests. Even amid the deepening of the Cold War, by which time the Communist Party had lost much of its influence on the left, the lines between card-carrying Communists, socialists, trade unionists, and liberals with various agendas including pacifism and civil rights remained amorphous, their causes frequently overlapping. That was especially true in the years before Joseph Stalin's atrocities in the Soviet Union became well known, crumbling Communism's mythology in the eyes of all but the most blinkered fellow travelers in the West. It was the broad spectrum of the left that had nurtured folk music and helped keep it alive, before and after World War II, and Odetta would have been exposed to a lot of leftist orthodoxies as she became more entrenched in the folk scene.

In one of her first performances as a folk singer, Odetta sang for the International Ladies' Garment Workers' Union in Los Angeles, with Hamilton backing her up on harmonica. The group was then staging pickets and boycotts in an effort to unionize several Los Angeles garment factories. "They were immediately taken with her, particularly the left-wing groups," Hamilton said. "Because the civil rights [era] hadn't happened yet but it was bubbling just underneath. It was about to happen."[21]

An older white couple, Seema and Jack Weatherwax, both Communist Party members, lived in an apartment on Commonwealth Avenue in East Hollywood, where they were neighbors with Odetta and her extended family. The neighborhood had grown blacker than it had been before the war, with most of the whites and other minorities having moved away. "It was not Watts, not a black ghetto, but practically all the people who lived there were black," Seema Weatherwax remembered. "There were some large families, like Odetta's, who lived in three or four houses. These were modest homes, not expensive. About one-third of the people owned their own homes and the rest were renting, and they were charged higher rents than whites for comparable housing." Sometimes on Friday and Saturday nights, Odetta invited friends over to drink wine and hear her sing. "Her voice and her presentation were wonderful, full of power," Weatherwax said. "I thought, 'My god, why isn't she known more?'"[22]

The Weatherwaxes supported an array of progressive causes, from the peace movement and labor strikes to pickets aimed at businesses that refused to hire blacks. It's likely that they had many political discussions with Odetta, though Odetta never espoused any hard-core Communist views.

The biggest influence on Odetta's politics was Paul Robeson. By any realistic measure, Robeson was one of the most gifted Americans in history—and one of the most unfairly maligned. A pro football player, lawyer, actor, singer, and orator, he attained a popularity that was highly unusual for a Negro in the 1930s and '40s, filling stadiums with his bass-baritone and showing up in polls as one of the most admired Americans around the world. He used his bully pulpit to advocate fiercely for blacks, who he said were second-class citizens in the US, and he called for a "dictatorship in the South" to secure Negro rights.[23]

After World War II, Robeson praised the Soviet system for its treatment of blacks and implied that American Negroes weren't interested in a fight against Russia—a sentiment that, with the intensifying Cold War, brought him withering condemnation from many black leaders as well as white. (It didn't help that the Associated Press misquoted Robeson, attributing to him a much broader sentiment, that blacks would refuse to fight in a US-Soviet war.) The Truman administration revoked his passport, and Robeson became one of the early victims of the blacklist, his concert work drying up, though he did manage to find sympathetic audiences. Robeson would later defiantly tell the House Un-American Activities Committee, "I am being tried for fighting for the rights of my people," and his plight served not only as an inspiration but also as a warning to black activists of Odetta's generation that they could pay a steep price for standing up against oppression. Of Robeson's influence, Odetta said, "Paul Robeson was the one that politicized me. Through his works and his words, I found that it was necessary for me to be responsible to my brothers and sisters all over the world."[24]

In her early days as an amateur folk singer, Odetta got involved with the Fellowship of Reconciliation, a pacifist group that had been founded by religious leaders such as A. J. Muste and social activists, including Jane Addams, to oppose US entry into the First World War. As with many left-wing organizations of the early 1950s, it had a far-reaching agenda, one that encompassed nonviolence in general and opposition to war in particular, including military escalation against the Soviet Union. During the Cold War, however, any group like the Fellowship that spoke out against a military buildup was an easy target for Red-baiters. While it's true that peace groups had often made common cause with the Communist Party in the 1930s, many, including the Fellowship, had parted ways after the Communists were too quick to follow orders from Moscow. The Fellowship, in fact, had officially barred working with the Communist Party beginning in the 1940s, but that didn't mean there weren't Communists within its ranks. For American blacks, however, the group's pull usually had less to do with a Communist political agenda than with other more pressing concerns.

Bayard Rustin, director of the Fellowship's civil rights department, had spoken in Los Angeles about local racial problems such as "the inability of Negro boys and girls to swim in the pool," according to the *Los Angeles Sentinel*, a black newspaper.[25] In 1947, the Fellowship, along with the Congress of Racial Equality, had spearheaded the first Freedom Ride in the South to protest segregation on interstate buses—a protest that cost Rustin thirty days on a North Carolina chain gang. It was a precursor to the more activist agenda of the next phase of the civil rights movement, and Rustin would later plan the March on Washington with Martin Luther King Jr., calling on Odetta to lend her voice to that seminal event.

In 1952, the Fellowship was helping raise money for the defense of Julius and Ethel Rosenberg, the young married couple from New York's Lower East Side convicted the previous spring of passing atomic secrets to the Soviets. While their attorneys spent two fruitless years trying to get the Supreme Court to review their death sentences, the Rosenbergs maintained support in some left-wing circles among those who thought they were innocent or that their civil liberties had been violated. "I remember being involved with the injustice to the Rosenbergs," Odetta recalled. "And I remember taking petitions around and having petitions signed to save the Rosenbergs."[26] Odetta's comment, decades later, suggests that rather than having a staunch commitment to the case, she approached it as would a young woman getting involved with a cause that other progressives were championing.

What's clear is that her deepening involvement in folk singing and the left-wing movement played a seminal role in one of the most important decisions she ever made. In the summer of 1952, she was still appearing with Turnabout Jr. during the week while working weekends as a counselor at a progressive summer camp connected with the Fellowship outside Los Angeles. One Friday after her Turnabout show, she drove back to camp, headed into her bunk, and surprised her all-white group of girl campers, who hadn't gone to bed yet. "OK. Let's get some scissors," she said. "I want you to cut my hair." They went into the bathroom, began snipping, and as Odetta's long straightened locks fell to the floor, the girls grew agitated. "They started getting scared because it was so short," Odetta recalled. "[I said,] 'Never mind. It's OK.' They cut and cut and cut. And then I went into the shower, washed my hair, and came back. It was nappy, short." She tied the decision to her newfound appreciation of black culture, "learning the folk songs and the stories that came along with the songs, which was a history of us, and was definitely not in our history books, and I often said it straightened my back and it kinked my hair."[27]

Odetta's niece, Jan Ford, believes her aunt experimented with leaving her hair unstraightened, or "natural," as far back as high school, but if that's the case, the decision this time was permanent. And political. "Oh, yeah, nothing but political" was how Odetta characterized it many years later.[28]

Odetta's immediate inspiration for what Americans would come to know a decade and a half later as "an Afro" came from a chance encounter at Los Angeles City College, where Odetta continued to take classes but would never earn a degree. There she bumped into a black dancer named Jeni LeGon, who'd been getting ready to do a program at LACC on Africanesque dances and had washed her hair and left it long and kinky. LeGon was originally a tap dancer who got her start at age sixteen in the chorus of the Count Basie Orchestra, and she later tapped her way to history, becoming the first Negro woman to sign a contract with a major film studio, MGM. But like most blacks in Hollywood, she played mainly stereotypical roles, usually finding herself in a maid's costume. She quit Hollywood in the early 1950s, opened a dance studio in Los Angeles, and took an interest in African and Caribbean music.

It was one thing, however, for a Negro woman in the US to sport kinky hair for a theatrical performance with an African theme, another entirely to adopt the hairstyle in her everyday life. Hair straightening was so ingrained in African American culture by that time that it was rarely questioned, at least publicly. It had begun at a time when enslaved black people with lighter skin and straighter hair—usually the mixed-race descendants of slaves raped by their owners—were often favored with domestic work in comparison to the enslaved people with darker skin and kinky hair who were relegated to the fields. The unmistakable message was that people with straighter hair and lighter skin were "good" because of their physical proximity to whiteness, while those with more African features were "bad."

By emancipation, straight hair had become a standard sought by freed blacks looking for acceptance in the wider white world. Some black churches, mindful of public relations and social strata, were even said to have had a "comb test" to keep out the kinky-haired. By the twentieth century, straight hair was seen as one more aspect of "proper" grooming that would help blacks to advance in society.[29]

That's not to say that hair straightening, also practiced to a lesser degree by men—who otherwise wore their kinky hair cropped—was never a matter of debate. In the 1920s, the Jamaican-born black nationalist Marcus Garvey demanded that his followers stop using skin lighteners and hair straighteners and famously thundered, "God made no mistake when he made us black with kinky hair. . . . Take the kinks out of your minds instead of your hair!" Carter G. Woodson took up the cause in the 1930s. "The face-painting, hair-straightening Negro, then, goes a step beyond the white man who dubs the race an inferior group," he wrote. "Such a Negro in addition to acknowledg-ing this inferiority purchases the badges of it." But their pleas mostly went unheeded.[30]

A huge economy had formed around the culture of hair straight-ening, keeping many black barbershops, salons, and cosmetics com-panies afloat. Madam C. J. Walker earned one of the earliest fortunes as an African American by advertising her patented hair-care prod-ucts in black papers across the country, including combs and lotions used for straightening. The black press, which played a heroic role in the advancement of black culture and civil rights, said relatively little about black subservience in matters of hair. The hair straight-ening industry, in fact, fed the coffers of black papers by supplying a significant percentage of their advertising for combs, heaters, wigs, attachments, hair straightening creams, and "hair culturists" adept at removing kinks. One early 1950s ad in the *Los Angeles Sentinel* for Aida's Hair Pomade showed a black woman with kinky hair on one side and long straight hair on the other, treated, side, with the caption: "Keeps your hair BEAUTIFUL in HOTTEST weather." For men, an ad on the next page featured Marques Haynes of the Harlem Globetrotters as pitchman for Perma Strate, which promised up to six months of "soft, straight, attractive" hair for every application.[31]

James Baldwin, who was a few years older than Odetta, wrote of the shame blacks felt about their hair and skin, beginning in childhood:

> One's hair was always being attacked with hard brushes and combs and Vaseline; it was shameful to have "nappy" hair. . . . The women were forever straightening and curling their hair, and using bleach-ing creams [on their skin]. And yet it was clear that none of this ef-fort would release one from the stigma and danger of being a Negro; the effort merely increased the shame and rage.[32]

Jan Ford, in recalling her aunt's lonely stand on the issue, said that growing up, the idea of deemphasizing one's blackness was so routine that it didn't have to be taught. "We were just raised [to] straighten your hair, look presentable," she remembered. "Your natural state, like with no makeup or your natural hair . . . none of that was being natural."[33]

Odetta, who wasn't given to boasting, would later lay claim to being the first black American woman to embrace natural hair in a public way. "I was the only black going around with nappy hair then . . . and I looked so exotic, so unlike other black American women, that people assumed I was an African."[34] Dancers such as LeGon and Pearl Primus would occasionally put their hair in a natural state on stage, but photos of both from the 1940s and '50s show them with straight hair. Odetta's haircut may seem like no big deal today, but for a young woman whose size, color, and natural hair didn't measure up to white society's definitions of beauty, it was a courageous statement of individuality and pride. And it sent a message to anyone who beheld her: I am no longer willing to be who you want me to be; I'm going to write my own narrative.

When Odetta returned home from camp, her mom didn't mince words. "Lord, look at that fool," Flora said, but neither did she press Odetta to pick up a jar of hair straightener. Jo Mapes recalled of her friend's political awakening: "She was going through changes, becoming Odetta, but she was always just 'Detta to me."[35]

Others weren't so forgiving. Some barbers arched an eyebrow when Odetta sat on the chair, forcing her to make a quick judgment. "If the barber looked like he questioned it, I all of a sudden thought of an appointment to go to, because once you cut it, there's nothing you can do about it," she remembered. And others too looked askance. "There was a lot of times when I would get on a bus and people would snicker and laugh, and it was very difficult at the beginning."[36]

But Odetta pushed on. Ford said her aunt was often teased, and once a man came up to her on the street, intent on causing a scene because of her Afro. "And this guy, a white guy, told her, 'This is what we do to blacks,' or whatever word he used, and he lassoed her with a rope," Ford recalled. "And she beat the shit out of him."[37]

While it's hard to imagine the outwardly gentle young Odetta displaying her fury quite as forcefully as Ford remembered, one thing is certain: the young woman with the natural hair and prodigious singing voice wasn't about to be pushed off the course she'd so boldly set for herself.

CHAPTER THREE

THE TOAST OF NEW YORK

Despite the Weavers' success, folk music was still largely a bottom-up phenomenon in the early 1950s, driven by small clusters of teens and twenty-somethings in song circles, regional folk music clubs, square dance societies, and progressive organizations. Big record companies hadn't yet found a way to reliably monetize folk music, nor were they especially trying to at that point. With the Communist scare in full swing, having already ruined or dampened the careers of performers like Pete Seeger, Josh White (who voluntarily testified before the House Un-American Activities Committee), and Burl Ives (who testified and named names), it would have been hard to fathom who would take up the call in their place. That it was a black woman with natural hair, barely a year removed from picking up a guitar for the first time, is remarkable. Then again, Odetta was brimming with such talent that she would have been hard to ignore.

She began generating buzz in the overlapping worlds of folk music and progressive politics by the end of 1952. At the hootenanny in Topanga Canyon, Seeger had become an instant fan. Although his star was then dimming because of the McCarthy-era witch hunts, he remained a force in folk music, and he began spreading the word about Odetta wherever he went. "She was astonishingly strong and direct and wanted her songs to help this world get to be a better place," he recalled.[1]

Whatever the extent of Odetta's shyness or self-hatred—and it seems to have been quite severe during her early years—she fought through it. Still unknown in early January of 1953, she performed before an audience of 1,300 people during a meeting of the Southern California Peace Crusade at the Embassy Auditorium on Grand Avenue in Los Angeles. The group was a local branch of the American Peace Crusade, another organization that would face accusations of being a Communist front. Speakers that night reported on the recent Peking Peace Conference, presenting favorable reports about Communist China and charges (disputed to this day) that the United States was employing germ warfare against North Korea. "Oletta [sic] Felious, young Negro singer, thrilled the Embassy audience with songs of peace," reported the next day's *Daily People's World*, a Communist newspaper published in San Francisco. Misspelling aside, it was her first write-up as a folk singer. That meeting, and Odetta's performance, would later draw the attention of the House Un-American Activities Committee, though there's no evidence the committee ever pursued Odetta directly and she was never called to testify. Very early in her career, still feeling her way, she avoided saying anything overtly political on stage, preferring to let her music do her talking, which may have saved her a trip to Washington.[2]

In June, with a few more gigs under her belt, Odetta returned to the Embassy, this time to sing in front of a crowd of two thousand, as the opening act in a concert by her hero Paul Robeson. "He had heard about me on the grapevine," Odetta recalled, and Robeson had asked for her to appear, a passing of the torch to a new generation of black radical singers, though neither could have fully known it at the time. Robeson sang "Old Man River," "Water Boy," songs in Yiddish, and "American working class songs," according to the *Daily People's World*. "Odetta Felius [sic] opened the program with songs and guitar accompaniment," the paper said. Although the concert was advertised as benefiting local Negro causes, it took place only five days before the Rosenbergs' execution, when left-wing groups were in a fever pitch trying to convince President Dwight Eisenhower to issue an eleventh-hour pardon. It's highly likely that Robeson addressed the situation during the show. Odetta, in fact, recalled it later as a benefit concert for the Rosenbergs, which is doubtful, considering that the Communist newspaper failed to mention it. "It was the only time my knees shook," Odetta remembered, although that too seems unlikely given her early problems with stage fright. She would later take "Water Boy" and make it one of her signature songs.[3]

However Odetta felt about Julius and Ethel Rosenberg, she later said the FBI had kept a file on her, which "likely came out of [my] involvement in collecting signatures to save the Rosenbergs."[4] It's not clear whether Odetta ever saw an FBI file. Whatever its contents, the FBI appears to have destroyed it in the 1990s.

By the time of the Robeson concert, Odetta had already gone to San Francisco to visit Jo Mapes and her daughter, Hillary—Odetta's goddaughter—who had been born the previous year. The real beginning of Odetta's professional career came when she and Mapes took in a show at the Hungry i, a bohemian basement club on San Francisco's Columbus Street run by a flamboyant former concert violinist named Enrico Banducci. The club would later become a launching pad for envelope-pushing comedians, including Mort Sahl, Lenny Bruce, Woody Allen, and Dick Gregory. But on this particular night, a young balladeer named Nan Fowler graced the stage.

Convinced of Odetta's blossoming talents, Mapes decided that her shy friend needed a bit of a push if she was going to get paid for her singing. At one point, Mapes excused herself from the table and, without telling Odetta, went to talk to Banducci, informing him that "there was a folk singer in the audience who is on tour."[5] Banducci fell for the pitch and invited Odetta to sing a few songs. On the spot, he offered her a job.

Odetta returned to Los Angeles, quit her housekeeping job, and moved up to San Francisco, living at first with the Mapeses. When she reported for work at the Hungry i, however, she ran into a roadblock: the club's regular headliner, a black folk singer named Stan Wilson, refused to share a bill with her, perhaps out of a fear of being overshadowed. Odetta was relegated to Wednesday nights, Wilson's one night off, earning $10 a week—not even enough to join the local musicians' union.

She eventually found another gig at a jazz club called Cable Car Village at California and Hyde streets. When the smooth-talking emcee tried to get Odetta to add extra sets on the house, she refused—she'd performed for too many union groups by then to take that kind of treatment sitting down—and the engagement ended after just three nights. But sitting in the crowd for one of those shows was Peggy Tolk-Watkins, owner of a new club called the Tin Angel, who offered Odetta her first steady job.

The Tin Angel had just set up shop in a converted warehouse across from Pier 23 on the Embarcadero, the San Francisco Bay waterfront that had once been the region's shipping and transportation hub. *Embarcadero* means "place to embark" in Spanish, so it's a fitting starting point for Odetta's career. The piers, ferry boats, and short line railroad that once gave the waterfront life had fallen into decline following construction of the Golden Gate Bridge and the migration of shipping traffic across the Bay to Oakland. But the trains still ran on the tracks outside the club, its whistles providing an unsolicited counterpoint to the music emanating from the stage.

Tolk-Watkins, a lesbian poet, painter, and raconteur, is remembered as one of the real characters of North Beach bohemia. She drove to work in an old Ford sedan covered in pink and blue polka dots and was rarely without a cigarette in one hand and a martini in the other. She painted the Tin Angel's walls red, blue, and green and decorated the club with assorted kitsch, artwork, and a player piano, giving it a decidedly campy feel. She'd pilfered the club's namesake mascot, a two-and-a-half-foot-tall tin angel, which hung over the club's door, from a defunct church in Brooklyn, New York.

Odetta opened at the Tin Angel on August 25, 1953, a Wednesday. It's here, from witnesses, music reviewers, and a live recording from the period, where we begin to get, for the first time, a sense of her fledgling stage act and the extraordinary impact it had on her audiences. Her repertoire already included work songs ("John Henry," "No More Cane on the Brazos"), spirituals ("Children, Go Where I Send Thee," "I've Been 'Buked and I've Been Scorned"), British ballads ("I Know Where I'm Going"), and songs from Lead Belly ("Rock Island Line") and Woody Guthrie ("The Car-Car Song").

It wasn't only Odetta's selection of material that set her apart from many other white folk singers in the early 1950s. It was also her extraordinary interpretive ability. She could evoke a small child asking a parent a million bedtime questions or a convict singing while toiling on a road gang and do both equally convincingly. Her deep contralto, especially on songs about black prisoners or railroad workers or forlorn slaves, seemed to roar from the depths of her being.

Her rendition of "Take This Hammer," set to driving guitar, built tension so dramatically that by the time she ended the song, interspersing verses with guttural cries to mimic the crack of a nine-pound hammer, her listeners could actually begin to feel the pain and sweaty exhaustion of a convict laborer.

> *Take this hammer—hah!—and carry it to the captain—hah!*
> *Tell him I'm gone boys—hah!—tell him I'm gone*

The force of her singing contrasted, in an almost bewildering way, with her bashfulness on stage. Odetta's spoken introductions to songs, delivered in a near whisper, came across almost apologetically. In fear of the audience, or engaged in an inner struggle against her sense of inferiority, she sang with her eyes closed beneath a short halo of natural hair.

One reporter, who showed up a bit later during her Tin Angel run, described a typical scene: "The large woman came out of the back room marked 'private' and walked between the scarred tables onto the stage. She sat on a stool, tuning her guitar . . . her eyes downcast. 'This is the story of a man and a machine. The man's name was John Henry,' she spoke so softly . . . barely audible." But after she started to sing, "[a]ll of a sudden the room was filled with a voice so magnificent and powerful . . . beyond any description."[6]

That snapshot is echoed by Pauline Oliveros, who went to Odetta's debut performance and later became a noted avant-garde composer. "She was so very modest, almost self-effacing in her presentation, but her voice was so very powerful," Oliveros recalled decades later, the memory still intense. "So when she sang she was really transformed from this young person who seemed almost reticent to present herself."[7]

Jo and Paul Mapes were there too. Once again, without Odetta's knowledge, Jo had seen to it that her old friend got some attention. Jo had dialed up the *San Francisco Chronicle* and one of its music reviewers, Robert Hagen, had picked up the line. "There's going to be a new singer" and "you must go down and hear her," she told him.[8]

Hagen arrived a bit late, as Odetta was in the middle of shouting a cappella the prison song "Another Man Done Gone," with just her hand claps keeping time. Hagen was so impressed that he invited her to his office the next day to find out more about her. When Odetta showed up, wearing the large hoop earrings that would become one of her trademarks, he was surprised to learn that she hadn't arrived straight from Alabama but had actually grown up mostly in Los Angeles.

His review appeared in Friday's paper. "After hearing her sing 'Why Can't a Mouse Eat a Street Car' and such folksy items as 'I Was Born Ten Thousand Years Ago' and 'You Gotta Haul That Timber Before the Sun Goes Down' in a low-down voice that sounded like an impossible amalgamation of Bessie Smith and Lead Belly, I was permanently convinced that Odetta is that rare but happy occurrence in the music business—a natural." He described her as looking like a young Bessie Smith, "if she had worn a crew cut."[9]

If attention was Mapes's goal, she succeeded admirably. By Saturday night, the club was packed to the rafters for Odetta's 9 p.m. show—a terrifying prospect for a stage-shy singer. "I drove up, I got there, and I looked into the door, and I saw all those people," Odetta recalled. "Scared me half to death. I turned around to walk back to the car."[10] But she steeled herself and snuck into her dressing room, literally a broom closet.

It just so happened that Herbert Jacoby, co-owner of the posh Blue Angel nightclub in New York, was vacationing in San Francisco and had gotten wind of the glowing review in the *Chronicle*. He decided to see what the fuss was about. Jacoby, a gay Frenchman with a long, birdlike nose, knocked on the broom closet after the show. "We'd like to have you at the Blue Angel someday," he said. Odetta hadn't heard of the famous club, so her nonchalant reply—the equivalent of "Sure, sounds great"—might have come off as quiet confidence. A week later, Jacoby called Tolk-Watkins and told her they had a sudden opening. Could Odetta fill in? Barely weeks into her professional career, she was headed to New York.

The Blue Angel was a swanky after-theater club on East Fifty-Fifth Street with a red carpet at the entrance, a beautiful hatcheck girl, and a main room with pink leather banquettes and walls of gray tufted velour. (Lenny Bruce was said to have likened the decor to the inside of a coffin.) Jacoby and his partner, Max Gordon, made sure audiences were racially mixed, an uncommon feature in the early 1950s; white and black performers were equally welcomed and treated well, largely due to Gordon, who often booked black singers into his downtown Village Vanguard before moving them to the uptown venue. By the time of Odetta's appearance, Josh White, Pearl Bailey, and Harry Belafonte had already had successful runs at the Blue Angel. "Oh, I had graduated from the deep dishmop sink at the Tin Angel to a real dressing room and this place!" Odetta remembered. "I mean, it was a classy jernt!"[11]

She debuted at the Blue Angel in the middle of September. She made no changes in her act for her nattily attired new audience, performing a mix of work songs, spirituals, and children's songs, and attracted immediate attention, not all of it for her singing. *Billboard*'s reporter called her "a kinky-haired, pleasant, round-faced, chubby gal." Indeed, early in her career, writers would wear out thesauri describing her hair and weight. Aside from the superficiality of the entertainment press, whose mostly male reviewers often reduced women to the sum of their measurements, none had come upon a black female with natural hair. The put-downs quietly trampled Odetta's soul, but she wouldn't say so publicly until much later. This reviewer nevertheless concluded that she showed considerable potential: "There's a peculiar quality in Miss Felious's voice that should interest record people. Audience reaction was only tepid. But this could change, once the nervousness and minor amateur traits are eliminated."[12]

The gossip columnist Walter Winchell weighed in too. "The Blue Angel's new stardust is a blues thrush named Odetta Felios [*sic*]. She landed in N.Y. after being 'discovered' in a San Francisco spot on her 2nd week in Show Biz." Winchell was far from alone in flubbing her last name. Robert Dana of the *New York World Telegram and Sun*, calling her "Miss Felois," described Odetta as a "buxom Negro lass" and pronounced her "probably the most exciting folk singer to hit town since Harry Belafonte switched from bop to folk tunes."[13]

One night, Jacoby brought Belafonte to Odetta's dressing room. If the meeting was memorable for Odetta—she recalled her mouth nearly agape at the sight of him—it was equally so for Belafonte. He'd started out as an actor in the mid-1940s, then begun crooning standards like "Pennies from Heaven" and "Stardust" with a jazz band and recording Tin Pan Alley ballads with an eighteen-piece orchestra. By the early 1950s, his movie career had just begun to take off, and he'd started recording folk songs like "Shenandoah," but as a singer, he still channeled Bing Crosby more than Lead Belly. *Down-Beat* had dismissed him as "synthetic in folk singing."[14]

When Belafonte saw Odetta at the Blue Angel, he was astounded. "From the very beginning, she was just an absolute marvel," he recalled. "She was such an imposing figure. She was very majestic, and then when she opened her mouth, out came that voice, which was unlike any other anybody had ever heard."[15]

Belafonte has usually been cast as a major influence on young folk singers, which he would soon be, but it was Odetta, he says, who set him on his path. "My real thrust into the music of the peoples of the world was deeply, deeply stamped right when I first heard Odetta sing. . . . When I listened to Odetta sing, 'Look over yonder, hot sun turnin' over,' that shout, that drive released a mechanism in me, because there was the place I belonged. Would my instrument take me?"[16]

By the time his first LP, *Mark Twain and Other Folk Favorites*, came out the year after he first heard Odetta, he'd started to form the style that would bring him superstardom. "I told [RCA's] executives I wanted to try a new approach. Most of my singles had been saturated in lush orchestrations that I felt overwhelmed the songs. I knew that was the style of the times but I wanted a more bare bones accompaniment."[17] He would go on to record a number of songs from Odetta's repertoire, including "Another Man Done Gone," "Bald Headed Woman," and "Water Boy," which imitated Odetta's arrangement.

News of Odetta's prowess spread quickly in New York. According to Odetta's last manager, Doug Yeager, her Blue Angel shows attracted most of the city's major folk talent. "Harry Belafonte came almost every night, so did Pete Seeger, so did Josh White—I mean, she was like the toast of New York," Yeager said.[18]

She remained at the Blue Angel until late October, having made, at the age of twenty-two, a significant, if brief, ripple in the belly of the entertainment world. She returned to San Francisco and the Tin Angel, which was more than eager to get her back.

Odetta continued to hone her singing and repertoire. She had been taking guitar lessons from Rolf Cahn, who, like Frank Hamilton, played a major role in her early development as a performer. A flamenco guitarist and guitar teacher, Cahn was the ex-husband of Barbara Dane, a gifted young white blues and folk singer in the Bay Area. Jo Mapes described Cahn as "a short, intense, young German Jew who had gotten out of Berlin just in time, loved flamenco, but played it like a Prussian march." Odetta recalled that during her early San Francisco days, Cahn helped her to understand guitar rhythm and dynamics and how to add tension to a song. Others said he did far more than that. "The person who taught her her original repertoire was a guy named Rolf Cahn," recalled Ed Pearl, who would later open the Ash Grove nightclub in Los Angeles. "Basically, after he and Barbara separated, he became Odetta's teacher and he taught her Barbara's repertoire. I mean, Barbara laughs about it and so do I. But I'm just telling you the truth."[19]

That's probably overstating matters some. But Dane, interviewed in her early nineties, was mum when asked about it, politely declining to speak about Odetta.[20] According to an interview Dane gave to *Sing Out!* in the 1960s, however, the most important songs that Cahn taught Odetta were three old Negro spirituals: "Oh, Freedom," "Come and Go with Me," and "I'm On My Way." Dane often performed them individually to close out sets in Bay Area dives in the early 1950s, she told *Sing Out!*

Odetta never acknowledged her source—which isn't surprising, given how common sharing was among folk musicians—but she did recall the remarkable thing she did with the three songs Cahn had shown her. "At one point I was sitting with the guitar and these three songs just seemed to come in together," she said. "It was a stroke of, maybe I was open and the muse found a lovely spot in me and out came what is called the Freedom Trilogy."[21] Odetta's "Freedom Trilogy" would become, perhaps, the most important soundtrack of the civil rights movement aside from "We Shall Overcome," the old spiritual reworked by Pete Seeger, Zilphia Horton, Guy Carawan, and Frank Hamilton.

There were plenty of reminders for Odetta, even in liberal San Francisco, that blacks and whites weren't quite living in the same

America. Despite California's antidiscrimination law, restaurants that didn't want to cater to blacks simply overlooked them or were evasive, rather than explicitly denying service. "Once in San Francisco," Mapes recalled, "Rolf and Odetta and I had gone to a restaurant, and while there were many empty tables it seemed that none were available. As we refused to leave, the manager was called. His eyes swept Odetta and he repeated that there [were] no available tables. Rolf said nothing, but he took off his glasses and handed them to me, all the while calmly looking at this tall man, a larger man, and we were seated immediately."[22]

Such encounters only served to strengthen Odetta's resolve to tell the stories of her people through song. They also help explain why Odetta remained unsure that she deserved the applause she was getting onstage. It was during her Tin Angel tenure that Odetta began collecting every news clipping with a mention about her, however fleeting, from a two-line gossip column tidbit or a quarter-page concert ad to a record or concert review. If she found four copies of an ad, she'd cut them out and paste them on construction paper for safekeeping. Later, when she went on tour, she made sure that friends or fans sent her the clippings, which she'd keep in ever-expanding files and boxes for more than forty years. It was as if she continually had to convince herself that she was indeed worthy of the attention coming her way.

In those days, she hated small clubs and the intimacy with the audience that they afforded, lest they get close enough to her to discover her hidden rage. The Tin Angel, at least, was dimly lit, but she closed her eyes when she sang anyway to avoid looking directly at the crowd. "I would finish singing and go off in my little [dressing room] and that was it," she recalled. "I didn't want to be bothered. I was really a semi-hermit."[23]

Peggy Tolk-Watkins gave her some early career advice. "Why don't you just use your first name?" she told Odetta. "Nobody is going to remember Felious." Given how often reviewers had already misspelled her surname, it seemed like sound advice. And Odetta thought it sounded "strutty." So from then on, she was simply Odetta. She wasn't the first performer to go by a single stage moniker; the cabaret singer Hildegarde in the 1930s and '40s and the actress Dagmar in the

'50s had both done it. But Odetta seems like a more direct link to the modern female singers, such as Cher, Madonna, and Beyoncé, who would later prune their names for the sake of marketing.[24]

In San Francisco, Odetta recorded an album for Fantasy Records, then just a regional label, and appeared very briefly on film in the widescreen *Cinerama Holiday*. For both, she teamed with Larry Mohr, a white twenty-two-year-old banjoist and singer from Detroit, with whom she performed frequently at the club, their interracial act going over well with their mostly young, progressive audiences. Their record, initially titled *Odetta & Larry* (his name was later scrubbed from the cover) included both solo songs and the duets they would sing in two-part harmony on stage. The LP attracted only a modicum of attention, with the folk music craze that Odetta would help ignite still a few years off. But it did make an impression on young folk fans who laid their hands on it, and several songs from the sessions, including "Cotton Fields" and "John Henry" would become staples of the revival, in part because of their renditions.

Cinerama Holiday was a travelogue set in Europe and the US, and Odetta and Mohr appeared during a segment on San Francisco, performing a sea shanty called "Santy Anno" at the Tin Angel. Odetta wouldn't actually see the film for a decade, ashamed of how her body might look on a wide screen. "I couldn't stand the idea of seeing myself sprawled from over there to over there," she later admitted.[25] But *Cinerama Holiday* brought her some added attention and the prestige of having a big-screen appearance on her résumé.

During her Tin Angel run, Odetta wasn't the only tall young black woman with a gap between her front teeth trying to make it on a San Francisco stage. On New Year's Day 1954, a St. Louis–born singer-dancer had debuted at the Purple Onion on Columbus Avenue, a basement cabaret a few miles down the road from the Tin Angel. She'd been performing around town under her birth name, Marguerite Johnson, but for her new gig the recent divorcée had been persuaded to use "Maya Angelou," combining her nickname and married surname into an exotic tongue-roller that suited her sexy calypso queen act.

"She was wearing a Trinidadian sort of outfit—the skirt looked like a sheet with the side cut out, and it allowed her to flash an extraordinary set of limbs," recalled Gordon Connell, who performed musical theater on a bill with Angelou at the Purple Onion that year. "She was six feet tall in her bare feet, and they *were* bare."[26]

It wasn't long before Angelou and Odetta discovered one another. "We were both tall black ladies, with attitudes," Angelou remembered. "And most people were really scared of us. We were young and black and female and crazy as road lizards." Angelou alluded to the difficulty she and Odetta had penetrating one another's defenses. "The amazement to me and to Odetta was we loved each other. We made sisters. And to be a sister of an African American woman is no small matter. To be a true sister of anybody is no small matter. But to be, in the 1950s, black and turned away from almost everything, and to say I have come here to stay and to be a sister of somebody who had courage is no small matter. She was my sister friend."[27]

As was the case with Belafonte, Odetta's singing clearly struck Angelou powerfully, as she much later recalled.

> Odetta, with her training [in] European classical music, sat on that stool, on that kitchen chair and sang old time songs. . . . True sophistication is to go from simpleness through all the affectations and back to utter simplicity. And that was Odetta. She sang the old songs and gave it to us and said look at the beauty of this. For that reason, I am Maya Angelou. For that reason, I tell the truth. . . . I've tried to tell the truth in my books and my poetry and some music and the way I live my life. And . . . much of that . . . the credit, can be laid at the foot of that sweet black woman who could take the rafters off the windows, sitting on a kitchen chair.[28]

On May 17, 1954, the Supreme Court handed down its unanimous ruling in the *Brown v. Board of Education* case, declaring racially segregated schools "inherently unequal" and overturning the 1896 "separate but equal" precedent from *Plessy v. Ferguson*. Chief Justice Earl Warren's opinion noted that "segregation of white and colored children in public schools has a detrimental effect upon the colored children. The impact is greater when it has the sanction of the law, for the policy of separating the races is usually interpreted as denoting the inferiority of the Negro group."

For Odetta, it was confirmation of what she'd always felt, the more-subtle forms of racism having taken a great toll on her psyche. Though she couldn't have known it then, the *Brown* decision was a turning point in the civil rights movement that would come to enlist her voice and presence so often. After the ruling came down, Odetta and Angelou headed to a Berkeley bar and shared a toast.

Less than a week later, Odetta was fired from the Tin Angel. As Odetta told the story, Peggy Tolk-Watkins had been lamenting that she needed a new act to get some press attention. When she called the club one night when Odetta was supposed to be on stage, the bartender told her that Odetta was nowhere to be seen. "Tell her when she comes in, she's fired," Tolk-Watkins said. Odetta blamed her tardiness for her routine of waiting until the last minute to get ready for a show—a measure of her anxiety about performing. The firing, she said, taught her a lesson. "I figured never would I give anybody that privilege [to fire me]. I would never do it to myself. They would have to do it on their own and that's when I started pulling myself together to be on time."[29]

No more hiding in a broom closet for Odetta. Whether she liked it or not, her talent had made people stand up and take notice.

CHAPTER FOUR

GETTING POLITICAL

With the end of her Tin Angel stint, Odetta sang again for the Turnabout Theatre, becoming a star of the adult version of the show, this time delivering her growing repertoire of folk songs instead of classical tunes to audiences in Los Angeles and then in San Francisco, after the troupe decided to cut stakes and move north. The Turnabout accounts for almost all of Odetta's concert work in 1955 and the early part of 1956. But in September of that year, her talents, and the growing interest in folk music, brought her the break she'd been looking for in the person of Dean Gitter, who paid Odetta a visit one afternoon at the three-room railroad house in Berkeley where she was living. "She played, I talked, and before I got up to leave she had agreed that I would be her manager and I would produce her first three albums," Gitter recalled.[1]

The somewhat convoluted story of Gitter's role in Odetta's career starts at Harvard University, where, at the age of twenty, he had just earned an English degree. A fellow graduate, Tom Wilson, had borrowed $900 to form a company in Cambridge, Massachusetts, called Transition Pre-Recorded Tapes. Wilson's idea, ahead of its time, was to sell prerecorded tapes to the masses, but in the terribly inconvenient reel-to-reel format that existed then. A tall, elegant black Texan, Wilson had been president of the Young Republican Club at Harvard and had graduated with honors and an economics degree. Before his early death, Wilson would become a top rock and pop producer, recording Bob Dylan, Simon and Garfunkel, and the Mothers of Invention, but he started as a jazz buff who preferred Sun Ra and John Coltrane to Pete Seeger.

The way Gitter tells it, he'd offered to put together a folk music line for Wilson and, after hearing the *Odetta & Larry* LP, had set his sights on signing Odetta for Wilson's new label. "I listened to that album and I fell out of my chair," Gitter said. "I never heard a voice like that."[2]

There are elements of Gitter's recollection that don't make sense. For example, a contract exists between Odetta and Wilson, signed back in March 1956, six months before Gitter met her. It calls for Odetta to record four LPs (with the material also to be issued on reel-to-reel) over three years. Gitter couldn't explain how that contract came to be, and he downplayed Wilson's role: "Tom did not negotiate that contract. I put it under his nose and he signed it. Tom never talked with Odetta, never met Odetta and didn't know anything about it except what I told him."[3]

Whatever the sequence of events, Gitter, who was newly married and looking, like Wilson, to make money in music, had driven cross-country to meet Odetta. That first day, Gitter said, "We sat together on her front porch for hours while she played through all of her repertoire." Two days later, they tried to find a recording studio. The first one Gitter called in San Francisco informed him that union rules prohibited it from recording blacks. "We had to go to a Jim Crow studio," Gitter said, one manned by black recording engineers. The session lasted more than eight hours, and Odetta, accompanied by Lou Gottlieb on bass, recorded sixteen songs.[4]

On September 22, Gitter left Berkeley and drove back to New York. He arrived about 7 p.m. on the twenty-fourth, and by 10 that night he had turned up at the Bronx apartment of his friend Kenny Goldstein, who was already becoming known as the nation's top folk music producer. He played the Odetta tapes for Goldstein, who pronounced them "sensational." At midnight, Gitter called Tom Wilson in Boston to deliver the news, and Wilson dropped a bombshell about his company. "We're broke," he said.[5]

By the first week in October, Wilson had transferred the contracts of all his artists, including Odetta, to Gitter, who assumed title to recordings of Odetta and a few other singers, as well as Transition's debt. With Goldstein's help, Gitter began shopping the tapes to all the folk-oriented record companies in New York, including Riverside (where Goldstein worked), Elektra, and Tradition, a label started by the acting-singing brothers Paddy, Tom, and Liam Clancy, later part of the seminal Irish folk revival group the Clancy Brothers and Tommy Makem. Everyone agreed that Odetta was destined to be a star.

On October 5, Gitter spent all night writing Odetta a four-page, single-spaced letter in longhand, explaining all he was doing on her behalf in trying to secure a new record deal for her. The letter was among several that Gitter would later provide to a court after things went south in their partnership. But at the beginning, Gitter was full of enthusiasm. "I believe that you in time are going to make Belafonte look like an amateur," he wrote, "so believe me when I say that I am going to conduct the affairs between us in such a manner that when March 1, 1959 rolls around, you will be tickled pink to extend our agreement."[6]

It appeared that Odetta and Gitter, who was also a folk singer and actor, had struck up a friendship during his brief stay in Berkeley. He ended the letter by saying: "Just to be consistent with my usual practice of putting most important things last: How are you, honey? Stay well and hungry and write soon. Love and stuff, Dean." Six decades later, Gitter made a point of insisting there was nothing but a business relationship and a shared passion for the arts between them, though he acknowledged that Odetta thought there was more, which he chalked up to "strange fantasies about who she fell in love with."[7]

Gitter had appeared in the play *Finnegan's Wake* with Tom Clancy at the Poets' Theatre in Cambridge, and he ended up selling the Odetta tapes to the Clancys, who began preparing them for release. Back in California, Odetta gave notice at the Turnabout Theatre. Then she boarded a train bound for Chicago to perform at a new club there called the Gate of Horn.

Albert Grossman had opened one of the nation's first folk music nightclubs in the basement of the run-down Rice Hotel on the corner of Dearborn Street and Chicago Avenue, where he would book established stars like Josh White and the bluesman Big Bill Broonzy and up-and-coming young folk singers like Bob Gibson.

Grossman, with sleepy owl eyes, chubby cheeks, and a crew cut (which would continue to lengthen throughout the next decade until his hair tickled his shoulders), had grown up in Chicago and earned a degree in economics. He was one of the first people to realize that a business could be built around folk music. Grossman had named his club, modeled on the basement jazz lounges of Paris, after a line in Homer's *Odyssey*, which contrasts a gate of ivory from which deluded fantasies arise with one made of horn that allows only the truth to pass.

Whether Grossman, soon to become the most important music manager of the era, represented truth or a ruthless quest for money and power wound up being one of the more fascinating parlor debates about the 1960s music business. "It wasn't the folk music, because Albert knew nothing about folk music and could have cared less when he opened the Gate of Horn," said Gibson, who performed frequently at the club and later hired Grossman as his manager. "He knew that a listening room could work." Frank Hamilton, who moved to Chicago from Los Angeles and became the house backup guitarist at the Gate, held a jaundiced view of Grossman. "Al could be charming," he recalled. "But I don't think he had really terrific values as a person. I think he liked the music enough. But it was more the glamour and the fact that he could see this was going someplace, this folk music revival, and he could make it happen."[8]

Grossman had written to Odetta and told her about his new club. When her train pulled into Chicago on October 30, she went directly to the Gate of Horn for her sound check. Standing outside waiting for her were Josh White and Bill Broonzy. White had just finished a run there, and Big Bill lived in the Windy City. They'd gotten word that Odetta would be performing and felt protective of a fellow black musician. "They wanted to make sure their little sister was going to get on ok," Odetta recalled.[9]

Odetta opened for Gibson her first night. By the following week, she was the headliner, with Gibson and Paul Clayton getting second and third billing. As usual, she made an immediate impression. "Odetta toplines with a set of pipes as direct and powerful as a blowtorch and as deep and resonant as an old master's bass viol," *Variety* said. "Accompanying herself on the guitar, this femme is superb with the blues and the spirituals, the powerful gutsy songs. . . . Odetta goes off to thunderous applause."[10]

It had been a little more than a year since the lynching of the Chicago boy Emmett Till in Mississippi and the open-casket funeral his mother had insisted upon in his hometown, which drew the national press and brought the horrors of Southern Jim Crow home to Americans, awakening many to injustices that had been all too easy to ignore. Soon after, inspired in part by Till's gruesome death and the easy acquittal of his murderers by an all-white jury, Rosa Parks had refused to give up her seat to a white person on a bus in Montgomery, Alabama, sparking the bus boycott that brought Martin Luther King Jr. to prominence.

In her early Gate of Horn shows, Odetta began to sense the political moment and what she might do with it. Though she started out tentatively, she began speaking about the history behind the spirituals and slave and prison songs. Her secret fury still hid behind the guise of her singing, and her perfect diction and thoughtful manner commanded attention.

In Chicago, she appeared several times on Studs Terkel's popular radio show on WFMT, which mixed folk music, blues, and jazz with topical conversation, lubricated by Terkel's inquisitive mind and liberal politics. "She's a powerful singer," Terkel told his listeners, "but seems even more so because of the time in which we live." He asked Odetta about "Another Man Done Gone," the chain gang song she delivered nightly at the Gate in dramatic fashion by removing the guitar from her shoulder and laying it on the stage, before belting out the a cappella number, her hand claps echoing like nine-pound hammers or overseers' bullwhips. "There was a time when the prison farms, or state farms, chained the men to the beds at night and to each other during the day, during work hours," Odetta told Terkel. "When a man escaped . . . blood hounds were put on the trails and usually the prisoner who tried to escape was killed in some fashion or another."[11]

Odetta changed a verse in the song, first collected by John Lomax from Alabamian Vera Hall in 1940. Instead of singing, *He killed another man, He killed another man*, an apparent reference to the convict's crime, Odetta made it, *They killed another man, They killed another man*, keeping the focus on the barbarous system itself. For a woman endeavoring to break free from her own chains—"society's foot on your throat," as she'd put it—there was a metaphorical power in her renditions of chain gang songs, as if by her extraordinary telling, she was taking a sledgehammer to iron shackles.

Americans of an earlier generation had briefly been made aware of the reputation of Southern chain gangs for brutality. The 1932 movie *I Am a Fugitive from a Chain Gang*, based on the memoir of a Georgia chain gang escapee named Robert Edward Burns, had caused an uproar over the inhuman treatment of Southern convicts, many of them black, who were worked as legally sanctioned slaves under threat of death for the slightest misstep. The outcry had supposedly led to reforms, but Northern newspapers in the 1950s occasionally followed the stories of escapees who fled to cities like New York and Chicago, echoing fugitive slaves from a century earlier, with tales of unspeakable horrors perpetrated by sadistic guards.

While Odetta didn't go so far as to tell her audiences that the justice system in the South that had put so many black men behind bars was a sham, she was nevertheless cluing them in to the fact that there was more to be learned than they'd gotten in history class. When she became the prisoner, or the railroad worker in "John Henry," or any of the other desperate characters she inhabited, she allowed her audiences to empathize, however briefly, with their plight, making it more likely that the history might genuinely sink in. "There was a period in my early career when I needed to learn what to say and what to leave out," Odetta remembered, "but I felt I had to say a lot because our schools certainly weren't teaching us anything about ourselves."[12]

Dean Gitter had been in Chicago for Odetta's opening. And in early November, after her two-week run ended, he headed back to New York and Odetta back to Berkeley, where she received a letter from Gitter written on November 13 that began: "Hello Baby: Forgive the long delay in writing, but my affairs—long neglected while I was in Chicago—closed in on me last week and I've been up to my ears in work." He told her that he was embarking on a plan for her called "Operation Stardom," which would begin, he said, with "a concerted assault, no holds barred, teeth bared, on the entertainment hub of America—New York City." He was talking to concert promoters such as Max Gordon of the Village Vanguard and Blue Angel and Art D'Lugoff of the Village Gate, had spoken to *Finian's Rainbow* lyricist Yip Harburg about possible opportunities on Broadway, and was trying to get her a national TV appearance. He signed it "XXXOOOXXXOOOXXX, Dean."[13]

The next day, Tradition Records released Odetta's first solo LP, *Ballads and Blues.* The striking red-and-white album cover featured a closeup of Odetta's face deep in the throes of singing. As with all her early records, the producers avoided showing her very far below the shoulders, an apparent effort to deemphasize her large body. Purposefully or not, these portraits only accentuated Odetta's natural hair, as it framed her quite striking features, providing an indelible image of black beauty that didn't try to cater to white tastes.

The LP, with Gitter as producer, included all sixteen tracks she'd recorded for him in San Francisco. The record reflected Odetta's wide tastes in folk music, from "Santy Anno," the sea shanty she'd sung in *Cinerama Holiday,* to the calypso tune "Shame and a Scandal," to Lead Belly's "Alabama Bound."

Aside from her astounding voice, it was her ability to build tension in a song—the result of her operatic training and the tutelage of Rolf Cahn—that immediately set her apart from just about anyone else then singing folk music. Her "Joshua Fit De Battle of Jericho" was so powerful that when she sang "well them walls come tumbling down," it seemed as if she could have done the deed herself with her voice alone. Josh White had introduced the song to the folk world, but his rendering had been far more polite.

The centerpiece of *Ballads and Blues* was Odetta's crowning masterpiece, the spiritual "Freedom Trilogy" she'd learned as individual songs from Cahn. Once again, she ratcheted up the tension masterfully from a dirge on the slave lament "Oh Freedom" through the hopeful awakening of "Come and Go with Me" and on to the stirring promise of "I'm on My Way." While the component spirituals had already begun to appear on the front lines of civil rights protests in places like Montgomery, Odetta's inspired coupling brought to bear the whole history of the black struggle to make a profound statement about the crescendo of change just beginning to swell across America.

I'm on my way and I won't turn back
I'm on my way and I won't turn back
I'm on my way and I won't turn back
I'm on my way, great God I'm on my way

The meaning of the song in the context of the quest for civil rights was crystal clear. As Chestyn Everett, a columnist for the *Los Angeles Tribune*, a black paper, would put it: "'I'm On My Way,' as Odetta sings it, is our serious nomination as a replacement for the socalled [*sic*] Negro anthem. The prophetic fervor, the indestructible faith and determination of a people is mirrored in Odetta's rendition of this song—a true revelation!"[14]

The LP hit critics like a thunderbolt. Robert Bagar's review in the *New York Journal-American* was fairly typical.

With undisguised excitement the people at Tradition records are touting this lady as the coming "Queen of American song." Also they name her a direct descendant of the fabulous folkists Ma Rainey and Bessie Smith. Want to know my opinion? I think they're right. It is out of the kind of singing and the kind of songs sung by such artists as Odetta that a rich lore is created, and from that a country's musical personality.[15]

The record immediately changed the game for folk musicians coming of age then. Many of the folk artists—most of them men—already well known by the mid-1950s were earnest performers in the vein of Burl Ives, who expertly resurrected old songs in a pleasant manner that didn't have a particular edge to it or tell you anything about the inner life of the songwriter. Pennsylvanian Ed McCurdy was a former vaudeville performer who had success singing folk songs in New York nightclubs and would later become a minor TV star, and Paul Clayton from Massachusetts was a folklorist and singer who specialized in sea shanties and ballads. (Bob Dylan would base "Don't Think Twice,

It's Alright" on Clayton's "Who's Gonna Buy You Ribbons When I'm Gone?") Englishman Richard Dyer-Bennet gently fingerpicked a guitar and sang songs like "John Henry" but with a pretty voice that sounds (to modern ears) more suited to sentimental love songs.

Kentuckian John Jacob Niles, one of the most audacious of the early folk revival minstrels, played a lute and sang in an eyebrow-raising falsetto. He gathered material on song trips through the Southern mountains, where he'd visit county judges, school superintendents, jailers, and truant officers, who often knew the best local singers from whom he could "collect" songs. He also wrote songs such as "Black Is the Color of My True Love's Hair."

Belafonte, a genuine star and sex symbol, remained the pacesetter in sales, and Seeger, though still hounded by the blacklist, was a huge influence on the younger generation of folk fans, though, again, not the kind of singer who could inspire, especially on vinyl.

When it came to folk material that, either explicitly or not, addressed the civil rights struggle, Josh White had long led the way, bravely singing about Jim Crow, often at great personal risk. During his prime, in the mid-1940s, when he'd held court at Café Society in Greenwich Village, he'd sometimes had to beat back attacks from racist whites angry at his renditions of tunes such as the antilynching song "Strange Fruit." But while hard-core lefties sympathized with his cause, the nation at large wasn't much interested then in doing anything about the nation's festering racial inequality.

By the mid-1950s, White had come to be seen as something of a relic. His voluntary testimony in front of the House Un-American Activities Committee had torpedoed his reputation on the left, even though he hadn't named names, while it didn't completely remove the taint from his appearance in the anti-Communist pamphlet *Red Channels*. And while White had come up from the South and learned firsthand from a number of traditional bluesmen, including Blind Lemon Jefferson, his act had become very polished from his many years in the nightclubs, and that didn't resonate with younger folk music fans. White would enjoy some success during the coming folk revival, but he wasn't the tastemaker that he'd once been. "The perception was that Josh had adapted too completely to nightclub work," the folk singer Dave Van Ronk recalled. "Josh had smoothed all the rough edges from his act, and he was essentially a cabaret singer. And we were not interested in that at all."[16]

The dimming of White's star left the door open for other black folk singers to push the national consciousness toward acceptance of blacks as full citizens, and Belafonte and Odetta, along with black artists in a variety of fields, would do much to help make that happen.

In early December, with her album generating considerable buzz, Odetta arrived in New York. On the tenth, she signed a contract making Gitter her personal manager. It was an ambitious deal, covering five years with two options for five-year renewals, his management fee expected to rise as her bank account fattened.[17]

There was reason once again to believe that folk music was on the rise, half a decade after the Weavers' successes. The previous year, Bill Hayes had scored a number-one hit with "The Ballad of Davy Crockett," and Tennessee Ernie Ford had done the same with the Merle Travis song "Sixteen Tons" (and Ford and the actor Fess Parker also had hits with their own versions of "The Ballad of Davy Crockett"). Then, in 1956, Belafonte notched his first number-one album with *Belafonte*, which led off with Odetta's arrangement of "Water Boy." Belafonte followed that months later with *Calypso*, history's first million-selling LP. Despite Gitter's optimism about Odetta's future, however, he wouldn't stick around long enough to find out whether she too could become a star.

CHAPTER FIVE

THE FUSE IS LIT

A merica in the late Eisenhower years was a nation in transition, from what had been a rigid, top-down society to something more egalitarian but also more uncertain. Amid whirlwind economic prosperity, the family circle was beginning to weaken: more women started working outside the home, and men spent longer hours at the office, many commuting to work from newly manufactured suburbs, their unquestioned authority in the nuclear family diminishing. Young people had less structure in their lives—greater opportunities, to be sure, especially if they were white, but also more doubt, not only about their own futures but about a country riven by issues of class, race, and ideology and a world consumed with war, both hot and cold. They seemed to be soul-searching for meaning as never before.

Many parents had blamed rock 'n' roll for what was deemed an epidemic of youth rebellion in the mid-1950s, with dozens of cities putting curfews in place to get kids off the streets. "Never before in our history have we Americans experienced such a wave of distrust of our teen-age youth," read an article in the *Los Angeles Times*. But the rock fad merely tapped into an angst that was already there. Unlike swing, the youth obsession of a previous era, rock was do-it-yourself music, spurring teenagers to buy their first guitars and make some noise of their own. Now, in early 1957, with the first phase of the rock 'n' roll revolution showing signs of waning—teen heartthrobs like Pat Boone and Tab Hunter were all over the radio, and by year's end, Elvis would be drafted and Little Richard would retire to join the church—young people were looking for something new that spoke to their doubts and desires and finding it in another do-it-yourself genre: folk.

In New York City, the epicenter of the coming folk revival, the youth movement planted its first flags in the ground. At 110 Mac-Dougal Street in Greenwich Village, twenty-nine-year-old Izzy Young opened the Folklore Center, ostensibly a store selling sheet music, folk music books, and instruments but more importantly the place where musicians would gather to jam, share the latest gossip, or score a gig if they were lucky, perhaps even one sponsored by the gregarious Mr. Young himself at his shoebox establishment. Not far from the Folklore Center, in Washington Square Park, gaggles of devout "folkniks," as Young called them, began congregating with their guitars, banjos, and mandolins on weekends to play blues, ballads, and old-time music.

Despite whatever misgivings these young people may have harbored, when they were playing music, the city was brimming with youthful energy and possibility, and that's what Odetta found when she packed up her belongings in Berkeley and went to live with Dean Gitter and his wife, Margery, in a two-room basement apartment at 327 West Fourth Street in the West Village.

As in Los Angeles and San Francisco, she found plenty of comrades-in-arms eager to trade songs, political philosophies, and more. In coffeehouses, bars, and church basements, music, poetry, and literature cross-pollinated and roused one another. "We all had an audience for whatever we were doing, whether it was a jazz or classical musician performing, or an opening for an off-off-(way off) Broadway play, or a reading from a book or poetry recital, or folk musicians having a hootenanny," the jazz musician David Amram, who later became a good friend of Odetta's, recalled. "Pete Seeger, Odetta and I all played with musicians from every style because there were no cultural commissars telling us what was Correct and what was Verboten."[1]

Odetta wasted little time in establishing her reputation in New York, a city she would call home off and on for the rest of her life. Her first gig after arriving from Berkeley was a "Folk Song Fest and Calypso Carnival" at the Brooklyn Academy of Music. Also on the bill were the Kentucky balladeer Jean Ritchie and Oscar Brand, the

Canadian-born folk singer who hosted a seminal radio show, *Folk-song Festival*, on New York's WNYC. Brand served as emcee for the concert, and he recalled going backstage before the show and hearing Odetta singing scales in grand fashion, which was hardly typical for the city's young folk singers. "We talked for a while and I said, 'Do you sing opera?' And she said, 'No, I sing . . . folk,'" Brand remembered. "And she walked out on that stage and that audience had never known her or seen her or anything, including me. And she just blew them out of that place, with the voice and that personality. She was a person that was more of a spirit than any kind of human being."[2]

In the audience were Selma Thaler and her husband, Ed. He was a newly minted doctor, and she was years shy of starting a therapy practice and pregnant with their first child. The Thalers, both from Brooklyn, had met Odetta a few times in Berkeley, and when Selma heard about the concert on Brand's radio show, she decided to try to reconnect. She invited Odetta to dinner at their two-room apartment near Highland Park, and after some initial awkwardness, they were still listening to blues and folk records at 3 a.m., talking and telling funny stories, eliciting Odetta's contagious childlike giggles. They became lifelong friends, which Thaler agreed was difficult for Odetta: "She was able to trust us. It was not easy for her to trust people and she could trust us. And she knew she was loved and not judged."[3]

Odetta would spend a lot of time with the Thalers at their apartment whenever she was in town. "She would offer to wash the dishes after we would eat and she would sing German lieder," Thaler said. "That's what she was trained for—she could have been one of those." Thaler's daughter, Carrie, born the following year, remembered Odetta as a great hugger of children and an even better listener through the decades, someone who prized her special friendships, once she allowed someone to get close to her. "Odetta was someone that, and I don't think I'm unique in this, I always felt really good to be around her," she recalled. "And I think a lot of people may have felt that way."[4]

In the Village, many of the new record companies that were starting to put out folk material were within walking distance, including Vanguard Records on East Eleventh Street, Elektra Records on Bleecker Street, and the Clancy Brothers' Tradition Records, which had just released Odetta's LP, on Christopher Street. Liam Clancy remembered what it was like in the cozy Village scene in 1957:

> One evening the great Odetta phoned and invited me to a Bob Gibson concert at a church hall on Bleecker Street. . . . I was shy about it, but what a thrill it was. . . . After the concert she and I went down the street to Izzy Young's Folklore Center, where the banjos and guitars were goin' at it. Paul Clayton was there singing whaling songs with his friend Jo El. It turned into a party, as it always did at Izzy's place. Odetta sang "The Lass from the Low Country," and Paul and I did some sea shanties. I walked Odetta home and we had a long talk. She sang me some songs in that powerful voice of hers (even though she tried to sing sotto voce) that shook the walls . . . as if they were the walls of Jericho.[5]

Odetta found kinship in this early circle of folk music enthusiasts, which included the people who ran the record companies and genuinely loved the music—before big business got deeply involved. She was especially taken with the young and rakish Clancy Brothers, who sang about revolution in Ireland in ways that hit home for black Americans. As her friend Maya Angelou would note of one of the Clancys' songs, "Wearing of the Green": "If the words Negro and America were exchanged for shamrock and Irish, the song could be used to describe the situation in the United States."[6]

The Clancys often hung out at the White Horse Tavern, a gritty Hudson Street bar that had attracted a literary crowd, including Dylan Thomas and Jack Kerouac, and where "people would sit around and sing all night," Odetta recalled. "I'm glad it was through them [the Clancys] that I was baptized, rather than going into Warner Brothers or RCA, where there's nothing but bean counters telling you to smile, even when you're hurting."[7]

By the spring, the Gitters, along with Odetta, had moved to a five-room apartment at 144 East Twenty-Second Street, where it turned out blacks were not entirely welcome, the kind of Northern racism often underplayed in histories. Dean Gitter had become friendly with Earl Jones, a six-foot-six black actor who moonlighted as a floor sander. Jones had done some work on the Gitters' previous apartment (along with his son, a young thespian named James Earl), and he visited a few times at the Twenty-Second Street place. "One afternoon, I got a visit from a representative of the august realtor who managed the building," Gitter recalled. "He told me that it was alright for the 'nigger gal' to stay in the apartment, but 'the big *shvartze*' [Yiddish slang for a black person] was frightening the old Jewish ladies who lived in the building and must not visit us again. I threw him out."[8]

Albert Grossman, visiting from Chicago, stayed in the third bedroom that spring. One night, they had a dinner party, and Bob Gibson came with a friend who wanted to meet Grossman: a young singer named Mary Travers, whom Grossman would later tap for Peter, Paul and Mary.

New York had no club devoted to folk music in early 1957. The high-end cabarets mostly offered pop music and jazz. Aside from the Gate of Horn in Chicago, in fact, only a handful of clubs around the nation, including the Hungry i in San Francisco and Storyville in Boston, regularly featured folk musicians. That would very soon change.

In mid-August, one of the first of the new wave of folk clubs, the Café Bizarre, opened its doors at 106 West Third Street in what was said to have been a former stable once belonging to Aaron Burr. Odetta headlined on a bill that featured several others, including a young merchant seaman, Dave Van Ronk, who had never performed before on stage. Van Ronk recalled what Odetta did that night, which was certainly beyond the call of duty for the night's main attraction.

> I still do not know what I sang or said, but I remember very well what happened immediately afterward. I was shaking like someone who has narrowly missed a fatal car crash, and just as happy, when up came Odetta herself with a great big smile on her face—and she has a smile that could melt diamonds. "That was wonderful," she said. "Do you do this for a living?" I told her, no, I was a merchant seaman on the beach and I meant to ship out again as soon as my money ran low. Well, she said, if I was interested, she could take a tape of mine out to Chicago to Albert Grossman, owner of the Gate of Horn.[9]

In what became a legendary episode, Van Ronk's tape never quite made it to Odetta or to Chicago, but Van Ronk thought it had, and after hitchhiking to the Gate of Horn, he endured a failed, soul-decapitating audition for Grossman. With Odetta's encouragement, however, Van Ronk soon took up folk singing full-time, becoming one of the more influential performers in Greenwich Village, even if he never quite became a star.

Van Ronk said Odetta's music "had made an incredible impression on us," and his wife, Terri Thal, recalled Odetta's gesture to a then-unknown singer as "a generous, wonderful thing to do." Odetta made a similar impression on a young Grace Slick, who, while still in college, snuck into her dressing room at a Village club around this time and played and sang for her. "She encouraged my moderate ability and gently warned me that being a musician was a sort of hit-and-miss occupation," recalled Slick, the future Jefferson Airplane singer.[10]

By the end of August, Gitter had booked Odetta on a fall tour of colleges. And he got her her first national TV spot, on NBC's *Today Show*. It would have seemed a perfect showcase for Odetta's powerful work songs or spirituals, yet even though McCarthyism was ebbing—a disgraced Joseph McCarthy himself had died at age forty-eight a few months earlier—television in the summer of 1957 wasn't quite ready to embrace folk songs with a message. A limousine picked up Odetta and Gitter at his apartment at 6 a.m. and took them to NBC's studio on Forty-Ninth Street. But the cohost of the show, Jack Lescoulie, "didn't know what to make of Odetta, didn't know what to make of folk music," Gitter said. "And she sang, 'The Fox,' [a cute English folk song] which was all the *Today Show* could stand."[11]

A short time later, Gitter abruptly parted ways with Odetta and left for England, nine months after becoming her manager and outlining an ambitious plan to make her a star. Gitter offered various reasons for the decision. He said that he'd already been accepted a year earlier to the prestigious London Academy of Music and Dramatic Arts to study Shakespearean acting and had delayed his admission for a year just as the opportunity with Odetta had arisen. "But as the end of the year began to approach . . . I realized that I really didn't want to be a manager," Gitter said. "To me it smacked of flesh-peddling."[12] On another occasion, he said that as much as he admired Odetta's talent, he concluded that he couldn't make a living at folk music, which was true of most people in the business then. Margery had just given birth to their first son, Jonathan, and Gitter, about to turn twenty-two, felt he had to provide for his family, although going to acting school hardly guaranteed him a future income.

As for who would manage Odetta then, Gitter said he quickly settled on Al Grossman. "And I arranged to give—GIVE!—the contract to Albert Grossman, who had never managed anybody, but he did have the Gate of Horn, so he was becoming one of the most important figures in folk music, even then."[13]

According to their official agreement, signed September 20, 1957, Gitter transferred all his managerial rights to Grossman. As compensation, he asked for a 20 percent cut of the fall concert tour he'd booked for Odetta through the end of November. Odetta, Gitter said, felt betrayed by his decision to leave. "Albert related how really personally pissed Odetta was with me," Gitter said, with Grossman telling him the end of their partnership "sounds more like a love affair with you screwing her."[14]

If Odetta was blindsided by Gitter's exit, she did already seem taken by Grossman's can-do attitude and forceful personality. "One sensed that Albert was brilliant, a man of impeccable artistic taste," she recalled.[15] For Grossman, it meant that he now had the top new folk singer as a client. He immediately booked Odetta at the Gate of Horn, this time for a five-week run starting in early September. Her shows there at the beginning of the year had generated buzz, but now she'd begun attracting a serious fan base.

With Odetta's first Tradition record selling briskly, Grossman rushed her into the studio to record her second solo LP, released by Tradition in late October of 1957. In an early example of Grossman's marketing genius, it was entitled *Odetta at the Gate of Horn*, even though the entire recording was made in a New York studio. As Odetta began to gain fame, Grossman would enjoy a growing reputation as folk music's éminence grise. While it's certainly true that serious folk fans would have heard of the club, there's no doubt that the record helped put it on the map. It would often be said later that Grossman had "discovered" Odetta at the Gate of Horn, but as to who helped the other more, a good argument can be made that Grossman benefited from the relationship far more than she did, as she helped spearhead the ascendance of folk music around the country.

Charlie Rothschild, who would start working for Grossman's managerial firm a few years later, maintained that Grossman helped guide her early career in important ways. "He was a very good businessman and he did wonders for his acts, including Odetta," Rothschild said. "When he met Odetta she was probably making peanuts and he generated a good income for her and got her exposure." Yet it's arguable how much of that exposure would be due to Grossman and how much would come from word of mouth and the unusual power of her music. Rothschild agreed that Grossman wound up reaping big benefits from the client Gitter had handed him. "I would assume," Rothschild said, "Odetta attracted a lot of people to Albert." As Odetta herself would note in looking back at this period much later, "Albert started his business on my back."[16]

In terms of content, *Odetta at the Gate of Horn* picked up right where *Ballads and Blues* had left off, with another selection of the ballads, convict songs, slave songs, and spirituals she was singing in her live shows. They included the old Negro spiritual "He's Got the Whole World in His Hands," which would forever be associated with her, and "Take This Hammer." Odetta used the liner notes of the album to assert that her music had a clear political message if her listeners would pay close attention to the words. Of the lyric "I don't want your cold iron shackles" in "Take This Hammer," she wrote that it represented "what man has done to man"; and of the line "hurts my pride—hurts my pride," she commented that it "continues to do in one form or another."[17] Instilling black pride would be a constant theme of her work, whether by showing off the inherent beauty and power of black music born of slavery and Jim Crow or by using the history of folk songs to show that her people had a real past worth remembering.

Critics were quick to heap praise on the record. "When Odetta lets out all the stops of her strength and feeling on the work songs 'Timber' and 'Take This Hammer,' one is aware of listening to an extraordinarily gifted singer," Robert Shelton wrote in the *New York Times*, the first of his many plaudits over the years.[18] Odetta's two records on Tradition would more or less carry the small label for a time. Still, although her popularity was building in folk circles, Odetta's sales were modest when compared with Harry Belafonte's record-breaking LPs on RCA. While RCA had a huge marketing department and connections with radio deejays to boost airplay, Tradition relied mostly on word of mouth to generate sales—not a recipe for hit songs or albums.

In November, Odetta embarked on the college tour Dean Gitter had booked for her. It included stops at Yale, Princeton, Oberlin, and other schools, with a total gross of a little more than two thousand dollars. The college folk circuit was then in its infancy, but Josh White and Pete Seeger had both had successful college shows—and interest among students was swelling. It was on these campuses that the fuse was really lit for the folk revival. "In going to different university and college campuses, to see the kids who are playing banjos, recorders, guitars, 12-string guitars, who are sitting and entertaining themselves, it's quite a lovely thing to see," Odetta told an interviewer a short time later. "And it's growing and growing."[19]

As Odetta saw on her campus tours, young people were ready to ditch "Heartbreak Hotel" and "Tutti Frutti" for more thought-provoking fare. "Her voice is thoroughly disciplined and the vocal pyrotechnics that she displayed would put Little Richard to shame," wrote June Starr, Oberlin class of 1958, in her review of Odetta's concert on November 16. She reported that "a wildly enthusiastic audience greeted the first appearance of Odetta at Oberlin. From the opening choruses of 'Santy Anno' to the final encores we were unquestionably hers."[20]

By Christmas Eve, Odetta was back for yet another run at the Gate, with Chicago quickly becoming, for a time, her new home base. It made sense now that her new manager and one of the top folk clubs in the nation were both there. It was also a good midway point for shuttling between gigs on both coasts.

Early on, she usually stayed at the home of Dawn and Nate Greening, folk music enthusiasts who lived in nearby Oak Park. Dawn was a founder of the Old Town School of Folk Music, which had started informally in the Greenings' living room and had just opened for business on North Avenue, amid increasing demand for teachers of folk music. Aside from offering classes on guitar, banjo, and folk dancing, the school would become an informal gathering place for visiting musicians such as Josh White, Pete Seeger, and Big Joe Williams, and it would help cement Chicago's folk scene the way Izzy Young's Folklore Center did in New York.

A warm, friendly woman whom students at the school would affectionately call "Momma Dawn," Dawn Greening had met Odetta during her first Gate of Horn show and they grew close after some typical hesitation on Odetta's part. "She didn't believe that my mother was as nice as she seemed," recalled Dawn and Nate's daughter Lesley Greening Taufer. "She said, 'I never ever believed that your mother was real.' And then of course she did."[21]

The Greenings were avowed "anti-segregationists," their son, Lance, recalled. But it seemed that wherever Odetta went, she had to deal with racial hostility. Some of the Greenings' neighbors didn't take kindly to having a black woman in their midst. Oak Park had already made a name for itself as a racially unfriendly enclave. When Percy Julian, a black research chemist who had helped pioneer the synthesis of testosterone and other hormones, had moved his family to Oak Park in 1950, several attempts were made to burn down the home, including an attack with dynamite hurled from a passing automobile. "Every time [Odetta] came to town she stayed with us," Lesley Greening Taufer said. "And our neighbors would peek through the curtains at us, and my mother would take Odetta's album cover and stick it in the window."[22]

The TV networks would play a critical role in raising the consciousness of the nation about the black struggle, and in April of 1958, they featured Odetta for the first time in a civil rights context. She appeared on CBS for a Saturday morning program entitled *Odetta Sings*. Produced by the network's public affairs department, the program, according to one black newspaper, was intended to stress "the lasting contribution of the colored race to America's civilization."[23] It was just the kind of opportunity that would have appealed to Odetta, one in which she could sing songs that spoke of the black experience. While the appearance was briefly noted in the black press, however, it was hardly a prime-time slot. Those would come soon enough.

She claimed by then to have a repertoire of 150 songs, according to a short profile in *DownBeat* that May. Her concert work was increasing, and she was mostly doing stage shows at places such as the Berkeley Little Theater, Jordan Hall in Boston, Orchestra Hall in Chicago, Reed College in Oregon, and the University of Wisconsin in Madison.

As the summer approached, though, any thoughts of a clean break from Dean Gitter evaporated. He filed suit against Odetta in Massachusetts, claiming that Grossman had never paid him the commission he was owed for the fall 1957 college concert tour. The suit also claimed that Odetta had reneged on a record deal Gitter had made on her behalf the previous June with Riverside Records. He was seeking 20 percent of the concert gross and fulfillment of the record deal, which could mean far more for him since it gave him a share of the royalty. As court papers later revealed, Odetta had cashed nine checks totaling eight hundred dollars as an advance against royalties of the Riverside record, but Grossman had balked at the contract Gitter had signed.

In August 1958, Odetta wrote her lawyer Samuel Freifeld in Chicago, dismayed at the legal imbroglio with her former manager and friend. "With the possibility of ending the recording contract with Dean, my mind goes back to the hope and enthusiasms of two young people with faith and respect for one and the other just about two years ago. I am saddened by the failure of our friend and business relationship."[24]

It wouldn't be the first time Odetta would feel let down by what she felt were the cold calculations of people in the music business at the expense of the caring human relationships she so desperately longed for. "There have been some few difficulties concerning records in my life and it looks from here as if it will never be straightened out, but I'm sure it will," she told an interviewer in September, without giving any details. "And I really don't know right now where anybody stands."[25]

In November, the Kingston Trio's version of the old murder ballad "Tom Dooley" skyrocketed to number one on the *Billboard* charts—the event considered the Big Bang of the folk revival. Young, clean-cut, and hip, the Trio became the first teen idols in the brief era when folk music reigned in American popular culture. The number of folk clubs soon exploded, as did the number of amateur guitarists and banjoists performing at local hootenannies with dreams of making it to the top. The record companies, too, already witnessing the success of Belafonte and other purveyors of folk, realized that the music was fast becoming mainstream and that meant a new search for talent with hit potential.

Odetta told an interviewer that she wasn't interested in the great fame that now appeared possible for folk singers, though subsequent events make it seem as though her avowals were a bit defensive, as if she were subconsciously bracing for rejection. "I don't want stardom. I don't want stardom," she said. "There's too much for one to do and to experience for say a stardom like Mr. Belafonte, who has a great responsibility. If he comes up with a hit, somebody in some office is saying, 'Ok, where is the other one?' These are no conditions to work under." She added that starting a family was too important to her to sacrifice on the altar of fame. "Because a career minded person, I'm not," she said. "I couldn't get along with just a career."[26]

CHAPTER SIX

TV SENSATION

Dave Van Ronk once estimated that the Red Scare delayed the folk revival by a decade. If true, the postponement had one unintended but far-reaching consequence: it meant that folk music and the civil rights movement would peak at the same moment in time. Had folk taken off earlier, it might have run its course as a pop fad and not played such an indispensable role in the freedom struggle. Odetta would figure prominently in both.

In May of 1959, she teamed up with Count Basie for a benefit performance at Hunter College in New York, sponsored by a group called the Youth March for Integrated Schools. The concert raised money in support of a civil rights bill pending in Congress that Senator Paul Douglas of Illinois, a liberal Democrat, had introduced. Two years earlier, Douglas had spearheaded the Civil Rights Act of 1957, which had created a civil rights division in the Justice Department to prosecute voting rights violations in the South—the first significant federal legislative action on civil rights since Reconstruction. Now, Douglas's new bill called for expanding the Justice Department's civil rights enforcement powers to other areas, including school desegregation, which, despite the *Brown v. Board of Education* ruling, was "slowly grinding to a halt," according to one recent report.[1] The bill, like all other civil rights legislation over the next several years, would face a stiff wall of opposition from the Southern wing in Congress, leaving activists to continue pressing their case in local disputes and in the court of public opinion.

The committee for the Hunter College show comprised a who's who of civil rights leaders, from A. Philip Randolph of the Brotherhood of Sleeping Car Porters and Roy Wilkins of the NAACP to Martin Luther King Jr. and his chief confidante in the entertainment world, Harry Belafonte. For Odetta, it marked the first time that Belafonte enlisted her aid in the civil rights cause, something he would do repeatedly as both movements gathered force. "People had heard about this nappy headed little girl talking about the history," Odetta recalled. "They would call upon me to do benefits. So it was like we were all developing at the same time."[2]

In Odetta, Belafonte could hardly have found a better representative of the hopes and dreams of African Americans. Her queenly deportment, radiant smile, and Afro all exuded pride in race, while her mighty, impassioned singing evoked the soul-striving of her people and a clarion call for justice. If she was more likely to talk then about chain gang labor than to get on a box and demand rights for blacks, her very presence—and talent—made it harder to ignore the second-class status of America's Negroes.

That spring it was becoming clear to everyone paying attention to folk music that Odetta had assumed the mantle as its most inspirational figure. Not long before the Hunter College benefit, Odetta had taken the stage for the first time at New York's Town Hall on West Forty-Third Street, long one of the city's most important concert venues. Founded by suffragists, the fifteen-hundred-seat theater was the place where Margaret Sanger had once been arrested on stage for daring to discuss birth control and where Marian Anderson had made her New York debut while still barred by the Metropolitan Opera. More recently, it had played host to Duke Ellington, Mahalia Jackson, and Thelonious Monk.

In the reviews for the Town Hall show, one sees the mainstream press, while fumbling to describe Odetta in a white-centric way, nevertheless beginning to come to terms with her power and artistry, conveyed with increasing confidence on stage, and what she might mean for the emerging civil rights movement. "Odetta is a Negress who seems six-foot tall and has a baritone voice," wrote Jay S. Harrison, music editor for the *New York Herald Tribune*. "Her bearing is that of a princess, her manner that of an intensely devoted executant who has something to say and the wherewithal to say it." He continued:

> Bessie Smith and Lead Belly seem her closest models, and like them the sorrow of her race is in her voice; the protest too, at the misfortune of being ever in the minority, ever against the world. And the pride, also, that comes of physical strength and unashamed feeling. . . . Odetta . . . gave us the picture of a strong and indomitable people.[3]

Unfortunately, she had little time to bask in the attention just yet. The day of her Town Hall show, Riverside Records sued her in New York, in a companion action to Dean Gitter's lawsuit, over her failure to fulfill her recording contract. In the months since Gitter had sued Odetta, folk music had clearly taken off, and Riverside sensed an opportunity to cash in on the deal that it had made in good faith with Gitter. Calling Odetta "a singer of great and unusual talent" whose recording would be lucrative, Riverside was seeking $25,800 ($212,000 today) in damages and restitution.[4]

On the cusp of stardom, with her shows nationwide selling out and her records selling briskly, Odetta now found herself caught up in a legal battle pitting her against a record company and her former manager. The suits were certainly proof that the stakes in folk music were growing bigger every day. They would drag on for several years.

A week after getting served, Odetta returned to Chicago and tried to divert her attention by getting married. She'd only met Danny Gordon, a native of Queens, New York, seven months earlier while performing at Cosmo Alley, a new folk club in Los Angeles. Leo Vincent Daniel Gordon was a lithographer by trade, Odetta hazily recalled later, but his artwork doesn't seem to have made any lasting impressions on anyone.

A tall, handsome African American who possessed a silver tongue, Gordon introduced himself by telling Odetta that he loved music and that his two favorites were Frank Sinatra and Odetta. Danny and Odetta appear to have become quickly inseparable, and in the months before the marriage, Gordon, who was in the midst of finalizing a divorce, moved into Odetta's small apartment at 1252 North Wells Street on Chicago's Near North Side and started working for Albert Grossman, a job Odetta surely arranged for him. When they took their vows before Judge Abraham Lincoln Marovitz in Cook County on May 1, Danny was thirty-one, and Odetta, twenty-eight.

Gordon got decidedly mixed reviews from Odetta's friends, who knew she had a propensity to fall in love quickly. On the one hand, they found him quite charming. Selma Thaler described her initial impression of Danny as "very intelligent, very sensitive. He was bright . . . he was smart, he was with it." "He was a lot of fun and everybody loved him," Lesley Greening Taufer recalled. One can imagine Gordon saying all the right things to woo Odetta, who had been conditioned from the beginning to doubt her looks and self-worth.[5]

But Josh White Jr., who became a folk singer like his dad, immediately had doubts about Gordon's sincerity. "I think we were all a bit surprised when she got married," he said. "I don't know for some reason, if it was just me or others, didn't think it was going to last." And Peter Yarrow of Peter, Paul and Mary, who met Danny a bit later, smelled trouble. "I never had a good feeling about Danny Gordon," he recalled. "I felt that he was using her, that he was playing her, so to speak."[6]

Gordon often talked big, like the many times he showed up at the Greenings' home with his latest get-rich-quick idea. "One time he came to our house with a thing called a zoomer-ing that he found in China that was going to take over the world like the hula-hoop," Lesley Greening Taufer said. The fad never materialized. "He would come in with all sorts of schemes about how he was going to make a million," she added, "and I think that kind of did 'Detta in eventually, the schemes and her money disappearing and her money supporting him."[7]

The newlyweds decided they wouldn't mix business with pleasure, although it didn't quite work out that way. "If he managed me we'd have to break the contract or get a divorce," Odetta told an interviewer, "and I'd much rather stay married." A photo of the bride and bridegroom appearing in *Jet* magazine shows a beaming Odetta in a white dress and Danny in a dark suit and tie sharing a post-wedding toast with Al Grossman and Barbara Siegel, a publicist. Gordon has a cigarette in his left hand, which is around Siegel's shoulder. There was a reception that night, but with Odetta's increasingly loaded calendar, not a lot of time to enjoy their wedded bliss. "Congratulations and long life to Danny and Odetta on their marriage in Chicago," Izzy Young noted in his "Frets and Frails" column in *Sing Out!* "Shortly afterwards Odetta flew to Boston for a return engagement at Storyville."[8]

Odetta's music was beginning to exert a magnetic pull on those it touched. It had inspired Dave Van Ronk and Grace Slick, and brought Danny to her side, and it was Odetta's gigs at Storyville that year that convinced the jazz club's owner, George Wein, to create the Newport Folk Festival, the nation's premier folk gathering, in Rhode Island. "If I had to pick one person responsible for the establishment of the Newport Folk Festival in 1959, it would be Odetta," Wein recalled. "We had Sunday afternoon sets at Storyville in those days and I saw that hundreds of young people were filling the club, buying $1 ginger ales, just to hear this magnificent artist whose beauty and power of self-presentation reached deeply into their musical minds."[9]

Wein, a jazz pianist who ran the popular Newport Jazz Festival, had been unaware of what was taking place on Boston's college campuses, where excitement had been building over folk music. He had been planning to feature some folk artists at that year's jazz festival, but he realized folk was becoming a big enough draw to warrant a separate festival of its own.

Grossman had accompanied Odetta to her Storyville gigs, and during her shows, he and Wein discussed the folk scene. These conversations led Wein to tap Grossman to coproduce the festival with him. While in Boston, Grossman had also gone to a new folk club in Cambridge called Club 47, where he saw an eighteen-year-old Staten Island–born beauty named Joan Baez, who had also been inspired by Odetta, perform some of her first shows. He invited Baez to come to Chicago and sing at the Gate of Horn.

In mid-June, Baez appeared at the Gate, her first gigs outside Boston, with the *Chicago Tribune* calling her "a Mexican songstress with sad eyes, long tresses, and a steady guitar." At the club, Baez met Odetta for the first time, and her reaction says a lot about the almost spiritual force Odetta was beginning to exert on the younger generation of singers. "When I first met her, at the Gate of Horn in Chicago, my knees went to jelly, and that doesn't happen to me very often," Baez recalled.[10]

Baez, whose family moved around, depending on where her academic father was working, had discovered Odetta a few years earlier during high school in Palo Alto, California, shortly after hearing Belafonte and Pete Seeger. She'd grown up listening to the Negro spirituals her mother loved, particularly from Marian Anderson. But Odetta became her new "heroine," and she cut her teeth on songs from Odetta's two Tradition records, like "Oh, Freedom," "Another Man Done Gone," and "Lowlands."[11] Baez described their first meeting at the Gate—in rather colorful language:

> One night the Queen of Folk, Odetta, came to the club. I was a nervous wreck waiting to see her and was at the bar when I realized that she had arrived. . . . She was as big as a mountain and black as night. Her skin looked like velvet. She wore massive earrings that dangled and swung and flashed, and her dress looked like a flowing embroidered tent.[12]

Baez dealt with her nerves by bounding up to Odetta and singing a spot-on version of "Another Man Done Gone." "She looked surprised and then pleased, and then she enveloped me in her great velvet arms. I felt about six years old, and my heart didn't get back to normal for a week."[13]

When the Newport Folk Festival got underway a few weeks later, Odetta picked up Baez at her parents' house in Belmont, Massachusetts—Joan Senior had extracted a promise that Odetta would look after her little girl—and off they drove, with Danny behind the wheel and Bill Lee, Odetta's new bass player, in the back seat. The festival took place over two days, July 11–12, in Freebody Park, and it featured a mix of young urban folk singers like Bob Gibson and the Kingston Trio and traditional artists, including the bluegrass Stanley Brothers from Virginia and the blind gospel guitar virtuoso Reverend Gary Davis of South Carolina. In addition to concerts, there was a workshop and a seminar, where musicians and folklorists discussed musical origins and demonstrated performance styles.

Despite rain and fog, the turnout exceeded expectations. "Devotees of folk music are flying here from Florida, Tennessee and even as far as the West Coast," the *Newport Daily News* reported. "Odetta, the renowned California vocalist, is at the Hotel Viking," the newspaper noted. In the festival program, Seeger and Odetta got top billing, their two blurbs appearing together on the first page of artist bios. They also closed the Saturday night concert, with Odetta taking the stage right before Seeger and giving what Robert Shelton of the *New York Times* called "the crowning performance of the week-end."[14]

Odetta—or at least her music—became entangled in one of the event's minor contretemps, a debate about whether traditional artists were getting short shrift in favor of more popular urban folk song interpreters. At her concert, Odetta gave what Shelton called "a commanding performance" of "Another Man Done Gone," her a cappella showstopper. On Sunday morning, the folklorist and song collector Alan Lomax told the audience assembled for the seminar entitled "What Is Folk Music?": "Last night we heard Odetta sing 'Another Man Done Gone.' The woman from whom the song was collected lives in Alabama, her name is Vera Hall, and she's a dishwasher. She's the one we should be hearing." But others countered that not every traditional artist was necessarily ready to perform in a festival setting. "How do we know that Vera Hall could do as well here as she has recording in her own home?" the poet Langston Hughes, a member of the festival board, told a reporter.[15]

While it's probably true that Hall learned a good deal of her repertoire in her rural community and not from records and books, the line of demarcation between traditional musicians and folk song interpreters was fuzzy at best. Many of the celebrated prewar bluesmen, for instance, were well known in their communities for performing songs they'd heard on records or from other musicians who'd heard the records. Lomax himself had had to teach Lead Belly some of the songs for which he became famous, including "Take This Hammer." And Woody Guthrie's background had been a lot more middle class than many people assumed.

Debates about the relative authenticity of various folk singers would become an ongoing sideshow to the folk revival, and Odetta would remain a frequent target. The definitions of authenticity were always muddy, but often boiled down to geography and a kind of unspoken misery index. Odetta's operatic training and perfect diction certainly created the illusion of a middle-class childhood, far from the struggling communities that bred traditional artists, and her press materials, which tended toward the pretentious, didn't help. "A true artist, Odetta is a perfectionist and her own severist [*sic*] critic," read a typical early press release from Grossman's management firm.[16]

Her detractors, including the young Minnesotans who started the influential *Little Sandy Review* to critique the latest folk records, would seize on her presumed background and her seriousness as signs of inauthenticity. "One gets the feeling of an enormous dishonesty in all that this woman sings," it complained. "She doesn't really sing a song; she beats it to death with a club."[17]

But to her growing multitude of fans—and that would include most of the young folk singers who became stars during the next few years—Odetta practically walked on water. It began with Baez, who made her Newport debut that year singing duets with Bob Gibson. Odetta introduced Baez to other musicians and "was really my black angel," Baez recalled. She hoped some of Odetta's majesty would rub off on her. She copied Odetta's dangling earrings, and back at the Viking Hotel, she even tried to steal Odetta's leftover roast beef sandwich, which she spied on a tray outside her room. "I tried to eat her sandwich and the meat had gone bad. I guess I thought, *Ooohhh, Odetta's roast beef sandwich!*" Baez said.[18]

With Gibson at the festival's Sunday night concert, a barefoot and muddy Baez sang "Virgin Mary Had One Son" and "Jordan River" and launched her career. In addition to her precocious talent, Baez would offer the coming legions of young white folk fans a sex appeal that Odetta couldn't. George Wein noted Baez's "modest but alluring stage presence," and the press would brand her the "Barefoot Madonna." If Odetta was the reigning Queen of Folk, then Baez was now the Virgin Queen in waiting.[19]

In addition to Odetta and Baez, another big winner at the festival, which had attracted upward of fourteen thousand people—or, as one critic noted, "the impressive equivalent of between four and five sell-out concerts at Carnegie Hall"[20]—was Al Grossman, who had programmed the event and returned to Chicago with even more clout.

With Odetta's star rising, he would soon try to broaden his client roster beyond her and Bob Gibson.

———————

A few weeks after Newport, Odetta released *My Eyes Have Seen*, her first LP for her new label, Vanguard Records. Founded by two brothers in New York City, Seymour and Maynard Solomon, Vanguard had specialized in jazz and classical music early on but was increasingly making inroads into folk. The Solomons, reliable left-wingers, had recorded both Paul Robeson and the Weavers, even as the artists had continued to suffer the effects of the blacklist.

My Eyes was Odetta's first record with Bill Lee, a young jazz veteran from Georgia who would be her traveling companion for the next several years. The album also included the backing of a chorus on a few songs conducted by Milt Okun, who had already arranged music for Belafonte and would later create Peter, Paul and Mary's sound. While Vanguard was no Columbia or RCA in terms of its power in the industry, it was a definite step up from Tradition. Belafonte seemed determined to help Odetta achieve the stardom he thought she deserved. He wrote the liner notes and, in a signed introduction, paid tribute to his own musical debt to her: "Odetta is a vast influence on our cultural life. We are fortunate indeed in having such a woman in our musical world. Those of us who call ourselves artists can learn much from her strength, simplicity, warmth, humor and complete humanity."[21]

Like her Tradition records, *My Eyes* was a mix of spirituals, work and prison songs, ballads, and a children's song. It opened with "Poor Little Jesus," a traditional black spiritual, but one that Odetta slyly adapted to modern times. With the civil rights struggle in mind, she added a line that she knew would resonate with anyone sympathetic to the cause.

> *Poor little Jesus, mmmm-mmmm,*
> *Laid him in a manger, yes, my lord.*
> *Well, they couldn't find no hotel room . . .*

In Jesus's case, of course, the inn in Bethlehem was booked, not segregated, but the line was lost on no one. While it wasn't Odetta's style in those days to sing more overtly political material in the vein of "Strange Fruit"—and the blacklist remained, even without McCarthy—she found other ways to raise consciousness about the black struggle, particularly in her song choices. Of the thirteen tracks on the record, four were convict songs, including two Alan Lomax had collected from prisoners at the Mississippi State Penitentiary: "Jumpin' Judy" and "Bald Headed Woman," which Odetta sang a cappella, with just her hand claps, as she'd done on "Another Man Done Gone."

Her recording of "Water Boy" (paired with "I've Been Driving on Bald Mountain") became an instant classic of the folk era and was almost unrivaled in its power. She learned "Water Boy" from the singing of Robeson, who in the 1930s had gorgeously rendered the traditional work song in typical art song fashion to delicate piano accompaniment. In Odetta's hands, it reclaimed its dusty Southern roots, the staccato strums of her guitar mimicking a chopping pick-axe, her throaty growls evoking the raw desperation of a chain gang convict sweating up a thirst in the hot sun.

The record ended with Odetta's moving rendition of "Battle Hymn of the Republic," a song written to inspire Union troops during the Civil War. Once again, the subtext would be obvious, having a young black folk singer singing a patriotic (and apocalyptic) song evoking the battle to end slavery—and a none too subtle statement that the work of Lincoln remained unfinished.

The LP garnered stellar reviews, though one critic noted that Odetta's fame was still limited to the folk faithful, and "this exciting performer . . . certainly deserves a wider audience."[22] That was about to happen.

In late September and early October, Odetta sold out the Ash Grove, a new folk club in Los Angeles, night after night. Ed Pearl, who opened the club in an old furniture factory on Melrose Avenue the previous year, just as the Kingston Trio was hitting it big, had to expand from four to six nights to accommodate the huge crowds for her, which included, according to *Sing Out!*, "mink coats and high school kids alike, working folks and the white-collar crowd, with a heavy sprinkling of liberals and the intelligentsia."[23]

On the day of her first show, after Pearl welcomed Odetta, her mother, Flora, and an assistant to the club, he went home to be with his family. He returned about 6 p.m. and checked on Odetta in the dressing room. "The room was beautiful," he recalled with a laugh. "They put pictures up, they had mirrors up. All the dust had gotten probably [vacuumed up]. She put a really nice cover over the regular couch covers so it wouldn't have dust on it." It was just Odetta being Odetta. "I mean she was a diva," Pearl said. "She was not one of the gang folk singers. . . . She practiced to sing absolutely perfectly, you know just exactly the right thing."[24]

Whatever Odetta was doing, scales and all, was working, and excitement was mounting. She may have been secretly fighting off nerves and getting her hate out, but on stage she commanded her audiences, who found themselves swept away by her charm and the visceral power of her voice. "She had a way, after a song or set, of just lowering her head and looking up with the most extraordinarily beautiful smile, her eyes a melt of love as she looked out at the audience," Lynn Gold Chaiken recalled.

The reviews from the period—and indeed throughout her early career—were so positively over the top that they almost defy belief. "Odetta has such charm, such ease, such artistry and understanding," one reviewer wrote, "that you're held quite spellbound while she is performing, with no sense of lapse of time—just a mild sense of loss when she finally exits." When she took a side trip during her Ash Grove run to perform at the Museum of International Folk Art in Santa Fe, New Mexico, a review in the local paper carried the headline: "Odetta Captivates Audience, Makes You Glad to Be Alive."[25]

———

It was only a matter of time before prime-time television came calling. By November, Odetta had signed a contract with Harry Belafonte's production company to costar on a prime-time TV special called *Tonight with Belafonte*. Odetta was excited but unnerved by the invitation. "Suddenly there was a television offer and the frightening thought that millions would hear me," she said.[26]

When CBS and Revlon had approached Belafonte about hosting a variety show, they were in dire need of some good publicity. As the network and sponsor of *The $64,000 Question* and *The $64,000*

Challenge, both had been tarnished by the TV quiz show scandals, when it was revealed that contestants on some shows were fed answers or received easier questions in an effort to boost ratings. Television executives and sponsors, including Revlon founder Charles Revson, had been defending themselves in congressional hearings in October and November, and it was in that atmosphere that Revlon agreed to give Belafonte $200,000 ($1.7 million today) and complete creative control to produce what was reportedly the first prime-time TV special by a black production company. Spend what you want, Belafonte was told, and keep the rest.

"I started envisioning a portrait of Negro life in America told through music," Belafonte recalled. "What better way to promote understanding than with music that reached millions of Americans in sixty minutes?"[27] Belafonte, in addition to his hit albums, had become a Hollywood star, and he said it was assumed he would tap a black starlet like Lena Horne or Dorothy Dandridge, with whom he'd made three films, as his costar. He recalled what happened when he met with Revlon and CBS executives to tell them his plan for the show.

> When I put it together and sat before the supreme forces on Madison Avenue and they said, "Well, tell us, what will we see. Who will be with you?" and I said, "Well, first and foremost will be Odetta." And there was this moment of silence. And one of the principal forces said, "Excuse me, Harry, but what is an Odetta?" I said, "It is not a what. It is a human being. It's a she, it's a who." "And what does she sound like?" "Paul Robeson. Her voice is enormous. And the depth and range of it is never-ending." "Uh, huh," they said. "And what does she look like?" I said, "She's a Nubian Queen. She is the mother of history, of all of Africa. Her beauty reigns as supreme."[28]

And, as a final dagger to the cosmetics company, Belafonte said he added: "And there will be no need to make her up." It's a great line, and while the story was probably polished over time, the larger point is that Belafonte was set on making a statement to the nation about the black experience that was far removed from Hollywood, and Revlon and CBS had no veto over his choices.

Dandridge would certainly have been the safer pick. She was the nation's first black female movie star and sex symbol. Earlier in the year, Hollywood mogul Samuel Goldwyn's wife, Frances, had praised Dandridge's popularity with the white public as "very healthy. It makes our concept of beauty more interesting."[29] It was about to get even more so.

Odetta flew in from Chicago, and Belafonte put her up at the Beekman Tower Hotel at Forty-Ninth Street and First Avenue. During rehearsals at CBS, he told a TV critic for the *Daily News*, "It isn't enough just to parade a host of big names in front of a TV camera, all dressed up and set in a resplendent scene. It isn't enough if they don't have something worthwhile to say and entertaining to do."[30]

The one-hour show aired live at 8:30 p.m. on December 10, 1959, commercial-free other than two Revlon ads that bookended the production, and it was seen in living rooms that Thursday night from Boston to Biloxi, from San Francisco to Selma. The civil rights undercurrent was apparent from the start. It began with Belafonte, lithe and handsome in an open-collared shirt, singing "Bald Headed Woman," which he'd heard on Odetta's new record. Behind him in the shadows, muscled members of a chain gang moved in unison swinging imaginary hammers to the beat of what sounded like the cracking of a bullwhip. He then sang "Sylvie," a Lead Belly song he'd recorded about a man working in the field and asking his wife for water.

Next a lone spotlight shone on Odetta wearing a dark loose-fitting dress, and she began singing "Water Boy," or, rather, she unleashed it. Accompanying herself with her large National acoustic guitar, eyes closed, brows knitted in concentration, she brought the full tragedy and anger of chain gang life to bear.

> *There ain't no hammer*
> *On this mountain*
> *That ring like mine, boy*
> *That ring like mine*
> *I'm gonna whoop this rock, boy*
> *From here to the Macon*
> *All the way to the jail, boy*
> *All the way to the jail*

But there was something else. Near the end of the song, when she shouted "Water Boy!" in her huge, full contralto, in between whacks on her guitar, the camera pulled back, seeming to recoil from her strength. It was a mesmerizing performance, and one of the most memorable moments from the show. "Her presence was very strong and very charismatic," recalled Robert De Cormier, the show's musical director and Belafonte's longtime arranger.[31]

Other surprises awaited Americans who tuned in that night. An interracial group of children heard Belafonte sing one of Lead Belly's children's songs, "More Yet," and Odetta sing "Three Pigs." When Belafonte began "Pick a Bale of Cotton," another song associated with Lead Belly, he was surrounded by an interracial troupe of twenty-five dancers. One of TV's unwritten but widely accepted rules then forbade blacks and whites from performing together. Having black acts and white acts on a variety show was fine, but they had to be kept separate to appease stations in the South. "Revlon could not stand that, and I don't think CBS could either really," De Cormier said. "They tried to get Harry to make it all black, which they would have accepted. But they were really concerned about having blacks and whites together. But Harry absolutely refused to give in on it."[32]

There were other scenes of black life: Belafonte putting music to the Langston Hughes poem "I Wish the Rent Was Heaven Sent," the blues duo Brownie McGhee and Sonny Terry performing an instrumental dance tune; and Odetta singing the Negro spirituals "Joshua Fit De Battle of Jericho" and "Glory, Glory," the former backed by an interracial chorus. The show's unlikely hit, however, came from a nonsense song that was almost a throwaway: "Hole in the Bucket," about a man trying to get out of doing the chores. "It was just a simple kind of a riddle song that didn't have any power of melody and storytelling," Belafonte recalled. "It was so simple and so childlike in its content, yet when she and I did it—we did it on stage as well as in the show itself—audiences loved it. And I think it was what we brought to it that captured the audience's fancy."[33]

Reviewers loved the show, and most singled out Odetta. "Belafonte . . . introduced to network TV audiences the little-known folk singer Odetta," wrote Fred Danzig, the television reporter for United Press International. "Today, this woman must be regarded as a star."[34]

The black press could scarcely believe what Belafonte had pulled off on network television, a show in which whites and blacks stood side by side celebrating black America. Unsurprisingly, they too singled out Odetta's performance and what it meant for their race. "I hope you caught the hour-long spectacular on television last Thursday night when Harry Belafonte displayed his great showmanship . . . and introduced Odetta, who makes the Mahalias and the Rosettas get back," wrote L. I. Brockenbury in the *Los Angeles Sentinel*, referring to the gospel stars Mahalia Jackson and Sister Rosetta Tharpe. "Some people may not like her looks—her hair has never seen a hot comb, she has strictly African features," Brockenbury added. "But when she opens that mouth to sing, she is beautiful to these eyes. She should serve as an inspiration to all who would feel they can't get ahead because of their looks, the texture of their hair, or the color of their skin."[35]

It's hard to overemphasize how radical it was seeing a black woman with kinky hair on American television. It just didn't happen. Even the half dozen black women in the interracial troupe of dancers on the show all had straightened hair. "She was making a political social statement about black people," Belafonte recalled, looking back on the show at age ninety. Odetta "wasn't trying to compete with the culture of the day. She was saying something else altogether: 'My blackness unadorned is in itself its own adorning.'"

The black folk singer Jack Landrón, who began performing in the late 1950s as Jackie Washington, explained that in Odetta, blacks found someone who was not only supremely gifted but unafraid of her heritage. "You have to understand, there was never any particularly prideful thing about being black in America," he recalled. "You were a second-class citizen. You never opened up magazines or went to movies and saw yourself reflected in a positive way. The whole thing of straightening one's hair and wearing it in styles that was more like the women in the dominant culture or [the] men. Odetta was new."[36]

Odetta's appearance on the national scene would prompt soul-searching kitchen-table debates in black homes around the country, like those of Carlie Collins Tartakov, an education professor, remembered a pair of aunts having about Odetta's hair. One agreed with the long-accepted notion that it was "an embarrassment for us to let other people see us without some disguise on our hair." The other argued: "Wouldn't it be nice if we hadn't 'bought into' the Europeans [*sic*] conception of what is beautiful? If we could just wear our hair any way we wanted?"[37]

It wasn't only blacks, of course, who were thrown for a loop by Odetta's first star turn. Janis Fink, then nine years old and a few years away from becoming the precocious teenaged folk singer named Janis Ian, discovered Odetta that night in East Orange, New Jersey, and was forever changed. "I was taking a shower when I heard the most incredible voice coming from the living room," she recalled. "Throwing a towel around me, I raced out of the bathroom, yelling, 'Who is that? Who is that?' That's Odetta, my mom replied. I stared at the television screen. Even in black and white, she was absolutely beautiful. Dressed simply, with large hoop earrings framing her face, her hair in the first Afro I'd seen."[38]

After the show wrapped, Selma Thaler, along with her husband, Ed, who'd come to the studio for the taping, went with Odetta to the cast party at Belafonte's gorgeous apartment on Seventy-Fourth Street and West End Avenue, the same residence Belafonte and Martin Luther King Jr. would use as an unofficial New York headquarters for King's Southern Christian Leadership Conference in the coming civil rights fight. For most of the party, Thaler was blind as a bat, because her hard contact lenses had disappeared up under her eyelids, but she remembered the celebration as "thrilling" and said Odetta was very happy with her performance. The show had been a game changer, not only for American culture but for Odetta personally. As Charlie Rothschild recalled, "It catapulted her into another arena."[39]

The next morning, Odetta was getting into a taxi in Midtown Manhattan when she was intercepted by some fans who congratulated her on her performance and began peppering her with questions about her professional and private life. "I was in the spotlight and suddenly all I could think about was fleeing for privacy," she told a reporter soon after.[40] For Odetta, the push and pull of fame would be a constant struggle. Although she continued to claim fame didn't interest her, she still saved every news clipping about her that she could find and she would clearly enjoy the perquisites of celebrity: the limousines, the first-class hotels, the special treatment accorded to the famous. At the same time, she could feel overwhelmed by the attention, and her hermit side would force her to run for cover.

CHAPTER SEVEN

THAT LOVELY ODETTA . . . PLAYING A MURDERESS

A few days after her TV triumph, Odetta returned to Chicago, where Al Grossman had booked her again into his Gate of Horn for three weeks. Reservations poured in. Her record sales shot up. And Langston Hughes soon offered her a role in his new play, *Tambourines to Glory*, but she would ultimately have to decline. That's because a call came from Hollywood. Film producer Richard Zanuck had seen the Belafonte show, and from his office at 20th Century Fox had sent for a kinescope of the program. He would soon summon Odetta for a screen test for a new film called *Sanctuary*, based on the writing of William Faulkner.

While all this was going on, Odetta suddenly had a falling out with her biggest benefactor—Belafonte himself. "Something has just come to my attention which is hard for me to conceive," he began an angry letter to Odetta on December 16, 1959. It involved Miriam Makeba.[1]

Makeba, the young South African singer, had recently fled to the US after making an appearance in Lionel Rogosin's apartheid documentary *Come Back Africa*. Since then, Belafonte had helped Makeba escape a usurious contract she'd inked with her South African record company, giving it 65 percent of her earnings. And he'd also shamed Rogosin and Village Vanguard owner Max Gordon into ripping up a managerial contract they'd gotten her to sign only weeks earlier when she was appearing at the club. Belafonte had taken Makeba under his wing professionally, given her money and advice, and promised to help promote her.

Before Odetta had left New York and headed back to Chicago, she had invited Makeba to dinner and, without telling her, had brought along Al Grossman, who had made his own pitch to become her manager. Belafonte was furious. "I am left with no recourse but to let you know how terribly disappointed I was to know that you, too, were capable of precipitating the same kind of conduct of which I am sure, for many years, you have been the victim."[2]

It's not known to what extent Odetta knew of Grossman's intentions, but it's quite possible her involvement was innocent enough. Belafonte's protectiveness regarding Makeba, who would owe him a big debt for igniting her American career, is understandable given the racism and inequity he'd encountered in his own life. In hindsight, his indignation comes across as a bit idealistic, but honorable.

Yet an interesting side note comes from Makeba's own recollection of her arrival in the US and Belafonte's efforts to shape her for American audiences. Belafonte wanted her to get her hair straightened so he could present her as a pop chanteuse, she recalled in her autobiography. He arranged an appointment at a Harlem salon, but Makeba rejected her new hairdo and kept it short and kinky the way she'd always worn it back in Soweto. "This is not me. . . . I'm not a glamour girl," she said.[3] As Makeba's star rose, there were two prominent black female entertainers—one American, the other African—wearing natural hair, and others would soon follow.

The rift between Odetta and Belafonte didn't last long. Belafonte, in fact, had contracted for four more specials on CBS, and he wanted Odetta to appear with him again. But the two sides couldn't agree on terms, and the plan was scrapped. (So were all but one of the specials, after Revlon, bowing to complaints from Southern TV affiliates, asked Belafonte to do away with the interracial cast; he refused.)

Belafonte went on to win an Emmy for his performance in *Tonight with Belafonte*, the first black actor to take home the award. He and Odetta both received a Sylvania Award for the show. Given by Sylvania Electronics, then one of the top TV manufacturers, the award rivaled the prestige of the Emmys in the early days of television. However, when Odetta got word of her prize by mail during the third week of January 1960, a plain envelope arriving at her Near North Side apartment, she was affronted. "I was disappointed in the casual way I received the accolade," she told a reporter. "I had always dreamed of myself clad in a flowing gown, with a large orchestra playing suitable music as I walked down a long aisle for the presentation."[4]

As the new decade began, a slew of articles in newspapers and magazines touted the arrival of folk music as a genuine phenomenon. "Folk music is replacing rock and roll as the teenager's way of 'expressing himself,'" the *New York Herald Tribune* said. *Newsweek* noted that "it is not unusual to see artists like the Weavers, Theo Bikel, Pete Seeger, and Odetta fill halls with capacities of from 1,000 to 4,000."[5]

But Odetta's music wasn't getting played on the radio, something that would continue to plague her career. In March, Robert Shelton of the *New York Times* bemoaned the fact that while Belafonte and the Kingston Trio were getting plenty of the heavy rotation airplay that leads to hit records, Odetta was not. "Why is it that the most glorious new voice in American folk music is heard so rarely on the air? Odetta Felious Gordon, who calls herself Odetta, has a voice so large and a physical presence so commanding that recordings have yet to do her complete justice." One wonders why Grossman wasn't doing a better job promoting her to radio stations, though to be fair, the radio business at the time was highly corrupt and many well-deserving artists didn't get an honest shake. A House subcommittee at that very moment was conducting hearings on the under-the-table bribery of disc jockeys by big record companies in exchange for airplay, a practice known as payola. Shelton, meanwhile, observed that Odetta was "moving toward the heights of Negro song that have been scaled by Bessie Smith, Marian Anderson and Mahalia Jackson. Shouldn't the disc jockeys make a little time for her on their programs?"[6]

She fared better on television that year. On March 10, she appeared on NBC's *The Ford Show* starring Tennessee Ernie Ford. The title of the popular Thursday night variety program was a cute play on words since Ford Motor Company was the sponsor. (On Sunday nights, Chevrolet had to settle for *The Dinah Shore Chevy Show*.)

Odetta's appearance on *The Ford Show* was remarkable, though it's been overlooked in the annals of television. Just five weeks earlier, four students at North Carolina A&T, an all-black college, had staged a sit-in at a segregated lunch counter near the Greensboro campus, and their brave act of passive resistance not only had generated newspaper headlines and stories on the evening news but had also inspired sit-ins across the South in places like Nashville, Richmond, Atlanta, and Tallahassee. "It's important to remember that on February 1st of 1960, for all intents and purposes the civil rights movement began in Greensboro, North Carolina, when four men walked into the Woolworth's lunch counter and sat down," recalled Ernie Ford's son, Jeffrey Buckner "Buck" Ford. "And the next week there were more and the next week there were more and the next week there were more. This was a little more than one month away from Odetta guesting on *The Ford Show*."[7]

Ernie Ford and his wife, Betty, were big fans of Odetta's, having seen her perform in California shortly after the sit-ins began; Betty, more politically aware than her husband, had helped him understand the importance of having Odetta on his show at that singular moment. But when the show's producer, Cliffie Stone, and director, Bud Yorkin, presented the idea with the sit-ins gathering steam, it didn't sit well with the sponsor. Ernie Ford had shot to stardom when his cover of Merle Travis's "Sixteen Tons" topped the *Billboard* charts, but as a folksy Southerner who spoke in a countrified twang, Ford had crossover appeal. His show was as popular in Hattiesburg, Mississippi, and Lake Charles, Louisiana—the same kinds of markets that had complained about the racial content on Harry Belafonte's show—as it was in New York and Chicago.

"There was major objection, major resistance," Buck Ford said. "Ford Motor Company was at first unsure. It didn't take long, though, for somebody to convince them and to realize that this individual man is selling more freaking cars per week than your sales people that are working on the floor. And this [appearance] is happening, and this is a beautiful singer with a gorgeous voice."[8]

Ford didn't simply have Odetta on his show. As a white Southerner, he used her appearance to make an unambiguous statement to the nation about the civil rights struggle. He introduced her by telling his audience in his usual aww-shucks manner that her music was a welcome respite from the other sounds he'd been hearing on records (presumably rock 'n' roll), the "squealin' and skwawkin' and gruntin' and jumpin' up and down—it sounds like a lovesick hog in an empty pen."[9]

Odetta came on and sang with her eyes closed, as usual, beginning with the chain gang song "Another Man Done Gone," which must have reverberated quite differently for Mississippi viewers than for those in New York. Then, grabbing her guitar, she sang "Mule Skinner Blues," a tune well known to Southern audiences in versions by Jimmie Rodgers and Bill Monroe. When she finished, Ford joined her center stage, and that's when he took a stand. He grabbed Odetta by the hand, led her forward, held their clenched fingers aloft, and shook them in a display of solidarity as Odetta beamed, eyes twinkling. Then they sang two duets, on a medley of Woody Guthrie's "Pastures of Plenty" and Merle Travis's "Nine Pound Hammer" and on "I Was Born About 10,000 Years Ago," a bragging song Odetta and Larry Mohr had performed together back in her Tin Angel days. The interracial interplay was seen by millions.

Odetta returned later for the program's final segment, duetting with Ford on the hymn "What a Friend We Have in Jesus," backed by Ford's all-white choir. By the time the show ended and Ford gave his usual sendoff—"Good night and bless your little pea-pickin' hearts"—the pair had struck another blow on television for racial harmony.

Ford's stance was courageous, given that physical contact between blacks and whites on TV was just about as taboo as it had been a decade earlier when Sammy Davis Jr. had appeared on Eddie Cantor's *Colgate Comedy Hour*, and Cantor had wiped his guest's perspiring face with a handkerchief, which had led them both to receive a torrent of threatening hate mail. (And it would remain taboo eight years later when Petula Clark touched Harry Belafonte's arm on a prime-time special and caused a ruckus.)

Ford had featured the black singer and actress Ethel Waters on his show twice, when he'd also sung duets with her and grabbed her hand, but it had a much different feel. The gray-haired Waters had starred in a TV show portraying a mammy character named Beulah, so viewers would have associated her with the safety of the old social order, and her appearances had come before the civil rights movement had taken center stage. Odetta, on the other hand, was a young black woman with an Afro who sang about prisoners and chain gangs, as African Americans squared off with racist sheriff's departments over segregation.

As expected, Odetta's guest spot generated hate mail, but it died down pretty quickly, and, Buck Ford said, it made little difference to his father. He loved Odetta's music. "It was water off his back that somebody would tell him, 'You can't do this cuz, my God, Ford, she's a nigger!' It was about the music for him and he simply had never heard anything like her."[10]

The on-air chemistry between Ford and Odetta was genuine. After the live taping, Ernie and Betty Ford and Odetta retreated to the Fords' Hollywood home to watch the West Coast feed of the program. Once again, critics were quick to praise her performance. One noted that she "seems to have all the woes of all the downtrodden synthesized in her remarkable voice."[11]

———

Later that month, Vanguard released what would be the most overtly political album of Odetta's career, *Ballad for Americans*. The title number, which occupied all of side one, was a cantata composed by John La Touche and Earl Robinson and first made famous by Paul Robeson. It told the story of the nation from the Revolution through the Civil War, focusing on the ideals of freedom and liberty and what they meant for ordinary Americans—especially immigrants, women, and minorities. Robeson, taking the role of the singing narrator, first performed it on a CBS radio show in the fall of 1939 to huge acclaim, then recorded it for Victor Records and sang it in concerts around the US.

Debuting during the Great Depression and World War II, the piece melded the Popular Front emphasis on "the folk," with the patriotic fervor of a nation that would soon be at war against fascism. It was an unabashed celebration of the American experiment, but depending on one's political bent, it was also a none too subtle criticism that the United States hadn't lived up to the ideals laid out by the Founding

Fathers. It was so popular that during the 1940 presidential election, it was sung at both the Republican Party's and Communist Party's national conventions.

The idea of reprising Robeson's role must have enticed Odetta, who took it on at the suggestion of the Solomon brothers at Vanguard, according to Robert De Cormier, the musical director on the album. De Cormier directed the huge Symphony of the Air and an accompanying chorus, but Odetta was so nervous that she nearly scuttled the project. "I was frightened," she later recalled. "I'd sung with, at most, a string ensemble, but as those symphony men, about 100 of them, came into the studio with their instrument cases and took their places so solemnly and seriously, I thought I could never get up in front of them and sing. And as a matter of fact, I didn't."[12] When De Cormier saw Odetta shaking, he put a screen between her and the musicians so she couldn't see the orchestra, and she was able to continue.

The episode perfectly captured one of the chief contradictions in Odetta's story. Her self-doubt could be debilitating, but once she set her mind on performing, she projected incredible power and toughness. When she sang in the *Ballad*'s closing stanzas, "Our country's strong, our country's young and our bravest songs are still unsung, from her plains and mountains we have sprung to keep our faith with those who went before," no one listening could fail to hear this proud young black woman calling on Americans to uphold the promise of the Declaration of Independence that "all men are created equal."

On side two, she offered eight folk songs mostly in keeping with the same theme, including Woody Guthrie's "This Land is Your Land," a tune she would often tell concert audiences should be America's national anthem. However, she altered Guthrie's most famous line, singing "this land *belongs* to you and me" instead of "this land was made for you and me." It was a subtle change, but one she insisted on. "She thought it was arrogant to say this land was *made* for you and me," Selma Thaler recalled.[13]

The album was generally very well received, but the *Washington Post*'s jazz critic derided the record for its "liberal" message. The *Ballad*, however, did register with young idealistic folk fans. "During the early days of the civil rights movement, my friends and I used to sing it out loud on buses traveling to demonstrations," recalled Leda

Schubert, who was a fifteen-year-old living in Bethesda, Maryland, when she bought the record, shortly after it came out. She learned every word, she said, but didn't tell her parents, who'd owned the Robeson version, but had gotten rid of it during the witch hunts.[14]

On May 2, their rift behind them, Odetta, Harry Belafonte, and Miriam Makeba, who had declined to sign with Albert Grossman, teamed up for a benefit concert at Carnegie Hall. The show, which also included the Chad Mitchell Trio, raised money for the Wiltwyck School for Boys in Esopus, New York, a residential school for children with emotional and behavioral problems—"juvenile delinquents," in the dismissive parlance of the day—most of them from black and Hispanic families. It was a favorite charity of Eleanor Roosevelt, and she probably enlisted Belafonte's aid for the school.

RCA recorded the concert and released it as *Belafonte Returns to Carnegie Hall*. Odetta and Belafonte's performance of "Hole in the Bucket" was released as a single abroad and provided Odetta with a great deal of exposure around the world. It wasn't released in the US, probably because Odetta remained under contract to Vanguard—a shame since it wound up the most popular single of her career. RCA producer Bob Bollard, who worked closely with Belafonte, soon began trying to woo Odetta away from Vanguard.

The Carnegie Hall concert served as a dress rehearsal for Odetta's solo debut at Carnegie Hall just six days later. That performance benefited the Church of the Master in Harlem at 122nd Street, an integrated Presbyterian congregation that ran a community center, mental health clinic, and two children's camps. Odetta would perform hundreds of benefits over the years for causes that she believed in. Like her Town Hall show, this one proved, as if any more proof were needed, that she had ascended to the heights of folk music.

The civil rights movement, which had struggled since the Montgomery bus boycott almost five years earlier to gain traction in the American psyche, had by then taken a dramatic turn. With the sit-ins continuing, Martin Luther King Jr. had met with students to strategize, leading to the creation of the Student Nonviolent Coordinating Committee (SNCC), which would add youthful energy and daring to the movement and play a major role in the segregation and voting rights battles to come. King had resigned his pastorship at Dexter Avenue Baptist Church in Montgomery, Alabama, to focus his energies full-time on the Southern Christian Leadership Conference and the fight for civil rights.

But Southern leaders weren't about to give up Jim Crow without a fight. In Alabama, King had been indicted on what his supporters viewed as a trumped-up charge of perjuring himself on his state income tax, and a group calling itself the Committee to Defend Martin Luther King and the Struggle for Freedom in the South, chaired by A. Philip Randolph, had met at Belafonte's apartment to come up with a plan to raise money and awareness.

The group took out a full-page ad in the *New York Times* entitled "Heed Their Rising Voices"—also the headline of a recent *Times* editorial—denouncing violence and intimidation against civil rights leaders and students engaged in sit-ins and asking for donations to the cause and to King's defense. Noting that students had faced tear gas and fire hoses in Orangeburg, South Carolina; school expulsion in Montgomery, Alabama; and other abuses in a host of other Southern cities, the ad called on the nation to get off the sidelines and act. "Decent-minded Americans cannot help but applaud the creative daring of the students and the quiet heroism of Dr. King," the ad said. "But this is one of those moments in the stormy history of Freedom when men and women of good will must do more than applaud the rising-to-glory of others."[15]

On May 17, the sixth anniversary of *Brown v. Board of Education*, the committee organized two rallies and a fund-raising concert in New York with a number of stars on hand, including Odetta, Maya Angelou, Ossie Davis, Ruby Dee, and Sidney Poitier. The day began with about 400 people, including 150 students, taking a Circle Line boat from South Ferry to Liberty Island and the base of the Statue of Liberty. "This ceremony paying tribute to the Statue of Liberty is our way of re-affirming our faith in our country," Belafonte told the throng.[16]

After Belafonte sang "The Star-Spangled Banner," a Catholic priest, a protestant minister, and a rabbi all offered prayers. A student in a neat brown suit named Bernard Lee, who had been expelled from

Alabama State College for leading a sit-in at a snack bar in the Montgomery courthouse, read a proclamation as others laid bouquets and wreaths before Lady Liberty, a message of both hope and mourning for freedoms unrealized. "The colored people are neither bitter nor discouraged," Lee said. "We have faith in ourselves and a positive estimate for achieving our full status as American citizens under the republic."[17] A reporter for the *New Yorker* described what came next:

> Then the students filed up the steps to the ramp of the Statue of Liberty while Odetta—a large, solid black woman with close-cropped hair, as imposing and monumental herself as a statue—sang, "Oh, Freedom," a folk song that the Negro students from the South have been singing during their demonstrations. She stood with her eyes closed, singing very softly.[18]

On the boat back to Manhattan, the magazine noted, "the students—white and colored, from North and South—gathered in a group and sang the same song: 'I'm on my way/And I won't turn back.'"[19] Actually, what they were singing was the third portion of Odetta's "Freedom Trilogy," the rousing finale which served notice that a people still in fetters wouldn't stop until they were free.

A freedom rally sponsored by several labor groups, including the AFL-CIO, followed at noon and attracted thousands in the city's Garment District. Then a three-hour benefit performance was held that night by a mix of Hollywood and music stars, including Dorothy Dandridge, Alan King, Abbey Lincoln, Sidney Poitier, Sarah Vaughan, and Odetta at the Harlem 369th Regiment Armory, home of the segregated Harlem Hellfighters during World War I. Dandridge, one the show's emcees, introduced Odetta to the more than fifteen thousand in the crowd "as the number one female folk singer in the U.S.," one of the city's black papers, the *New Amsterdam News*, reported. "She proved it with selections that had the audience alternately in rapt silence and at other times clapping in spontaneous rhythm."[20]

The show raised ten thousand dollars for the defense of King, who had been scheduled to attend but instead had to appear in court in Montgomery. (In one of the few hopeful signs out of the South, an all-white jury would shockingly acquit him of his perjury charge later that month.) Just as importantly, the day's events had shown civil rights leaders the power of celebrity in bringing attention to their cause. Both the *New York Times* and Hearst newsreels had covered some of the events, and King and Belafonte absorbed the lesson.

Around the same time, with songs of freedom and the stirring of the civil rights movement ringing in her ears, Odetta flew to Los Angeles to audition for *Sanctuary*. A costume designer met her plane at LAX and took her directly to Western Costume on Melrose Avenue for a fitting. It was a taste of things to come. If Odetta wanted a movie career, she would have to conform to Hollywood's vision of the black experience, something she'd decried as a child and, she would find out, hadn't changed much in two decades. "When I got there," she recalled, "we went into this room . . . and this man started putting all these dumpy clothes on me. Then I thought *'Detta it's just a part.* Then one time, he put a sweater on me and he reached up and tore the sleeve down. I said, 'Now, you may make me raggedy, but you're not going to make me dirty.'"[21]

Thusly adorned, she did her screen test for the film's coproducers, Richard Zanuck and his movie mogul father, Darryl. It didn't go well, she recalled. Perhaps nerves or shyness played a role or those old feelings of humiliation had resurfaced. But it didn't matter. She got the part anyway. "You had this quality of transmitting the compassion you feel to the listener," Darryl Zanuck told her, perhaps chomping on one of his ubiquitous cigars. She would be portraying Nancy Mannigoe, a black, drug-addicted servant convicted of killing the child of her white employer, Temple Drake, in a screen adaptation of a couple of Faulkner tales—*Sanctuary* and *Requiem for a Nun*—set in the fictional Yoknapatawpha County, Mississippi. The gossip columnist Hedda Hopper summed up the irony of it all: "Richard Zanuck has that lovely Odetta, Negro folk singer, playing a murderess in 'Sanctuary.'"[22]

In late July, Odetta moved into the Chateau Marmont, the gothic fortress of a hotel on Los Angeles's Sunset Strip, to begin filming. From the start, the production was beset by tensions. Part of the behind-the-scenes drama arose from trying to satisfy studio censors with Faulkner's pulp fiction tale of a Mississippi debutante's kidnapping, descent into debauchery, and struggle to return to a more conventional life. Faulkner had written the novel *Sanctuary* for a quick paycheck during the Depression, and he produced, he said, "the most horrific tale" he could imagine, one involving rape, murder, prostitution, bootlegging, and voyeurism. A screen adaptation in the 1930s had been a catalyst for the infamous Motion Picture Production Code, and while the code by 1960 was seen to be on the wane, censors still held enormous sway over scripts and storyboards. "The simple truth was that under the then conditions . . . it was idiotic to have even considered making *Sanctuary*," the film's British director, Terry Richardson, recalled three decades later. "Now it might make a great movie, but at that time all that was vital had to be removed from the story."[23]

There was also reported turmoil involving the stars—the lusty Frenchman Yves Montand, Lee Remick, and Odetta—the kind that Hollywood gossip columnists loved to fuel. "They slammed the 'Sanctuary' set shut," the *Hollywood Reporter* dished later in the summer. "Yves Montand discovered he's playing third fiddle to Lee Remick & Odetta. Despite Montand's demands, script stays." Other reports said Odetta "spiraled from featured to fourth-star billing" and got an air-conditioned trailer like Remick's.[24]

The convoluted plot, involving composite characters, flashbacks, and other contrivances, is too complicated to summarize here, but Odetta's Nancy wasn't exactly the kind of role for which black actors and civil rights groups had long been campaigning. Blacks in Hollywood had been trying for decades to move beyond stereotypical roles as maids, butlers, and Stepin Fetchit–style dimwits. Sidney Poitier had probably managed this better than anyone, portraying a doctor, priest, and student in his 1950s films, although not without criticism that he was just the kind of conservative, self-contained black man that America could cotton to. The 1959 film *Porgy and Bess* had given blacks hope that a new era had begun in Hollywood. The black cast, led by Poitier, Sammy Davis Jr., and Pearl Bailey, had worked diligently behind the scenes to expunge racist dialogue, costuming, and characters. After its release, the *Chicago Defender* had pronounced the film "the Emancipation Proclamation of the Negro artist in quest of equality in Hollywood."[25]

But despite that hopeful assessment, good roles for African Americans remained the exception and not the rule in 1960. So if she wanted to break into film acting, Odetta had little choice but to work within the confines of the script. Her Nancy, a servant who had once been a drug addict, is condemned to die for murdering the baby son of Remick's Temple Drake to save the young married woman—and the baby—from returning to a morally bankrupt life with a French Creole bootlegger named Candy Man, played by Montand. That Nancy considers the death of an innocent baby a necessary evil to help Temple is hard to swallow—although it's straight out of Faulkner—but Odetta made the most of it. She managed to imbue Nancy with a quiet strength and nobility, and she winds up as the film's moral center.

When the film debuted early the following year, there were signs even then that Odetta, who had devoted her career to educating audiences about the *real* lives of African Americans, wasn't thrilled with the finished product. She asked 20th Century Fox to "tone down" the publicity about her, according to one report in the black press, saying, "For my first picture, I'd like my acting to speak for itself." Movie stills issued by the studio showed her attired in various maid and servant costumes, and one can almost sense her discomfort with the whole premise; in one particular shot, however, in which she waits on guests at one of Candy Man's swanky affairs, she manages an ironic half-smile. Many years later, she was more explicit in her criticism. "I would not do that film today," she said. "In this film, this black woman kills a child and gives up her life in order to save somebody's marriage. I could never do that again, never. My servant, she would die for me. Uh-huh."[26]

The critics mostly savaged *Sanctuary*. "The film dissolved into just another jugful of Hollywood's standard Southern Discomfort," *Time* said. "Zanuck's attempt to clean up Faulkner for the family seems a bit like trying to smear the whole of Yoknapatawpha County with underarm deodorant." But many singled out Odetta's acting, some even predicting an Oscar nomination. "The only admirable performance is given, with mahogany strength and beauty, by a Negro actress and singer named Odetta," the *New Republic* said. "Because of her impressive performance in the movie *Sanctuary*, folk singer Odetta is slated for more movie roles that will be exceedingly larger in scope," the *Chicago Defender* reported, although it offered no evidence to back up the claim.[27]

When she wasn't filming, Odetta had seemed to enjoy being back in Los Angeles, this time living like a Hollywood celebrity. The Chateau Marmont was always a scene, and she'd also spent time at Johnson's Bath House on Western Avenue, a spa that pampered black A-listers like Ray Charles, Dorothy Dandridge, and Willie Mays. She didn't completely neglect her singing career, though. In early October, she did a week at the Ash Grove, supported by a little-known folk singer named Peter Yarrow, doing his first club date outside of Greenwich Village. Yarrow, who'd been an art student at the High School of Music and Art in New York, had fallen under Odetta's spell and aimed to show her how smitten he was. "I made her a pair of earrings. I was in love with her heart, her soul. And they were big silver . . . and they looked so beautiful on her. And she tried them on and it started a friendship."[28]

By the time they met, they already shared a manager. Al Grossman had seen Yarrow perform that summer on a CBS television show called *Folk Sound U.S.A.*, the first TV folk spectacular if you didn't count Harry Belafonte's show, and offered to take on Yarrow, who didn't think he could do much better than having Odetta's manager on his team. "He was managing her at the time that he asked me if I would like to have him manage me," Yarrow said. "She was the queen. And we always called her the Queen of Folk Music."[29] Grossman would soon hatch the idea to build a hip trio around Yarrow, one that could capture the nation's attention—and rack up sales—like the Kingston Trio and the Weavers.

While Odetta and Yarrow were sharing a bill at the Ash Grove, Joan Baez's first album debuted on Vanguard—the label of Odetta and the Weavers—though Baez could have gone with a more commercial outfit like Columbia. *Joan Baez* would rise to number twenty on the *Billboard* charts, the first of her many hit records. "Manny and his brother were on the ball, but the shipping department wasn't quite together," Odetta recalled of the Solomon brothers who ran Vanguard, comparing her own records to Baez's. "Once she recorded for Vanguard, there was a backlog already before the record was out. They had to get off their duffs and get them out. The thing was that

along with the gorgeous voice, that she has that young pure looking white girl look, so of course, the whole industry and the rest of
the country would go along with that. But it's not like they put their
[praise] into something mediocre, she was splendid."[30]

Grossman had already made an aggressively seductive pitch to
manage Baez—famously telling her "you can have anything you want,
you can have any*body* you want"[31]—but he lost that particular sweep-
stakes to the low-key but earnest Boston concert promoter Manny
Greenhill, who fitted better with Baez's pacifist-humanist political
agenda and aversion to big business.

Seeing his future in the nexus of coffeehouses and record companies in New York, Grossman had sold his stake in the Gate of Horn
and decamped there, setting up an office at George Wein's Central
Park West apartment while Odetta was busy in Los Angeles for several months. It's hard not to see the significance in the move, given
that Odetta had chosen Chicago as her base after Grossman had become her manager.

But Danny Gordon and Odetta had plans of their own. In October, they announced they'd formed Dandetta Productions with the
goal of making movies and managing singers. According to a letter
from her attorney, they were dividing stock in the company equally
between them, although Odetta surely put up most of the money.
Danny was president, and a report in *Variety* named Grossman as a
vice president, but it's not clear whether he really had a formal posi-
tion in the company.

Although some of the details remain opaque, what's certain is that
despite vowing not to mix business with pleasure, Odetta and Danny
had decided to do just that. While Grossman nominally remained
Odetta's manager, Danny, who had little experience in the business,
took on a greater role in guiding her career.

He was probably responsible for floating items with gossip columnists that Dandetta would soon film *The Bessie Smith Story*, with
Odetta playing the lead. It makes sense that, having soured on her
first Hollywood experience, Odetta would want to assume creative
control over her future films. Disgusted with his own film choices,
Harry Belafonte had recently formed Harbel Productions for the same
reason. "I was tired of fighting Hollywood," he said.[32] But Belafonte,

who had more clout in the industry than Odetta, found that going it alone was far from easy, and his film career would soon stall.

Portraying Bessie Smith, who's generally considered the greatest blues singer of all time, would certainly give Odetta a meatier role than she was likely to get then from a Hollywood producer. There's no evidence, however, that Danny did much more than float the idea of a Bessie Smith film and announce that a script was in the works, as if that would bring, out of the woodwork, financial backers and a studio green light. Ash Grove owner Ed Pearl met Danny during this time and, like many of Odetta's friends, came away uneasy. "I did have a suspicion that he was taking her for money, that he was exploiting her for money . . . because he kind of talked like a city slicker," Pearl said.[33]

But the movie proposal marked a career-long fascination—obsession may be a better word—for Odetta with Bessie Smith. Reviewers had been comparing her to the prewar blues queen since she first walked on stage at the Tin Angel. But, more than that, there was something about Smith and other classic blues singers like Ma Rainey, their unrestrained sexuality and gutbucket lifestyles, that seemed to represent some kind of wish fulfillment on the part of the refined and proper Odetta. "I want to learn the freedom that Ma Rainey had in singing the blues," she told a reporter some years later, but she could just as easily have been talking about Bessie.[34]

While she waited in vain for the Bessie Smith movie to get made, her singing career continued to prosper—and intersect with the unfolding civil rights crusade. In November, when Ruby Bridges and three other little black girls in New Orleans attempted to integrate whites-only elementary schools six years after *Brown v. Board of Education*, they were met with hostile crowds that taunted and threatened them. US marshals were called in to escort the girls inside. As the events played out in front of the nation's eyes, Odetta appeared on *Jazz with Father O'Connor*, a TV show on WGBH in Boston hosted by Father Norman O'Connor, a Catholic chaplain at Boston University nicknamed "the jazz priest."

O'Connor asked Odetta to sing a song that could be dedicated to the girls riding in US marshals' cars to school. "The song was 'He's Got the Whole World in His Hands,'" O'Connor recalled. "Midway, tears started to fall down the brown face of Odetta, and for a minute I thought the program, which had 10 minutes to go, was quickly coming to an end." Odetta continued, he said, "but the tears kept falling." And when it was over, viewers phoned the station to find out what was going on. "Nothing more than a warm, intense woman," O'Connor told them, "feeling strongly about some children on their way to school."[35]

By Christmas, Vanguard released *Odetta Sings Christmas Spirituals*, which she'd recorded in New York in July before heading to the West Coast. Once again, she used her musical platform to promote black self-respect. It started with the cover, which Odetta insisted depict an image of a black Madonna and child. The idea of blacks reinterpreting the Bible to lift racial pride had gained currency in the black American Methodist Episcopal church before the turn of the twentieth century, when Bishop Henry McNeal Turner had declared, "We have as much right biblically and otherwise to believe that God is a Negro, as you . . . white people have to believe that god is a fine looking, symmetrical and ornamented white man."[36] By the 1920s, Marcus Garvey and his Universal Negro Improvement Association were leading a charge to convince blacks to tear pictures of white Madonnas and white Jesuses off the walls of their homes and replace them with Negro versions, and many blacks did.

For Odetta, who'd made racial pride of appearance so important to her image, the idea was perfectly in keeping with her goals. Recalling her mind-set in general for the LP, she said: "When we did the *Christmas Spirituals* record, it was time to make the point that there are things outside of what we've been told and taught."[37] Finding a black Madonna proved difficult however. Maynard Solomon spent four hours at the New York Public Library looking for options to no avail. After considering and rejecting several Madonnas, they appear to have decided to create their own. Using a photo of the gothic sculpture Nostre Damme de Grasse from a French art museum, they reproduced the image with a bronze tint in black and white, obscuring the baby Jesus's ruddy cheeks and giving him a decidedly African cast.

Odetta carefully chose thirteen Negro spirituals, once again with an eye toward messages that would resonate amid the conflict unfolding in the South. The song "Rise Up Shepherd and Follow" was originally a plantation song sung by slaves, who well knew, even if their masters didn't, the meaning of "there's a star in the East on Christmas morn; rise up shepherd and follow." When Odetta sang "If Anybody Asks You," the meaning was clear: "If anybody asks you who you are, you tell them you're the child of God." She also re-recorded "Poor Little Jesus," once again inserting the line about segregated hotel rooms.

Odetta concluded a whirlwind year by appearing Christmas night on the *Ed Sullivan Show*. Sullivan was known in the industry for supporting black acts, and he made no exception for Odetta. Joining her on stage to introduce her, he grasped her hands in his and held them tightly, saying, "You know her from her albums. This is Odetta and she's going to sing two reverent Christmas songs." She performed "Shout for Joy" with only her hand clap, and Bill Lee's bass from offstage, as accompaniment. Then she grabbed "Baby," her acoustic guitar, pulled the strap over her head, and sang "Poor Little Jesus," including her lamentation that Jesus's family "couldn't find no hotel room," as the camera zoomed in on her face deep in concentration. That subtle but unmistakable comment about black civil rights was heard in prime time, in homes all over America.

It's not known whether her appearance led to any repercussions from Southern affiliates. In any event, as the civil rights movement gained momentum, images on television continued to be crucial in raising the consciousness of a nation contemplating the role of African Americans in society. Documenting segregation and the fight to end it was of course one vital thread in advancing the cause of civil rights, and the other was the mainstreaming of white acceptance of black culture and identity. In that role, Odetta continued to be a pioneer.

CHAPTER EIGHT

ENTER BOB DYLAN

In January of 1961, nineteen-year-old Bob Dylan arrived in New York City from Minnesota in the back seat of a Chevy Impala to fulfill his destiny as the greatest musical poet of his generation. He went to meet his idol, Woody Guthrie, by then suffering mightily from Huntington's disease and languishing at Greystone Hospital in New Jersey. If Guthrie was Dylan's present obsession, though, it was Odetta who had set him on his path.

Shortly before matriculating at the University of Minnesota, Dylan had unslicked his pompadour and traded in his rock 'n' roll electric guitar for an acoustic after hearing Odetta's *Ballads and Blues* album in a record store in Hibbing. "The first thing that turned me on to folk singing was Odetta," he recalled. "I heard a record of hers in a record store, back when you could listen to records right there in the store. . . . Right then and there, I went out and traded my electric guitar and amplifier for an acoustical guitar, a flat-top Gibson."[1] Dylan expanded on that first encounter in another interview:

What I was looking for were folk music records and the first one I saw was Odetta on the Tradition label. I went into the listening booth to hear it. Odetta was great. I had never heard of her until then. She was a deep singer, powerful strumming and a hammering-on style of playing. I learned almost every song off the record, right then and there, even borrowing the hammering-on style.[2]

As one of his biographers told it, he appeared completely changed by the experience, according to one of his old friends, John Bucklen: "Bob had become an apostle of a woman named Odetta. . . . For hours on end he rhapsodized about her earthy style, dropping her mysterious name as if she were an intimate acquaintance. Bucklen listened to Bobby strum through tunes like 'Mule Skinner,' 'Jack O' Diamonds,' 'Water Boy,' and ''Buked and Scorned,' equally fascinated by their beautiful melodies and 'the intellect of the songs.'"[3]

After building up a repertoire by listening to Odetta, Harry Belafonte, and Guthrie, Dylan sought Odetta's approval for his still-ripening artistry, by now a rite of passage for young folk singers. At some point, Dylan, before leaving Minnesota, had given a tape to his friend the blues singer John Koerner to pass on to Odetta at the Gate of Horn. Then, when Odetta was in Minneapolis, friends brought Dylan to sing for Odetta, either at a local café called the 10 O'Clock Scholar or at an after-concert get-together at a Minneapolis apartment, depending on who is telling the story. Most of Dylan's biographers put this meeting sometime in 1960, but it probably happened in May of 1961 when Odetta gave a concert at St. Paul Auditorium, her first appearance in the Twin Cities, at the same time Dylan was back home from New York visiting friends. He performed for Odetta, and she told him he had a chance to make it in folk music. "It was a big deal at the time," recalled Jahanara Romney, Dylan's then-girlfriend, whose given name was Bonnie Jean Boettcher (aka the actress Bonnie Beecher). "He was our friend, and Odetta was somebody we worshipped and adored from afar."[4]

Dylan would waste little time in 1961 making a name for himself in New York, and by the end of the year, he had a Columbia record deal and the attentions of the man who would soon become his manager: Albert Grossman. Dylan's fame outside Greenwich Village built slowly. In the meantime, Odetta remained folk music's queen, and with the release of *Sanctuary* in February 1961, her star continued to rise.

Her concerts became events. When she appeared again at Town Hall in New York in March, to provide what *Times* critic Robert Shelton called "the intense and heroic music-making that listeners have come to expect from Odetta," the program noted that her movie and TV work "have brought her to the largest audiences she has enjoyed. She has become one of the major concert attractions in the country, appearing in colleges, concert halls and summer music festivals throughout the United States and Canada."[5]

If the hype almost seemed hard to believe sometimes, those who attended some of her big concert hall shows in New York around then recall an almost rapturous embrace by Odetta's largely white audiences, put under a spell by her ability to embrace the characters she was singing about—and by the civil rights undercurrent to her act. Selma Thaler's daughter, Carrie Thaler, who was just a young child then, remained in disbelief when recalling what she had seen more than forty years ago. It wasn't just Odetta's artistic brilliance, but the metamorphosis she underwent to become the magnetic Odetta on stage that was hard to grasp:

> You know, the folk song would be about a broken-hearted lover and you could just see the people, whether they'd be Irish or from the islands or whatever, she just became that person, with dialect, body language and just something spiritual that happened. And there was an amazing transformation that would happen over the course of an Odetta concert and the audience just became transfixed and in love. . . . And then we'd go backstage and there would be 'Detta and I thought, *How could this be the same person?* I never could figure it out.[6]

The bluesman Guy Davis, son of Ossie Davis and Ruby Dee, also retained vivid memories of the spectacle at Odetta's big shows. "I remember her short Afro, I remember her pounding on the side of the guitar," Davis said. "I mostly remember after the event, when there were a lot of lights. We were in a really open area and a lot of people were around Odetta, and trying to be next to her, be near her and talk to her. . . . I just remember the crush of people trying to see her."[7]

Having grown up feeling marginalized, Odetta could perhaps be forgiven if she started putting on a few airs to befit "the great folk singer" and costar of *Sanctuary.* Some of Odetta's friends noticed the change. "As she grew more famous," Jo Mapes recalled, "she would become very noble and very serious and sometimes she would walk in or meet some new people I'd introduce her to, who would be awed by her, so she would be as awesome as possible."[8] Mapes, who by then had become a folk singer with a soprano that some compared with Joan Baez's, decided to use humor to try to bring Odetta back down to earth. "I used to call her Ophelia, which irked her at times. . . . I started teasing her once when she began to believe the grandness that was being spoken about her." Other times Mapes would change the words to one of Odetta's most solemn tunes, the traditional lullaby "Hush Little Baby":

Hush little baby don't say a word,
Papa's gonna buy you a mockingbird
And if that mockingbird don't sing,
Papa's gonna buy you a diamond ring

The third stanza went: "And if that diamond ring turns brass, Papa's gonna buy you a looking glass," but Mapes would jump in and ruin it. "I would zap her. . . . She would stop and sort of tense herself for what she was afraid was coming and that was the line I was gonna sing: 'Mama's gonna shove it up the jeweler's ass.'"

As much as a part of her wanted fame, Odetta struggled with the demands and media glare that came with it. Vivienne Muhling, then a concert promoter in Canada, had twice booked Odetta to sing at Eaton Auditorium in Toronto, and the two had been friendly. But things changed when Odetta arrived for a third concert at Eaton in the spring of 1961. "It was just after she made a film, which got her feeling that she was on the way to international [acclaim]," Muhling said. "And she came with an assistant, a maid or something the third time. And she really had lost her way as a human being." 20th Century Fox had arranged with Muhling to host a party to call attention to both the film and concert, and Odetta flat out wouldn't cooperate. "She got on her high horse and refused to go. She said no she was just going to do her concert, forgetting that she normally did publicity and media and all that, you know. . . . And it was quite unpleasant." Odetta may have bristled at the idea of promoting a film she secretly loathed. A year later, she apologized to Muhling, and they resumed their friendship.[9]

In May, on their second anniversary, Odetta and Danny finally took a proper honeymoon, in Mexico, where, to Odetta's displeasure, he put bullfights on their itinerary.

When Odetta landed back in Chicago, a script was waiting for her in the mail for the popular TV western *Have Gun—Will Travel*. As America moved further from its rural roots and embraced an urban and suburban lifestyle in the 1950s and early 1960s, westerns dominated the TV dial. It might seem like a contradiction, but it made perfect sense. The rough-hewn pioneer spirit of the younger nation had given way to a dreary conformity, with Madison Avenue holding sway over how people dressed, the cars they coveted, and the cigarette brands they craved. The family and company man, like the besuited Jim Anderson on *Father Knows Best*, became the model of 1950s manhood, and westerns, in addition to being very entertaining, offered a counterweight. Men needed an escape valve and an outlet for their repressed machismo, and brave, individualistic heroes like *The Rifleman*'s Lucas McCain and *Gunsmoke*'s Matt Dillon (one of the supposed inspirations for Bobby Zimmerman's nom de guerre, Bob Dillon, which he later tweaked to Dylan) drew legions of fans.[10]

It didn't hurt the genre that the US was locked in a bitter Cold War against the Soviets. Westerns presented an idealistic vision of America as a land where hard work, individualism, and integrity won the day and where good prevailed over evil because of the courage, strength, and unbending morality of rugged American men. Since westerns were set in a mythical nineteenth-century past, even a bit of racial tolerance or empathy was thrown in—occasionally. There were plenty of screaming, whooping, more or less cardboard Indian savages, but also a few Indian characters who elicited genuine sympathy because of ill treatment at the hands of white settlers. The same was true for Mexicans and Chinese, two other minorities who had significant roles in the real American West. Focusing on these ethnic groups in the setting of America's frontier history allowed shows to tackle the issue of racial intolerance without offending Southern stations, which would often refuse to run shows that broached the topic more directly.

Blacks, of course, played a prominent part in the saga of the West, but on TV they appeared only now and then in the saloons, corrals, trading posts, and one-horse towns where the stories were set. Black roles on prime-time television dramas overall were still very limited, a fact that black actors and the black press often bemoaned. The dismal reality in Hollywood had the comedian-activist Dick Gregory quipping before a congressional committee the following year that "the only show that hires Negroes regularly is Saturday night boxing."[11]

Of all the westerns, CBS's *Have Gun—Will Travel* took the most activist approach when it came to the treatment of minorities, a fact owing in large part to its star and guiding light, Richard Boone. The Los Angeles–born Boone, a seventh-generation nephew of Daniel Boone, had been a boxing champion at Stanford University and studied the Method at the Actor's Studio. Not handsome in the Hollywood sense, Boone made sure his character Paladin—named for the legendary chivalrous knights of Charlemagne, the Holy Roman emperor—was no typical western hero but a chess-playing, Shakespeare-spouting philosopher-gunslinger-for-hire with a soft spot for people battling powers larger than themselves. The laconic Paladin would rather be reading *The Brothers Karamazov* or brushing up on his Heraclitus than quick-drawing his Colt revolver but did so when a matter of honor or moral rectitude was at stake.

Boone favored New York stage actors with Method training, so he was going out of his comfort zone to cast Odetta, who had never taken acting lessons but had a way of inhabiting her characters in the same way that she did when singing about a convict or slave. Boone saw Odetta's guest spot—and television in general—as a means of advancing a civil rights agenda, his son Peter Boone recalled. His father had taken the family to see Odetta perform at the Ash Grove and was a "huge" fan, Boone said. "It was not an accident that she was on the show, I can assure you."[12]

Odetta flew to Bend, Oregon, in late July to film on location for an episode entitled "The Hanging of Aaron Gibbs," with Richard Boone directing. In the episode, Odetta portrays Sarah Gibbs, a woman whose husband is hanged at a mining settlement along with two other men after they try to steal the miners' payroll. As part of their getaway plan, the men had dynamited a mineshaft, which unintendedly had caused the mine to cave in, trapping and killing the miners inside. Sarah's attempts to bid farewell to her doomed husband and to recover his body after he's put to death are blocked by some relatives of the victims who are out for vengeance.

The filming took place in the midst of the Freedom Rides that spring and summer, when black and white activists rode interstate buses down South to challenge local segregation laws—and were met with mob violence and bombings—and there are more than subtle reminders of the civil rights struggle in the script. Sarah, an uneducated, dignified woman, tries to explain her husband's actions to Paladin as a by-product of their lack of economic opportunity and mourning for their young son, who had recently taken sick and died: "A man runs from trouble and finds trouble waitin' around the corner for him. It's hard for a man to go to field workin' after he's known better. He used to drag home at nights with his hands cracked open with blood."[13] At the mining camp, Paladin lays his hand on Sarah's shoulder, where it lingers just long enough to show genuine empathy and concern—an act he repeats once more later in the episode.

Viewers find out that Aaron and his accomplices did indeed blow up the shaft, though he maintains it was a terrible accident. After Paladin's prodding, the grizzled marshal of the settlement allows Sarah and Aaron to share a moment and a surprisingly tender kiss.

When Sarah asks to give her husband a Christian burial, one of the victims' relatives stands angrily in her path, saying, "Maybe you can find some way to get my brother out of that pit and bury him Christian." But Paladin sternly confronts him with a line that would have raised an eyebrow for viewers paying attention to the nightly news: "Are you the only human being in this world who ever had to fight hardship?" Paladin's defense of Aaron's right to die with dignity and religion seems to convince some of the family members. A woman gives Sarah a black shroud for Aaron's coffin, and some of the men help load it onto Sarah's wagon before she and Paladin depart, Odetta singing softly as they ride off into the sunset.

There's no doubt that the script, with its clear endorsement of black rights, caused some of the usual backstage turmoil, probably from the network, the sponsors, or both. "I remember there was some sort of controversy about that one, a certain amount of nervousness about it," the show's producer, Frank Pierson, recalled. "But when they heard that we were going with Odetta, it all quieted down."[14] The show would air that fall, and although *Have Gun—Will Travel* had fallen from third place in the Nielsen ratings to twenty-ninth, it attracted about 11 million viewers per week as the lead-in to CBS's most popular show, *Gunsmoke.*

Richard Boone was said to have been so impressed with Odetta's acting that he insisted she be included in another script to be filmed that fall, but for some reason, it didn't happen. Still, he recalled her appearance fondly: "I'll never forget Odetta's powerful voice, low and soft, singing in the gathering twilight of the Deschutes river country in Oregon."[15]

Despite the groundbreaking nature of much of the episode, one aspect conformed with Hollywood's vision of black Americans: Odetta had to cover her natural hair with a straight-haired wig. Although many freed blacks in the Northern cities were, by the 1870s, straightening their hair, many rural blacks who worked as sharecroppers and the like had little time for such fussing and kept their kinky locks covered in head rags. Nevertheless, the irony of Odetta donning a wig was considered so unremarkable in 1960s America that it got no notice even in the black press, which trumpeted her starring role, as it did whenever black actors managed to land parts other than the usual stock characters as maids and butlers.

Black newspapers, however, became endlessly fascinated with Odetta's hair. One article that year noted that Odetta, Miriam Makeba, and the jazz singer Abbey Lincoln "have cut their hair and leave it completely au naturel. Many fervent nationalists—bitter about racial assimilation—also leave their hair in a natural state. This growing group obviously does not need the services of professional hair straighteners." One far-fetched early 1960s rumor had it that Odetta turned down "a lot of money" to endorse a hair straightener because she refused to pose for photos with pressed hair. "I wonder how she would look with pressed hair," wondered a writer for the *Afro-American* in Baltimore, who apparently hadn't seen her on *Have Gun—Will Travel.* "But with her talent, who needs hair straightener?"[16]

Black identity was shifting in America by 1961, in no small part because of the exploding African independence movement, which had seen seventeen nations gain freedom from their colonial rulers the previous year alone. In an influential 1961 essay in the *New York Times Magazine*, James Baldwin wrote that the freedom for millions of black Africans meant that American Negroes were no longer willing to wait for their own liberation. With the sit-in movement in mind, Baldwin summed up black disaffection with a simple equation: "At the rate things are going here, all of Africa will be free before we can get a lousy cup of coffee." But a political awakening was only part of what was going on, he insisted. The rest was social. "The American Negro can no longer, nor will he ever again, be controlled by white America's image of him. This has everything to do with the rise of Africa in world affairs."[17]

Odetta was at the forefront of this movement. In addition to wearing her hair naturally—what some blacks began calling "an Odetta"—she had also taken to donning colorful African kaftans on stage. The kaftans partly reflected her wish to cover her large body, but they also signaled a telltale pride in her heritage and, together with her hair, gave her the look of an African princess. Andrea Benton Rushing, a black studies professor at Amherst College, recalled her shock at seeing Odetta for the first time in a New York concert in the early 1960s. "Helmeted in my chemically straightened hair because hot comb pressing was out of style, I saw Odetta at the Village Gate. . . . I was mesmerized by her stunning face framed in its short kinky halo. She had a regal poise and power that I had never seen in a 'Negro' . . . woman before."[18]

The hair revolution, in particular, was destined to proceed slowly and not without some pushback, however. An article in the *New Pittsburgh Courier* in the fall of 1961 captured the commotion that ensued when a well-to-do black woman walked into a social function in Camden, New Jersey, sporting kinky hair. "One of South Jersey's most dazzling personalities slipped through the entrance . . . in an exclusive gown creation, from one of Philly's super exclusive gown shops, [but] the mass shock wave came when they took one look at her coiffure, which wasn't a coiffure at all, but was in the first stage generally associated with drying out after a wash." Of this "back to Africa" hairdo, as the Philadelphia beauticians began calling it, the paper said that Odetta "may have slightly set off an idea."[19]

Given the societal shift going on and her bad experience in Hollywood, it's easy to see why, at the height of her fame, Odetta, along with Danny, continued to pursue her career in the movies on her own terms. "Acting is her second love but she has strong feelings about the kinds of roles she wants to do and will play no stereotyped 'Aunt Jemima' parts," one reporter wrote after interviewing her that year. Yet another item appeared in the gossip columns, this time from Dorothy Kilgallen, that "Odetta . . . will play the lead in *The Bessie Smith Story*, to be filmed in New York." However, it seemed the movie was no closer to being a reality than it had been the previous year.[20]

Odetta had begun to incorporate more straight blues into her concert act, in part to prepare for a Bessie Smith role but also to add variety to her repertoire. The first song she included was Smith's "Special Delivery Blues," which she'd set to a folk rhythm on her guitar. She also began singing "Weeping Willow Blues," another of Smith's classic blues shouts. And she began performing with a jazz outfit, the Fred Kaz Trio, to try to capture more of the original sound of Smith, who usually had piano and horn accompaniment. When Odetta debuted the new act as the second half of her show in late May and early June at One Sheridan Square in Greenwich Village—the club that had replaced Café Society—she earned a blistering review in the *Village Voice*. "With the addition of the Fred Kaz trio . . . the show fell apart. Odetta attempted old Bessie Smith and Ma Rainey blues numbers adapted to a modern style. Either she had not come to terms with this stylistic marriage, or the songs were beyond her present powers."[21]

She fared better in July, returning to the Gate of Horn, and backed again by the Kaz trio for a segment of her shows. But at the Gate, she was among friends, even if the club was in a new location on North State Street and no longer owned by Al Grossman. When she presented the blues program, billed as "The Bessie Smith Story," at the Monterey Jazz Festival in September, she again failed to hit her mark with her six-song set. Ralph Gleason of the *San Francisco Chronicle*, usually one of her biggest fans, noted that the very proper Odetta had a difficult time setting the mood for back-alley blues for the crowds that packed the Monterey County Fairgrounds to hear her. "Perhaps the formality of announcing her intention of singing songs from the repertoire of Bessie Smith and Ma Rainey set the stage awkwardly," Gleason observed. "Whatever the cause, her performance of this material did not come across as successfully" as he'd expected.[22]

By November, Odetta and Danny prepared to move to Los Angeles. His aversion to the cold weather and their movie aspirations probably precipitated their departure to the West Coast. They rented a home in the Hollywood Hills, at 1339 Miller Drive. Lesley Greening Taufer visited Odetta there after running away from home in Chicago as an eighteen-year-old and hitchhiking to California a couple of years later. "She lived in the Hills in a wonderful place," Taufer recalled. "It was the California Spanish style with a beautiful patio overlooking Hollywood and LA, and it was up high and it was really pretty."[23]

During her two-week visit, Danny wasn't around. He might have been traveling as he tried to build an artist management business of his own. As for Odetta, she would soon spend more of her time in a rented sixth-floor apartment on New York's Upper West Side, meaning she and Danny were rarely together. The address was 392 Central Park West, but the large red-brick high-rise building was on West 100th Street, almost at Columbus Avenue. She furnished it for $200 at an auction house, with the kind of decor one would expect for someone who was on the road a lot. "We had an apartment in New York because of [the] proximity of getting to [the] Northeast to beat the hotel racket and also when going in to New York to record," Odetta explained. "We rented a house in Los Angeles. Danny moved to and stayed in Los Angeles, and I would stay in the apartment in New York and get to Los Angeles every once in a while."[24]

She described herself in one interview around that time as "a rambler, really." As for a home life, "there's so little time now that I have for it," she told another reporter that year. "Dan and I have such a little time together." Asked about children, she no longer sounded like she was prioritizing starting a family over advancing her career. "It wouldn't be fair to them. They could not have a normal family life. Later on, perhaps we'll adopt children."[25]

In December, a few weeks after the Los Angeles move, Odetta flew to Europe for her first performances outside North America. In Manchester, England, she filmed a segment on a show called *Personal Appearance* for Granada TV. In London, she stayed at the Waldorf Hotel and hung out with British jazz journalist Max Jones, who interviewed her for *Melody Maker,* Britain's top music magazine, and took her for a visit to the city's famed Troubadour nightclub. At the club, Scottish folk singer Rory McEwen, a devotee of Lead Belly and one of the prime movers of the British folk revival, convinced her to borrow a guitar and sing "Gallows Pole" and a couple of other tunes.

Although only a few of her records had been released in England, the BBC had shown *Tonight with Belafonte* and her performance had made a big impression, as had the single "Hole in the Bucket" with Belafonte, which had spent four weeks in the UK Top 40. Whereas back home, many reviewers felt obliged to comment on her weight, Jones began his *Melody Maker* piece: "It is not every day that such a beautiful folk singer as Odetta Felious Gordon comes to town." Odetta would experience many of her overseas tours as soul-rejuvenating escapes from questions of race and the Hollywood ideals of beauty that followed her everywhere in the United States. To the people she would meet abroad, she recalled a few years later, "all of a sudden I was a beautiful woman, the feeling I hadn't had here [at home]. Over there you don't have to be a Lena Horne or a Marilyn Monroe. Here [in the States] that was a prerequisite and there was nothing else."[26]

From London, she flew to Rome and on to Africa to perform on the first night of a two-day arts festival in Lagos, Nigeria. The festival marked the opening of a new culture center in Lagos by the American Society of African Culture, which had been created by six black American writers and artists, including the novelist Richard Wright, as a cultural exchange between a decolonized Africa and the black diaspora in America. With Martin Luther King Jr. and other activists expressly linking African independence and American civil rights, black artists were eager to establish a connection and express solidarity with their ancestral homeland.

In addition to Odetta, the bill for the festival included jazz and blues heavyweights such as Lionel Hampton, Nina Simone, Randy Weston, and Brother John Sellers, as well as dancer and actor Geoffrey Holder. Before leaving on the trip, Holder had told the *New York Times* that he had "an extreme curiosity" about how Africans would view the black American arts.[27]

The overall answer, on this first offering in newly independent Nigeria, was not favorably. "We put on a poor show and they didn't let us get away with it," Holder recalled. The failure was epitomized by a "long, ambitious, solemn Uhuru Suite (by Randy Weston) calling on Mother Africa to shake off her shackles and rise," which played to "yawns, fish-eyes, and emptying bleachers." "Uhuru and 'Let My People Go' may be strong stuff at Washington Square folk song uprisings," Holder said, "but in Nigeria, 1962, freedom is something they have. Cheerleaders from Carnegie Hall they don't need." The *Daily Times* in Lagos reported that "appearances were too brief. The visitors showed little enthusiasm and were even sometimes quite stiff, at other times the painful conclusion was that they were condescending."[28]

Odetta was singled out as a big exception. Performing on the first night before five thousand people at King George V Stadium, she sang the "Freedom Trilogy" and "He's Got the Whole World in His Hands." "Odetta had me in tears," the Nigerian writer Peter Enahoro recalled. "When she sang 'Oh, Freedom,' I felt like a slave. She didn't just sing, she was the part and you could feel her straining, crying to the heavens above, tearing and wrenching her heart out. The 3,000 audience [*sic*] roared for more."[29]

However, the crowd didn't have much of a chance to enjoy her. Odetta sang only three songs "and walked briskly away" because she had to catch a flight back to Europe. A quick tour of Scandinavia followed, with shows in Denmark, Holland, and Sweden. At the Stockholm Concert House on December 19, she easily won over her audience despite the fact her records weren't much available there. Still, she recalled the trip as bittersweet, especially her brief Africa sojourn. Her future visits to Africa would go much better, but this one was tinged with disappointment, undone, it seemed, by unfair expectations and an intense longing to connect with the motherland. "I was all excited about going to Africa," she recalled. "My forefathers came from Africa; I was going to see what home was like." But, she said, when she got to Africa, "it wasn't home. It was a strange country, like any other strange country. I found myself thinking of an African, 'I wonder if your forefathers put my forefathers into that slavery bag.' That's when I stopped looking for it to be home."[30]

CHAPTER NINE

IN THE HEART OF JIM CROW

Still battling the lawsuit from Dean Gitter in early 1962, Odetta asked her record company, Vanguard, for an advance on future royalties to continue paying her Chicago attorney, Raymond H. Young, who had been repeatedly demanding money. She was near the height of her popularity and a major concert draw and recording artist with notable acting credits to her name, but Dandetta Productions, her and Danny's firm, was hemorrhaging money.

Other than trying to hype the stillborn Bessie Smith movie, Danny had promoted a few concerts for Joan Baez, the Clancy Brothers and Tommy Makem, and others in California, and had a small stable of artists in his management roster. But aside from Judy Collins, whom he briefly managed, none were the kind of performers one could build a business on, as Al Grossman had done with Odetta early on.

John Winn, a folk singer from Missouri who had been among Danny's first clients, recalled that things didn't go well from the beginning. It had started with an audition in Chicago, in which Danny had deferred to Odetta in choosing the talent. "I sang for Odetta," Winn recalled. "Danny said, 'What do you think?' and Odetta said, 'I think he's really good. Sign him.' So that was the beginning of the relationship."[1]

Danny tried to market the average-sized Winn, who had a trained tenor, as "Big John Winn," a kind of roving lumberjack-turned-songster. When Winn showed up to one of his first gigs, at a folk club in Minneapolis, the owner took one look at him and furrowed his brow. "You're Big John Winn? I was expecting someone wearing a checkered wool shirt with an ax over his shoulder." "I was a lyric tenor of the troubadour persuasion, so [Danny's] sales pitch did not show an understanding of the product he was selling," Winn said. "Not a good fit for me, so when his follow-up skills began to fade away so did my relationship with Dandetta Productions. I have no recollection of how it finally ended, but one day it clearly was not there anymore. He just seemed to disappear back into Odetta's shadow."[2]

Collins had a better experience, at least initially. A novice performer, she'd met Danny at the Gate of Horn in 1960 after first being floored by Odetta's act. "I'm sitting there and the lights go down and through the back entrance comes this gorgeous creature in this green silk long dress, and she had some kind of perfume that was so enchanting," Collins recalled. "And she came through the door and walked up onto the stage and began to sing and I thought I'd died and gone to heaven."[3]

Collins never signed a contract with Danny, but over drinks at the club, they agreed he would become her manager, Odetta's clout paving the way, and for about a year and a half, he "arranged a number of very good dates," Collins said. She realized at some point, however, that his knowledge of the folk clubs was the extent of his expertise, and she didn't need his services. Before it ended, the married Collins had to rebuff Danny's advances. "Danny asked me point-blank why he had been unsuccessful in establishing a more personal—meaning sexual—relationship with me," she recalled.[4]

Dandetta's financial troubles were reflected in Odetta and Danny's 1962 federal taxes, which would show that while Odetta earned $19,256 in record royalties that year, Dandetta lost $23,186 ($185,000 today). That left more than $20,000 in concert wages and other income, but with rents for two apartments, coast-to-coast travel, and other expenses, Odetta wasn't putting away any money during what would be her peak earning years, when she might have built a nest egg. "I don't know what [Danny] was doing, but he wasn't in show business," recalled Charlie Rothschild, who was by then road-managing acts for Grossman. "And then he said, 'I'll manage you and your career will be better.' . . . And all her monies and savings got pissed away."[5]

Gitter and Odetta finally settled their litigation in April. She agreed to pay him 20 percent of the gross revenue for her fall 1957 tour and to record one LP for Riverside, which also settled its lawsuit with Odetta. The settlement marked a sad end to Odetta's first managerial relationship and the personal friendship she and Gitter had shared. In the more than four decades in Odetta's life that followed, she doesn't appear to ever have mentioned Gitter in an interview, choosing instead to remember that his partner "Tom Wilson recorded me . . . when I cut tracks for the first record company that signed me."[6]

With the legal squabble behind her, Odetta made plans that month to begin recording what would turn out to be *Odetta and the Blues* to fulfill her obligation to Riverside. By then, she'd already agreed to leave Vanguard for RCA, for whom she also wanted to record blues. So, with largely the same tight backing group, anchored by trumpeter Buck Clayton, formerly of Count Basie's orchestra; clarinetist Buster Bailey, who once played with Bessie Smith; and stride pianist Dick Wellstood, Odetta recorded dueling blues LPs two weeks apart in Manhattan: April 11–12 at Plaza Sound Studios on West Fiftieth Street for Riverside and April 25–26 at RCA Victor Studio B on East Twenty-Fourth Street for an LP entitled *Sometimes I Feel Like Cryin'*.

By early 1962, the focal point of the civil rights movement had shifted to Albany, Georgia, where young activists in the so-called Albany Movement sought to overturn segregation in public facilities. Mass arrests of peaceful protesters, including Martin Luther King Jr., were chronicled in newspapers and on TV, with one commentator noting that the images presented a "deeply moving picture of American citizens rising up . . . to demand their simple constitutional rights."[7]

It was at that point that Odetta decided to do her first tour of Southern colleges. She'd been spreading her message of black pride and black history to audiences in the rest of the nation, but now she felt the time was right to make her presence felt in places where the stakes were higher. It took Britain's *Melody Maker* to point out the significance of her itinerary. "Folk singer Odetta is currently touring the South, singing Negro work songs, spirituals and Civil War songs!" the magazine reported.[8] While the tour would mostly take her to black colleges such as Kentucky State College, Le Moyne College in Memphis, and Southern University in New Orleans, she also performed for schools, and in towns, in the midst of segregation battles. In some cases, her bass player, Bill Lee, accompanied her, while in others she went by herself.

"When she first started out doing folk music, she had to travel down South singing by herself—no road manager, no other male person with Odetta," Josh White Jr. recalled. "And nobody fucked with Odetta. Nobody fucked with Odetta. Just take a look at her, then hear her sing. Do you want to mess with that? Hell no." To underscore how unsettling the South could be for a black performer, White recalled a trip with his father down to South Carolina when the younger White was a boy. "I remember, before I was double digits, going down to South Carolina either to do a gig and/or see his mother from Greenville. And I remember leaving New York City, driving out of Jersey and going down South and when we got to, I think it was in North Carolina, there was a big placard, with a Klansman on a horse . . . saying 'Welcome to Klan country.' And [Odetta] went down there by herself. Lotta respect for the lady."[9]

Odetta, a few years later, recalled why she headed to the South during a crucial period in the civil rights movement. "At one point I made the decision that we would play and sing to any students, segregated school or not," she said. "I felt that we could do that and we should do that, because there are all kinds of people to get to and perhaps do something." In January, she and the black folk singer Leon Bibb performed at the University of Texas in Austin. The school had accepted its first black student half a decade earlier, but blacks on campus were still trying to force the integration of university dorms and athletics, and that fall they would ask Martin Luther King Jr. for help, according to an article in the *Dallas Morning News* headlined "Officials at UT Disturbed by Report Dr. King Invited." In the city of Austin, public facilities and many private businesses remained segregated.[10]

In reviewing the concert at the university's Gregory Gym for the school newspaper, a student reporter steered clear of any overt references to civil rights, though the undercurrent was clear enough. "Powerful voices which emoted an understanding and feeling of the text from which they sang, as though they were singing of their

wanderings, found their way into every nook and cranny of the building—and into the receptive souls of their captive audience," wrote
Bill Hampton, later a longtime editor at the *New York Times*. He
particularly noted Odetta's rendition of Jimmy Driftwood's "He Had
a Long Chain On," which would have been heard as a freedom song
and which "was a tear-moving song that enrapt beautiful emotions
and left the audience moved."[11]

In February, when Odetta appeared at the University of North
Carolina, Chapel Hill, a similar situation prevailed. The school was
officially integrated, but the few black students on campus couldn't
participate in all school activities and much of the town remained
segregated. During Odetta's visit, a drive was in full swing to try to
integrate the Carolina Theater in nearby Durham, which catered to
students from the University of North Carolina and Duke University.

Odetta later recalled the segregation she and Lee faced in one of
the unspecified Southern towns—and their small act of defiance:

> They told Bill that he couldn't eat in the dining room [of the hotel]
> and by the time I'm hearing this, it's time for us to go to the concert.
> And Bill is saying that the clerk at the desk said that we couldn't
> use the front door. And I said, "Well I never thought that renting a
> room had anything to do with doors, front or back" . . . And so we
> go downstairs and this clerk is there yelling and screaming and Bill
> is putting down his bass. I said, "Hey, the only way he can argue is
> for us to sit up here and argue with him, right? So the thing to do is
> just to walk out." So we walk out of the front door.[12]

Their stand could easily have landed them in jail. But, perhaps owing to her childhood in Los Angeles, where the racism was less overt,
Odetta didn't have much stomach for the kind of boots-on-the-ground
activism—the sit-ins and Freedom Rides and confrontations with racist sheriffs' departments and theater and café owners—taking place
throughout the South. This hit home when, in the same town with the
segregated hotel, she and Lee went to a Negro restaurant and were
greeted by local blacks. "How proud they were that we were at the
hotel, and I remember the shame, you know, absolute shame I felt.
And it was with this experience that I said, 'Hey, forget, just forget

the segregated [schools], just forget it, because I'm not going to go back into that situation, though it needs to be helped, and I realize that there are kids there who are not necessarily of the opinion of the school segregation."[13]

Odetta, for the most part, would use her music, along with her commentaries about the songs, and her image to help move the nation toward a better path. She sang to inspire but, by and large, avoided directly confronting authorities down South as others did. So does that make her a civil rights "activist," a term so often applied to her in later years? That's a matter of interpretation.

The folk singers Len Chandler and Jack Landrón (Jackie Washington) clearly crossed the line into activism by going to the South for voter registration drives later in the 1960s, putting their lives in real jeopardy. Landrón, who dodged bullets on at least one occasion, didn't see Odetta as an activist. "I would say like with many artists, it was her talent, her being, her way of applying her talent . . . that was so important about her," he said. "The term activist is where I sort of hesitate with all these performers. . . . This is not to diminish her or anybody else'[s] interest or sincerity in wanting to change the situation in America. Everybody was impacted by it. But the term activist I hear applied to so many people, and I would not have called Odetta an activist." He went on: "Having lived in Mississippi for the better part of a year and doing the kind of stuff that was not dramatic or wonderful, that I was doing, then I ran into these people. Joan Baez would come to town, then do a concert and leave town! To me, this is not activism."[14]

There are nuances, of course. Baez frequently spoke out about civil rights and marched with King throughout the 1960s, not to mention staunchly opposing the Vietnam War later on. That's a different kind of activism from, say, the work of the four original members of the Freedom Singers, who started out protesting segregation in Albany, Georgia, and getting arrested, jailed, tossed out of college in some cases, before they formed a group under the auspices of SNCC to sing freedom songs across the United States. "I was dragged up the courthouse steps in Albany, Georgia," Rutha Mae Harris, one of the Freedom Singers, recalled. "We had workshops to teach us how to protect ourselves, so you know how to protect yourself when you're being dragged."[15]

But there's certainly an argument to be made that Odetta was indeed an activist, even if her work was more concentrated on influencing young minds in the North than in battling Southern racism firsthand. Odetta recalled a concert a couple of years later at Oberlin College where her songs actually moved spirits. "They had this Mississippi registration table for demonstration and this one student I knew was very interested in civil rights," Odetta said. "But his roommate was apathetic. This boy just couldn't get him interested. After the concert, he was one of the most interested at the table. Asked questions, nosed around, finally sat down and helped. So you never know what will affect them."[16]

Indeed, for the young, mostly white, mostly middle-class folk music fans who made up the lion's share of Odetta's audiences, her songs served to open eyes. The journalist Andrew Rosenthal recalled the impact of hearing her slave and chain gang songs as a teenager in the early 1960s:

> Her songs were at first difficult for my young ear: the power of her voice, and their unfamiliar rhythms. But in listening to Odetta, and asking my parents what her words were about, my eyes were opened to the crimes and tragedies embedded in American history. . . . "No More Auction Block for Me" led to conversations about slavery, about the "many thousand gone" in the Middle Passage, about the "driver's lash" that enforced the bondage of men, women and children. "Another Man Done Gone" shocked me with the atrocity of chain gangs and taught me about the lynchings that were a depraved public entertainment in the South. Each of Odetta's songs fed my dawning awareness of America's racial traumas and the civil rights movement that was spreading across the nation.[17]

They also had an impact on young blacks coming of age and trying to find their place in a white-centric society. Bernice Johnson Reagon, another member of the Freedom Singers, recalled what Odetta meant for a friend of Reagon's who was trying to break racial barriers. "A dear friend of mine who was in one of the early classes of African American students integrating the University of North Carolina to this day says that the singing of Odetta and Nina Simone kept her sane as she completed undergraduate work in a culture that was not yet welcoming to her development or her future," Reagon said. "In her dorm room their album covers helped to create a physical cultural force that helped her to survive."[18]

Odetta helped set Reagon on her path too. When Odetta's Southern tour brought her to Atlanta on March 3, 1962, to perform solo before a near-capacity crowd at Morehouse College, Reagon, then nineteen, was in the audience at the school's gymnasium. Newly suspended from Albany State College for her activism and now attending Spelman College, Reagon had agreed to become part of the inaugural group of Freedom Singers, who, encouraged by Pete Seeger, would go on to perform in forty-six states in the space of less than a year, logging fifty thousand miles in a Buick station wagon. The group needed a repertoire, and the historian Howard Zinn, who'd been advising SNCC, brought Reagon to hear Odetta. Doris Lockerman, an editor and columnist at the *Atlanta Constitution*, had previewed the concert thusly: "From the beginning, Odetta, the daughter of a Negro steel mill worker, had a voice like a weapon."[19]

Singing chain gang songs for an audience at a black college in Georgia, at that very moment the focus of the civil rights struggle, was far different from singing to whites in New York or Boston. "She had a powerful presence and was at the same time gentle, she looked beautiful and young, and her hair was cut short and natural," Reagon recalled. "When she began to sing, I could not believe what I was hearing! I was thunderstruck!"[20]

Odetta sang "Gallows Pole," "Cotton Fields," and "Prettiest Chain," a work song she'd once performed in Carnegie Hall. "And she hit the guitar," Reagon recalled of the Morehouse show. "Now in the course of the concert she also played the guitar, but she slapped the guitar. I thought I had died and gone to heaven. In Georgia, where I grew up in the country, the roads were built by chain gang labor. I knew the sound, because as the men worked, they sang. But I never thought I'd hear it coming from a concert stage. . . . She was just, the spring of 1962, what I needed to begin my life as a freedom fighter and as a Freedom Singer."[21]

The *Atlanta Constitution* reported that when Odetta had finished singing, "a shouting, screaming, standing audience demanded her reappearance again and again." "There is a personal magnetism and proud humility about Odetta that is impossible to catch on television or records," Stuart Culpepper wrote in his review of the concert. "It must be seen to be fully believed and appreciated. She sings with her eyes closed, head tilted back, completely, personally involved with each emotion in her songs. When finished with a number she greets the audience with a smile big and warm enough to heat the coldest room."[22]

Odetta's blues albums, hitting store shelves that summer and fall, failed to have a similar impact. Coveting, as Odetta did, a role as Bessie Smith, the idea of establishing her blues bona fides on record probably seemed like a smart move. However, attempting to do so just as folk music reached a boiling point in America was, at least in hindsight, ill-advised. And Odetta lacked the raw sensuality to pull it off.

Odetta and the Blues, her one entry for Riverside, debuted in July and featured songs from a who's who of prewar blues queens: Smith, Ma Rainey, Mama Yancey, Ida Cox, and Ethel Waters. The Dixieland jazz sextet behind Odetta lent the music authority, and her vocals boomed as ever on classic numbers such as "Weeping Willow Blues" and "Nobody Knows You When You're Down and Out." But reviews were mixed, at best, a far cry from the near universal acclaim for her folk singing. "One of the truly great blues singers comes flowing forth on 'Odetta and the Blues,'" Bob Scott of the *Los Angeles Times* raved. However John S. Wilson, music critic for the *New York Times*, wrote in *DownBeat* that "on a basic blues, she lacks the warmth and sense of involvement that make a blues singer. The result is that, although there are often suggestive reflections of Bessie Smith that spark out from her singing, she gives the impression of a rather steely Bessie Smith—an iron maiden rather than the very pliably fleshed Bessie."[23]

A single, featuring Rainey's "Oh, My Babe" and Waters's "Make Me a Pallet on Your Floor," went nowhere. Her fans simply didn't want to hear Odetta sing the blues. "The great Odetta . . . is currently under fire for doing a blues album that is closer to jazz than folk," *Time* noted that fall. Even Odetta's friends questioned her choices. "She wasn't a blues shouter," Frank Hamilton opined. "And she wasn't a Bessie Smith. That wasn't her bag."[24]

Sometimes I Feel Like Cryin', her RCA debut, arrived in September and fared little better with a different set of classic blues shouts. "Now, it seems, Odetta wants to be a blues singer," *DownBeat* sniffed. "Unfortunately, this talented young woman is not of the blues—or, as she sometimes sings it, 'ba-lews'—and, judging from this record, she never will be."[25]

Odetta later chalked up the chilly reception to her early blues records as musical typecasting. "Back then there were people who wanted to make sure that the music stayed where it was," she said. "But I'm not a purist in any way, shape or form."[26] Her critics, however, mostly got it right. Odetta had a voice that most singers could only envy, but at that point in her life, it lacked the intoxicating blend of warmth and melancholy that makes for great blues singing. Her folk singing could seemingly move mountains, but a blues siren she was not, despite her deep wishes to the contrary.

Her folk fans could take heart in her final Vanguard release, *Odetta at Town Hall*, out simultaneously with the Riverside and RCA LPs. While the album, recorded earlier in the year, broke little new ground, it was an excellent document of her live shows in 1962 and it garnered predictably stellar reviews. However, the over-the-top panning from the anti-Odetta faction at *Little Sandy Review* bears repeating, even if it failed to acknowledge that Odetta had been married for three years:

> There is a point at which dignity verges on grandiosity, and Miss Felious [*sic*] unfortunately hovers uncomfortably close to this point all too often. The theatricality of this Town Hall performance, like that of her Carnegie Hall album, leads one to surmise that all that is left for her is to appear at the Metropolitan Opera clad in Wagnerian horned helmet and chain mail. It little matters what type of music she sings, for her monstrous stage image pounds her material into whimpering insignificance. . . . Odetta fans may want to buy it for the applause.[27]

As mean-spirited as the review was, it brought out a larger point. Odetta's music was, by and large, very *serious*. And that wasn't what the youngest record buyers were looking for. Al Grossman seemed to recognize this. By 1962, he'd created a new folk hit-maker, Peter, Paul and Mary, putting Peter Yarrow together with two other hip young singers from the Greenwich Village scene, Noel Stookey (who used his middle name, Paul) and Mary Travers, whom Grossman had first met at Dean Gitter's dinner party five years earlier. Stookey, for one, wasn't sure at first about joining the group, but Grossman, aside from his talents as a persuader, had cachet. "Albert was the Village mogul; he was handling Odetta and producing things, he was the big time," Stookey recalled.[28]

By the time they recorded their debut record for Warner Bros., *Peter, Paul and Mary*, they had perfected an effervescent pop-oriented folk sound that lit up radio airwaves and sent record store cash registers a-ringing. In October 1962, the album landed at the top of the *Billboard* charts, on its way to selling more than two million copies, while the group's reworking of the Weavers' "If I Had a Hammer" made the top ten as a single.

If Odetta was going to get to that level in 1963, the move from Vanguard to RCA, the label of Elvis and Harry Belafonte, was at least a start. "Vanguard was a classically oriented record label, and the Solomon brothers put out good music [but] didn't know bubkes about oiling the wheel," Charlie Rothschild recalled. What Grossman had created with Peter, Paul and Mary, though, was a well-oiled, carefully stage-managed pop machine. "Albert understood that music was becoming an industry," the record executive Bob Krasnow recalled. Grossman had assumed the role of image maker, as much as a music manager. Travers, a sexy blonde, was told to stay out of the sun and instructed not to speak during concerts to add to her "mystical quality"—a requirement she and Yarrow argued about privately, but she went along with it for a decade. It's hard to imagine Odetta putting up with that kind of Svengali act. But aside from her failed attempt to present herself as a blues singer, Odetta's sound hadn't changed much in the decade she'd been performing. And if one thing was clear by the end of 1962, it was that the ground was shifting beneath her feet.[29]

CHAPTER TEN

MARCH MUSIC

In January of 1963, Odetta headed to Europe for a brief overseas tour. The first stop was Rome for two nights at Teatro Parioli. Al Grossman came along, and they were soon joined by two other new Grossman clients: Mary Travers and Bob Dylan. Dylan, still making a name for himself, had been in London filming a BBC teleplay, and he flew to Rome "just to see her concert," he told a reporter, although it's likely that Grossman arranged the trips to scout the European music scene for his growing roster of acts. Odetta sang to standing-room-only audiences and appeared on Italian TV, in a "brief, intense performance of the talented American colored singer," according to *La Stampa* newspaper.[1]

In Rome, Odetta, Dylan, and Travers went to a nightclub and inspected Roman ruins, and Odetta got to see an early glimpse of Dylan's magnetic appeal when a young Italian woman propositioned the singer to be her lover, according to one of his biographers. Dylan was in the early period of a songwriting explosion, and in Rome he was said to have written several songs including "Girl from the North Country." The tune came from the English folk song "Scarborough Fair," but the title likely derived from another old ballad, "Lass from the Low Countree," which Odetta recorded for her first Tradition record and sang during her Italian shows, translated in the program as "La Ragazza Della Vallata."

From Rome, Odetta flew to London, where she sang for ten nights at the new Prince Charles Theatre in London's West End. Dylan was in the audience for at least one of the shows, and it's likely that the entire posse was in tow. Odetta's first stage shows in Britain were generally very well received, although Britain's tabloids couldn't resist digs at her weight. The *Daily Mail* called her "Voice of Many Triumphs." "Monumental, wearing a straight flowered smock, with the face of a well-fed angel, the coloured American folk singer Odetta triumphed in her late-night show," the paper said. "Her voice is an extraordinary instrument, sometimes a mighty organ, sometimes a rusty shout, a tender fluttering croon or a Robeson moan." Not surprisingly, the critics didn't embrace Odetta's blues singing, which she did as a segment of her shows with the backing of British jazz musicians. "She has not the aggression of all the great blues singers," the *Daily Mail* said.[2]

Odetta already had a local reputation via her records, mostly her work with Harry Belafonte and the "Hole in the Bucket" single. Her music would soon make an impact on the budding British rock scene. The Kinks's first record, released the following year, would include two songs, "Bald Headed Woman" and "I've Been Driving on Bald Mountain," associated with her. Kinks founding brothers Ray and Dave Davies had sung "Hole in the Bucket" in live shows as part of an early quartet. And it didn't hurt that the Kinks' record producer, Shel Talmy, had seen Odetta perform at the Ash Grove a number of times. "All of us at the beginnings of rock-n-roll were listening to and to some degree, influenced by the roots blues and folk singers like Muddy Waters, Robert Johnson, Odetta, Brownie McGhee and Sonny Terry etc.," Talmy recalled.[3] After London, Odetta headed back to Rome to appear again on Italian TV before boarding a flight to Washington, DC, to perform for President John F. Kennedy.

She and a handful of other folk singers—Josh White, Judy Collins, Will Holt, Lynn Gold, and the Clancy Brothers and Tommy Makem—had been tapped for a CBS broadcast in January called *Dinner with the President*. The purported purpose of the show was the Anti-Defamation League's fiftieth anniversary and its presentation of the Democratic Legacy Award to Kennedy for his "dedication to democracy as reflected in his efforts to broaden the benefits of civil rights and to assure the application of constitutional principles of freedom to all Americans."[4]

Kennedy's role in the civil rights crusade and his actual guiding principles, whether moral or political, will endlessly be debated. After much cajoling from Martin Luther King and other black leaders, he had—only fittingly, his critics said—begun to use federal authority and the power of the presidency to advance the cause of dismantling Jim Crow. The Justice Department was working with Southern schools on desegregation plans, and Kennedy had issued a hard-to-enforce executive order banning discrimination by federally funded housing agencies, including mortgage lenders. Many, however, felt that he'd dragged his feet, failed to present the issue to the American people in moral terms, and stood by as blacks seeking to overturn the South's racist social order were met with violence. Nat Hentoff, in the *Village Voice*, wondered what the president was being honored for exactly. "The Bay of Pigs? . . . The carefully ineffectual Executive Order prohibiting racial discrimination in certain areas of federally supported housing? The management of news?"[5]

Why *was* Kennedy being feted before he fully committed to the cause of civil rights? The answer lies a decade earlier, when the Anti-Defamation League celebrated its fortieth anniversary and presented the same Democratic Legacy award on prime-time TV to President Dwight Eisenhower. On hand for that dinner were five members of the Supreme Court, which was then divided over the issue of school integration and pouring over legal briefs in the *Brown v. Board of Education* case. The justices and the rest of the nation watching at home that night heard speakers praise the court's role as a guardian of human rights, the actress Helen Hayes deliver a soliloquy as Harriet Beecher Stowe, and Eisenhower himself say that "no matter what happens here [in America,] the individual is dignified because he is created in the image of God. Let's not forget it."[6] The court went on, several months later, to issue a unanimous decision outlawing school segregation.

Now, with the civil rights struggle reaching a critical stage, and with folk music at the height of its popularity, the 1963 program was an unsubtle attempt to use folk songs to bolster the movement and passage of a civil rights bill in Congress. The songs amounted to a musical reminder to the TV-viewing public that the story of America had always been much more than a tale of blue-blooded white Anglo-Saxon

Protestants who rebelled against England. "It was the perfect timing because of all that was going on and it was a way of bringing us all together," Lynn Gold Chaiken recalled. "It was a reminder that, hey, we're all one, we're in these United States, we need to be united and we all come from a similar background, we're all immigrants."[7]

About a thousand people packed the ballroom of the Sheraton Park Hotel in Washington for the awards banquet, including President Kennedy, Vice President Lyndon Johnson, Attorney General Robert Kennedy, Secretary of Defense Robert McNamara, and several Supreme Court justices. As they enjoyed a dinner of filet mignon and filet of sole, they heard songs celebrating the nation's diversity and a narration by actor Robert Preston, reading a script by the poet Mark Van Doren. By highlighting songs of freedom sung by America's various immigrant groups through the centuries, the show sought to cast the fight for Negro rights as part of a universal quest. "Freedom is something we owe this nation for what it has given us," Preston pronounced.[8]

Holt, Collins, and Gold opened the program by singing "Shenandoah," a nineteenth-century rivermen's song (which, not coincidentally for the occasion, pays respect to Native American culture). Holt offered an Italian folk song, Gold sang a Jewish one, and the Clancy Brothers and Tommy Makem sang "We Want No Irish Here," after Liam Clancy noted that although his countrymen had gotten "a rather black welcome" when they first came to America, "I think some of them didn't do too badly"—eliciting a smile from the Irish Catholic president on the dais.

The theme later moved on to the Civil War and beyond, with Josh White singing several songs, including "John Henry" and "Free and Equal Blues," and Holt singing "Lonesome Valley," a spiritual that the Carter Family, the Monroe Brothers, and other hillbilly performers had recorded.

For the finale, Preston summed up the meaning in case it wasn't clear by then: "From our voices to our feet, perhaps when we sing it enough, we can dance to the tune. At least we can dream of it that way. But it will not happen so. Not for us. No, not completely. It is ours to aspire to, this work of bringing truth to the images we live by. . . . If we cannot answer the gift of the land, perhaps our children can. The songs of our intention are already here."

Then the camera panned to Odetta. She'd already elicited a stand-ing ovation from CBS employees during a run-through earlier in the day. And right before curtain time, she may have been reminded yet again that America was a nation in which blacks and whites were treated unequally. "Just before we went on to do *Dinner with the President*, we were all dressed and we had to go in and have TV makeup put on," Chaiken remembered. "And the woman who put on her makeup—I was waiting—was very rude to her. It may have been she was just in a bad mood, I don't know, but she was very different with me. I'm not saying she was racist; I only know I remember . . . that [Odetta and I] looked at each other."[9]

Odetta came out and sang the "Freedom Trilogy," a stunning performance given the political moment, and it stole the show. The audience, including the president, held in silence for the hour-long program, burst into applause. "What came through and who she was, it was beautiful," Chaiken said. "If one believes the artist is a mes-senger, she was that night and set the stage [for what was to come] given the full Cabinet and Kennedy were in the room and it was being broadcast live across the nation."[10]

At the end of the program, Kennedy approached the podium and accepted the award, saying:

> Almost two centuries have passed since a small, weak nation, a beachhead on a continent, began the great experiment of democ-racy, in a world where government . . . by the consent of the governed ha[d] been extinguished for 2,000 years. As Jefferson prophesied, there have been many years of desolation and destruction. It seems to me that it is our responsibility in this year of change and hope, to prove that we are equal to this great inheritance, to make it pos-sible for the four freedoms, which Franklin Roosevelt so eloquently described in another time of peril and danger 20 years ago, to make sure that those four freedoms, indeed the great concept of indivisible freedom, is made available to all of our people, to all of our citizens.

"After the show," recalled Collins, who'd just been released from the hospital following a bout with tuberculosis, "we all were put in a line to pass by and say hello to President Kennedy." As for what that might have been like for Odetta, having come from such humble beginnings, she was never much for telling tales and doesn't seem to have mentioned it to interviewers, other than to say she was honored to have been asked to perform for him. Collins, however, vividly recalled Kennedy's magnetism: "I felt the electricity that comes from certain people."[11]

Critics were mixed on the show's effectiveness. "Thanks to the CBS network the entire nation was able to sit in on this noteworthy affair and sample the many fine talents brought together to emphasize the varied strands that have gone into the fabric called America and to memorialize the aspirations and achievements that have given meaning to the land," Percy Shain wrote in the *Boston Globe*. Rick Du Brow of United Press International mostly panned it: "I'm afraid that aside from the rousing songs of that stout and great lady, Odetta, the chief effect of the concert was to provide acute indigestion: a gorgeous example of how determined culture, full of esoteric and marshmallowy loftiness about the meaning of it all, can make even preachments about liberty a comically pretentious bore."[12]

Part of the disappointment probably sprang from the president's remarks, which, while seeming to prod the issue of civil rights forward in unspecific language, fell far short of an explicit endorsement of the movement or offering the kind of moral imperative that black leaders wanted him to present. That would come six months later in a prime-time address, when Kennedy finally threw his weight behind a civil rights bill, called the fight to end segregation and discrimination an issue "as old as the scriptures and . . . as clear as the American Constitution," and asked the nation: "Are we to say to the world— and more importantly to each other—that this is the land of the free, except for the Negroes?"

Fresh from her latest TV coup, Odetta tried one more time in April to convince an audience that she could handle a blues repertoire. For what had become a yearly performance at New York's Town Hall, she appeared in the latter half of the show with a jazz quintet headed by Buck Clayton. But she earned perhaps the worst review of her career, from Robert Shelton in the *New York Times*, normally one of her biggest stalwarts. "The more Odetta has been moving in the last year, the less distance she seems to have traveled," Shelton wrote. "The contralto-guitarist gave a program of folk and blues songs at Town Hall last night revealing that she is groping for a new style." He concluded:

> Despite an obvious attempt to assimilate the manners of Bessie Smith, Ma Rainey, Dede Pierce and others, Odetta captured only the letter, but not the spirit, of those great women blues singers. Perhaps because Odetta is overcerebral in her approach, or unduly restrained. But her blues never scorched with the intensity or involvement their earlier singers had given them. . . . If it were not for Odetta's great artistry and depth, one would not have been so disappointed at where her groping has taken her.[13]

In 1963, folk made its most serious assault on the world of pop music. First the Rooftop Singers, a trio with former Weavers member Erik Darling, went to the top of the *Billboard* singles chart with "Walk Right In," a cover of an old Cannon's Jug Stompers tune. The Kingston Trio scored a pair of hits with "Reverend Mister Black" and "Greenback Dollar." And Peter, Paul and Mary went to number two with "Puff the Magic Dragon," a song Yarrow wrote based on an unpublished poem he'd read. By the summer, their version of Bob Dylan's "Blowin' in the Wind" was racing up the charts.

That was the situation in July when the Newport Folk Festival resumed after a three-year hiatus. (The tony town had briefly soured on music festivals after a drunken riot by young people during the Newport Jazz Festival in 1960.) Newport quickly renewed its status as the most important and influential folk music gathering in the nation, a place to be seen and heard, and a barometer of the state of the industry and where the music was headed.

According to her datebooks, on July 26 Odetta boarded a National Airlines flight from New York's Idlewild Airport to Providence, Rhode Island, and made her way to Newport's Viking Hotel, where all the musicians were staying. But at Newport 1963, she was a spectator and not a performer. It's not clear why she didn't appear that year, though it was presumably by choice. Still, if Odetta and Pete

Seeger had reigned supreme at the 1959 festival, with a strong cameo by a teenaged Joan Baez, by 1963 the new generation of folk musicians had come to the fore, led by Peter, Paul and Mary; Baez; and Dylan.

Dylan himself was becoming better known, more at first for his songwriting than for his singing, which was still an acquired taste, but that too was starting to catch on. He'd based the melody of "Blowin' in the Wind" on the slave ballad "No More Auction Block" that Odetta had recorded and introduced to the Greenwich Village scene, though at the time he wrote "Blowin' in the Wind," Dylan seems to have been listening to his sometime girlfriend Delores Dixon of the New World Singers sing "Auction Block" on stage nightly at Gerdes Folk City.

Other artists, including the Chad Mitchell Trio, the Kingston Trio, and Arthur Lyman would soon hurry out versions of "Blowin' in the Wind" that year, and the song would eventually become one of the most covered songs ever. Dylan and Peter, Paul and Mary were beginning to give Al Grossman something Odetta hadn't: hits and huge songwriting royalties. Odetta hadn't had a song on *Billboard's* Hot 100, which had debuted in 1958, nor had any of her records landed on the magazine's list of top one hundred LPs. With Peter, Paul and Mary, Grossman had jointly formed Pepamar Music, giving him a share of their songs, not only as their manager but as a music publisher, which was where a good chunk of the money was. Within two years, some 237 music copyrights would get filed on Dylan songs recorded by other artists, and Grossman had a healthy slice of that action too, eventually forming a publishing company with Dylan, Bob Dylan Words and Music. With Odetta not producing hits, and still under the sway of Danny, Grossman began shifting his energies elsewhere. "Albert was a pretty cold businessman," the folk singer Happy Traum recalled. "He went where the money is."[14]

At Newport that year, Dylan, Baez, and Peter, Paul and Mary shared the spotlight. The iconic image from the festival came on its opening night, after Dylan had closed the show and young concertgoers had demanded an encore. He was joined onstage by Baez; Peter, Paul and Mary; the Freedom Singers; Seeger; and the actor-folk singer Theodore Bikel; they interlocked arms to sing "We Shall Overcome" (as it happened, another song whose melody derived from "No More

Auction Block"). If Odetta indeed was there at the concert, one wonders what she thought of the scene unfolding before her.

With folk groups like Peter, Paul and Mary; the Kingston Trio; and the Limeliters selling so many records, Odetta realized that her approach to folk music, which hadn't changed in her decade-long career, needed updating. By the summer, she was performing and recording with a new backup unit consisting of Bruce Langhorne on guitar and a revolving cast of bass players. Langhorne, a baby-faced twenty-five-year-old, had been a sideman for two years to Brother John Sellers and a go-to accompanist to musicians at Gerdes Folk City in Greenwich Village. With mere stumps on his picking hand where his index, ring, and middle fingers had been before being blown off in a childhood cherry-bomb accident, Langhorne provided an angular, bluesy counterpoint to Odetta's steady rhythmic timekeeping, adding a swinging new dimension to her music.

Recognizing his immense talent as an improviser, Odetta gave him free rein to find the groove between her playing and singing. "The only restriction is that I listen to her," he told a reporter about their approach. Langhorne, one of only a handful of black musicians immersed in the folk scene, also shared Odetta's commitment to civil rights. Once, during an interview, Odetta was asked about the meaning of her work. "In some of my songs," she began, "I want to speak out against injustice, against prejudice, against men stepping all over each other, against—" Langhorne interrupted her. "Odetta, baby," he said, "we just call it 'The Fight.'" Langhorne was destined to become one of the most sought-after studio musicians in the folk world, playing alongside Peter, Paul and Mary; Baez; and Dylan, who used him as the inspiration for "Mr. Tambourine Man" after Langhorne brought a huge Turkish drum with bells to a recording session.[15]

Odetta and her new group, including jazz bassist Eddie De Hass, spent the late summer and early fall on tour with Peter, Paul and Mary and the young folk duo Bud and Travis, playing large concert halls and amphitheaters in the United States and Canada as part of a package produced by Al Grossman. On August 2, the tour landed at the Hollywood Bowl, billed as "Valley Teen Night," with young folk fans from the suburban San Fernando Valley taking chartered buses to the concert.

In the new pecking order, it was Odetta who opened the show before a crowd of seventeen thousand. With Langhorne weaving inventive blues lines behind her, there's no question that Odetta's sound was energized on songs like "He's Got a Long Chain On" and the old folk tune "900 Miles," and the sheer force of her singing was as impressive as ever. She dedicated the "Freedom Trilogy" to "many people here in Los Angeles and throughout the country who are striving towards civil rights for all and their many brave acts."[16] The crowd, enthusiastic but not particularly pumped up, called for an encore, and she sang "This Land Is Your Land" before exiting after about twenty-five minutes on stage.

Bud and Travis followed with their mix of music and comedy, and then Peter, Paul and Mary, pop powerhouses, closed the show with an hour-long set that sent their young fans into hysterics. "Two beards and a blond—Peter, Paul, and Mary—took charge of the second half of the concert, and their reception was tumultuous," the *Los Angeles Times* reported. These shows with Peter, Paul and Mary marked the first time since she'd first begun performing that Odetta was anything but the star of a folk concert, and it had to have stung, especially for a performer at the height of her musical powers. "I think that Odetta was feeling, perhaps . . . that her place in the cosmos of this music was diminishing," Yarrow recalled of that time. "And when that happens to any performer it's upsetting."[17]

On the other hand, Odetta and her music were gaining exposure to a new generation of fans who might never have heard of her. After dates in Winnipeg, Edmonton, Portland, and Seattle, the tour landed at the Carter Barron Amphitheater in Washington, DC, in late August for six shows. Peter, Paul and Mary were the ones "the people all came to see," the *Washington Post* reported, but Odetta once again opened the concert, and "from the growing applause it appeared they were pleasantly surprised at how stimulating traditional folk music can be."[18]

The Carter Barron gigs were timed to coincide with what would be remembered as the most important civil rights gathering in the nation's history, the March on Washington for Jobs and Freedom on August 28. That summer, the nation's attention had shifted to Odetta's hometown of Birmingham, where the commissioner of public safety,

Eugene "Bull" Connor, had unleashed dogs and high-pressure fire hoses on protesters, including school children, peacefully marching against segregation. With President Kennedy now, finally, behind the effort to get a civil rights bill through a divided Congress, an estimated 250,000 people converged on the Mall in a massive show of unity and resolve that resembled, in the words of a United Press International correspondent, "a gigantic revival meeting."[19]

They began arriving in the morning from all over the country, aboard twenty special trains, seven hundred buses, nine chartered planes, and by car and on foot. Most were black, but 10 to 15 percent were white. There were young and old, clergy and laypeople, men in pin-striped suits and beatniks with goatees and guitars slung over their shoulders.

Most of the black women were done up in their Sunday best, wearing dresses and chemically straightened hair, looking ready for church. However, a small but noticeable group, some of them volunteers for SNCC, wore overalls and short Afros, among the early signs that natural hair had begun to catch on as an emblem of protest. For some SNCC members, it was a matter of being practical: denim and unpressed hair was a more appropriate uniform for a protest or sit-in that might land one in jail. Others, such as SNCC field secretary Joyce Ladner, then a student at Tougaloo College in Mississippi, recognized their cultural antecedents, Ladner acknowledging she'd cut her hair "to emulate Abbey Lincoln and Odetta."[20]

No one could predict how the marchers would conduct themselves and whether counter-protesters would cause trouble. The police chief in Washington had on hand a force of nearly 6,000 men, including 1,700 National Guardsmen and 350 firemen with clubs. An additional 4,000 soldiers and marines waited on standby in case of riots. Several dozen members of the American Nazi Party, led by George Lincoln Rockwell, stood nearby the assembled masses around the Washington Monument grounds. "I can't stand niggers. I can't stand to hear 'We Shall Overcome,'" Rockwell said, but he and his men didn't stay for the main event.[21]

To enliven the spirits of early arrivals before the march began, organizers had planned a morning warm-up concert on a small stage by the Washington Monument, programmed by Ossie Davis, who emceed. Although the march is viewed today as a seminal event, the coverage was sporadic and no film or audio exists of the entire day's events. The various accounts that survive provide a hodgepodge of puzzle pieces that don't always fit together neatly. One newspaper said that Odetta first led the crowd singing "We Shall Overcome," but most reporting omits this and has Joan Baez beginning the concert about 10 a.m. with "Oh, Freedom," which she'd learned at age sixteen from an Odetta record, and following that with "We Shall Overcome," a song that Baez would release as a single that year, scoring a minor hit. Peter, Paul and Mary followed with their hits "Blowin' in the Wind" and "If I Had a Hammer."

And then Odetta arrived, dressed in a paisley jumper and yellow blouse and accompanied by Bruce Langhorne. "In her speaking," Baltimore's *Afro-American* reported, "she pointed out that so often she goes along feeling that she is less than a drop in the ocean, of how proud she was to be a part of this mighty downpour of fighting for what we shouldn't have had to ask for." Odetta then launched into her own version of "Oh, Freedom" and the rest of the "Freedom Trilogy." An ABC radio reporter described the scene:

> Odetta the folksinger is opening her vibrant voice now. "No more moanin' over me," she sings. Sitting on the grass listening is a young man in straw hat and overalls. He is from Clarksdale, Mississippi. It took him and 37 companions 40 hours to get here in a bus.[22]

As Odetta sang the last song of the trilogy, Josh White was inspired to join her. "White didn't wait for an introduction," the *New Yorker* said. "He merely unpacked his guitar, handed the cigarette he had been smoking to a bystander, and walked up to the microphone to join Odetta in singing 'I'm on the Way to Canaan Land.' In a few moments, Miss Baez was also singing, and then all the folk singers gathered at the microphone to finish the song."[23]

One marcher recalled the effect of hearing Odetta's voice radiating out over the expectant crowd. "Gathered around the grounds of the monument, where thousands were trying to hear Odetta sing 'Come Go to That Land,' and other freedom songs, everyone began singing and clapping in the spirit of her performance. A form of solemn serenity was engulfed by all." When the song ended and Odetta left the stage, a huge ovation erupted, with shouts of "More! More!" "The 50,000 souls crowded in the vicinity of the stand refused to turn her loose," according to the *Afro-American*. Ossie Davis called back Odetta, who asked the crowd to join her as she sang "No More Auction Block" a cappella, followed by another old spiritual, "If Anybody Asks You." "Odetta's great, full-throated voice carried almost to Capitol Hill: 'If they ask you who you are, tell them you're a child of God,'" the *New York Times* said.[24]

After White sang several songs, including "The House I Live In" and "Go Down Moses," Bob Dylan ambled up, a month removed from his success at Newport, and offered "When the Ship Comes In," with Baez supplying backup vocals. Later, Davis introduced Lena Horne, Rosa Parks, and others luminaries, and the eight-tenths of a mile march to the Lincoln Memorial began around 11:30, with Constitution and Independence Avenues becoming seas of humanity and poster board, marchers singing and holding aloft signs with slogans like "No U.S. Dough to Help Jim Crow Grow" and "Civil Rights Plus Full Employment Equals Freedom."

Shortly before 1 o'clock, Davis approached the microphone on the steps of the Lincoln Memorial to begin the music program leading into the speeches by civil rights leaders. A French radio feed managed to capture the scene, one of the only media outlets to do so. "I would first like to congratulate all of you on the orderly, dignified manner in which you introduced the march from the Washington memorial," Davis told the gathered masses, adding that they had shown the world "by your courage, your determination and your order that we mean business."[25]

Odetta was to sing first; however, she was stuck in a sea of humanity, and big crowds—and the intimacy they demanded, with their proximity to her hidden rage—still frightened her. "When the marching stars arrived at the memorial, Mary [Travers] of the folk singing trio Peter, Paul and Mary, was running about wailing, 'Odetta's in the middle of the crowd and can't get up here,'" according to an account in the *Lawrence Daily Journal-World*. But Odetta managed to work her way through, and Davis told the marchers that he was bringing up "an artist who will lead you in group singing." Odetta launched into

"He's Got the Whole World in His Hands," her voice ringing out over the Mall as marchers clapped their hands and sang along.[26]

He's got the whole world in his hand
He's got the whole world in his hand
He's got the great big world in his hand
He's got the whole world in his hand

The Freedom Singers came up after Odetta and sang "We Shall Not Be Moved" and "Ain't Scared of Your Jails," then Peter, Paul and Mary reprised their two songs from earlier, "Blowin' in the Wind" and "If I Had a Hammer." Baez sang "All My Trials," and Dylan followed with "Only a Pawn in Their Game"—his ballad about the shooting death of Mississippi civil rights activist Medgar Evers, a brave choice considering he could have done a more singable tune like "The Times They Are A-Changin'." Odetta and Langhorne returned at some point to sing the "Freedom Trilogy," just as Martin Luther King was making his way to the Memorial, according to Langhorne's recollection. "The old spirit of indomitable Negro slaves was recalled at the Lincoln Memorial when folk singer Odetta sent up a cry for freedom in musical terms," the *Pittsburgh Post-Gazette* said.[27]

Remembering the day and Odetta's rendition of "Oh Freedom" more than fifty years later, an infirm Langhorne got choked up and began to cry. "It just makes me realize that we are still fighting this basic battle between Neanderthals and Homo sapiens," he said.[28]

The folk singing program ended with Dylan, Baez, and Len Chandler singing "Keep Your Eyes on the Prize." Marian Anderson had been slated to open the formal program with the National Anthem, but she was late and organizers replaced her with a Virginia singer named Camilla Williams. (Anderson arrived in tears a short time later and was allowed to sing around 2:30, another offering of "He's Got the Whole World in His Hands," but by then "the audience was restless and inattentive, and it was a far cry from her famous 1939 performance at the memorial, when she kept a crowd of 75,000 spellbound.")[29]

The formal ceremony climaxed with King's crowning "I Have a Dream" speech coming after a series of speeches by civil rights and religious leaders and two gospel songs by Mahalia Jackson, "I've Been 'Buked and I've Been Scorned" and "How I Got Over." (Jackson was the only singer to perform during the formal part of the program.)

The president watched "some small portions" of the demonstration on TV, it was said at the time, and that included King's soaring oratory. "One cannot help but be impressed with the deep fervor and the quiet dignity that characterizes the thousands who have gathered in the nation's capital from across the country to demonstrate their faith and confidence in our democratic form of government," Kennedy said afterward, though the civil rights bill would remain stalled and wouldn't become law until after his assassination.[30]

The march marked the apotheosis of the marriage between folk music and civil rights. Odetta recalled it soon after as a life-changing experience. "It was the greatest day of my life," she told a reporter a few months later. "For the first time in my life I wasn't a performer working before an audience, separated from it. I was a part of it, and it was a part of me." Not insignificantly, it was one of the few times in her career that Odetta wasn't singing her songs of protest and perseverance for a mostly white audience. Jan Ford later recalled that Odetta was bothered that blacks didn't show up at her concerts. "When I was older and I noticed the audience at auntie's concerts, I noticed they didn't reflect me," Ford said. "When I asked auntie about this she told me that the black community had banned her music because it reminded them too much of slavery."[31]

As the black multitudes swayed to her music, allowing her freedom songs to wash over them like a joyous breeze, Odetta must have felt a special measure of pride. Looking back on the march long afterward, however, Odetta acknowledged that one aspect of the day had bothered her greatly. "When I got up to sing, I think all the film crew went to lunch because all the camera lights that were red before I got on went to out. . . . You know, that kinda hurt," she said. "I think many times we think in terms of popularity of the person and they will turn the camera on for somebody because they have a big following or they earn a lot of money and then they turn the camera [off] instead of just filming the whole thing."[32]

No TV network had extensive coverage of the morning music, and only CBS carried the formal ceremony. But the footage that exists backs up Odetta's claim: there's film of Peter, Paul and Mary; Dylan (or as some of the black press were calling him, "country and western star Bob Dillon"); and Baez performing full songs, but only a precious few seconds of Odetta singing the "Freedom Trilogy" by the Washington Monument.

All matters of race are tangled in America, and so it was on that day, too. Odetta wasn't alone in noting that the white stars got more attention from the media, though all the singers appeared to get genuine applause from an appreciative crowd of marchers. "I preferred to see Odetta up there," the black comedian and activist Dick Gregory recalled. "She is a virtuoso musician, and she lived what we were there for. What was a white boy like Bob Dylan there for? . . . If Bob Dylan and Joan Baez and whoever the hell stood out there with the crowd and cheered for Odetta and Josh White, that would be a greater statement than arriving in their limousines and taking bows." A. W. Godfrey, a white educator who also attended the march, recalled that "one got the feeling, however, that although the white participants [like Dylan and Baez] were honored guests, they are not family."[33]

It's pretty hard to fault Baez (who is half Mexican), Dylan, and the other stars who appeared at the march for a cause they fervently supported. In helping plan the event, Ossie Davis and Harry Belafonte, who was in charge of enlisting a strong Hollywood contingent, considered white celebrities an essential ingredient for sending a message to the establishment that middle-class America was behind the push for civil rights. Belafonte didn't think Odetta's omission from the TV coverage was about race, however. "I don't think she was left out of the equation because of her politics or because of her color," he said. "I think she was left out of the equation because if they had a chance to fill the space with a story on Bob Dylan, there was more payback for that."[34]

The coverage of the march was perhaps the final proof that a tipping point in folk music had been reached and young stars had eclipsed Odetta. Indeed, when *Billboard* had ranked the top-selling folk artists earlier in the year, Baez had placed second, behind Peter, Paul and Mary and just ahead of the Kingston Trio and Harry Belafonte. Odetta appeared in a separate list of "consistent selling" folk artists, along with Pete Seeger, the Clancy Brothers, and Woody

Guthrie. Bob Dylan was relegated to a third group of "folk artists to watch," although he would soon enough turn to folk rock and eclipse all the folk singers who had paved the way for him.[35]

Baez and Odetta both sang their versions of "Oh Freedom" at the march, but now it was Baez getting most of the attention. "In the world of show business, a frail, unstylish 20-year-old girl named Joan Baez is the most acclaimed folk singer today," the *Boston Globe* had declared that summer.[36]

"I would think that at some point it would have been difficult for her when I was so much in the limelight," Baez recalled of Odetta. "Cuz she was the Queen of Folk to me; that's how I thought of her, and then years later I realized I sort of had usurped the title. You couldn't usurp what she did." Baez didn't remember the handing-over of that crown ever being an issue between them, but Odetta did, and she carried a grudge around for years before finally baring her hurt to Baez, probably sometime in the late 1960s or early 1970s. "Finally we were together, and I said, 'I need to talk to you.' And I told her about the resentments that I'd felt, and didn't feel that she was the focus of it; but I really did resent that the whole of society did whatever it did or didn't do for me, and she said she understood. But I had to tell her because whenever I'd meet her there was this barrier that she didn't work for, she didn't earn it."[37]

Odetta continued to headline at nightclubs like the Village Gate in New York and perform at colleges around the nation, and the audience was often as doting as ever. She just hadn't found a way to make the leap to superstardom when folk music was at its commercial peak in 1963. In September, RCA released *Odetta Sings Folk Songs*, her first LP with Bruce Langhorne. RCA clearly had intentions of taking Odetta to the next level of popularity, bringing in the slick producing team of Hugo & Luigi (Hugo Peretti and Luigi Creatore), cousins who'd written or produced hits for Elvis, Sam Cooke, and the Isley Brothers.

With Langhorne as her foil, Odetta made some of the swingingest music of her career. The album included mostly reworkings of traditional folk, but songs such as "900 Miles" and "Yes I See" were given a driving pulse behind Odetta's muscular vocals. The LP also included her first recording of "This Little Light of Mine," the old spiritual that would forever become associated with her.

Odetta, still straightening her hair around age fifteen, at a party for the Turnabout Theatre in Los Angeles, mid-1940s. Her mom, Flora, front row, worked as a maid for the theater. Next to Flora is master puppeteer Harry Burnett, who sponsored Odetta's first serious singing lessons.

An early version of Odetta's first solo LP, *Odetta Sings Ballads and Blues*, 1956. With producers opting not to show Odetta's large body, the cover put the focus on her trailblazing unstraightened hair.

Odetta backstage at Mandel Hall, University of Chicago, 1957.

Odetta performing at the Old Town School of Folk Music, Chicago, 1958.

Odetta and Albert Grossman (far left). The future manager of Bob Dylan and Janis Joplin was handed Odetta as one of his first clients, and she later recalled, "He built his business on my back."

Odetta, Harry Belafonte (at microphone), and Sidney Poitier (second from left) take part in a rally at the Statue of Liberty organized by the Committee to Defend Martin Luther King in May 1960 after King was indicted on politically motivated charges of lying on an Alabama tax return.

Odetta performing in Amsterdam, December 1961.

Odetta with Bruce Langhorne singing near the Washington Monument during the March on Washington, 1963.

Odetta contemplates a new song, Middletown, New York, 1966.

Odetta Sings Dylan, 1965. "She made an album of all Dylan songs," Wavy Gray said, "and it helped to skyrocket the little fella."

Odetta on stage in Birmingham, 1965, still in the early stages of desegregation, where she received a key to the city of her birth.

Odetta meets Kenichi Takeda, a young fan in Tokyo, in 1967. Takeda would become so close to her that he called Odetta his "spiritual mother."

Odetta in Tokyo in 1967, at the time that she and Garry Shead became engaged.

In the early 1970s, Odetta's trailblazing Afro grew longer. With Janis Ian, 1972.

Odetta and the bluesman Louisiana Red, late 1970s. Odetta introduced Red as her husband, but they never officially married, and he would soon move to Europe without Odetta.

Odetta dining with President Bill Clinton at the White House in 1999 after Clinton presented her with a National Medal of the Arts and Humanities.

Till the very end, even as her health failed her, Odetta rarely turned down a benefit. Odetta, Pete Seeger (center), and David Amram (left) perform at the Beacon Theatre in New York City in 2008 to raise money for Seeger's Hudson River Clearwater.

Odetta at the Musicultura festival in Macerata, Italy, June 2008. She needed oxygen when she wasn't singing from the stage in her wheelchair.

Still, if RCA had hits on its mind, it's hard to tell from the record or the marketing plan. Odetta made a push into contemporary material, with a fine version of Bob Dylan's "Blowing in the Wind" (her more formal spelling), though its waltz-like tempo was unlikely to compete with Peter, Paul and Mary's more upbeat entry. But RCA opted not to release any material as a single to generate play on radio and jukeboxes, even the sprightly "900 Miles." RCA was the company that invented the 45-rpm single, an inexpensive and disposable format that appealed to young people and had become so crucial to pop music's ecosystem. It seems likely that Hugo & Luigi, who had offices in the Brill Building and were more at home with lighthearted fare like the Tokens' "The Lion Sleeps Tonight," simply didn't know what to do with Odetta. "I can't imagine the chemistry between Odetta and H&L," said Jack Somer, who would produce the rest of Odetta's RCA albums, "as she was a generous, loving fighter for freedom and justice, and they were . . . not!"[38]

Without heavy radio rotation, *Odetta Sings Folk Songs* managed to briefly crack the *Billboard* charts, peaking at number seventy-five on the Hot 100 in October. It was the only record of her career to chart, and one can't help concluding, at least in hindsight, that RCA and Odetta missed an opportunity. The alchemy of hit-making is complex, of course, but while Bob Dylan was beginning to crank out hits and Peter, Paul and Mary's rise was continuing apace, Odetta's career remained at a plateau, despite her enormous talent. "RCA wanted to do something with her, but they didn't have 'Puff the Magic Dragon,'" Charlie Rothschild said. "They didn't have a tune that could win over the public. They had her [exceptional] singing and she sounded great but there was no hook."[39]

———————

The euphoria felt by civil rights activists and their supporters over the triumphant March on Washington turned out to be short-lived. Two and a half weeks later, on September 15, a bomb made from what police said were at least fifteen sticks of dynamite exploded under the steps of the Sixteenth Street Baptist Church in Birmingham, just before the start of Sunday services. Four girls, aged fourteen and eleven, who were getting ready in the church basement, died in the blast.

Martin Luther King Jr. telegrammed Alabama's segregationist governor, George Wallace, saying, "The blood of our children . . . is on your hands." King and the other leaders of the March on Washington sent a letter to President Kennedy demanding that he lead the nation in an expression of "national mourning and legislative action."[40]

James Baldwin announced a protest march in Greenwich Village that Sunday. A group calling itself the Committee of Artists and Writers for Justice, including Baldwin, Ossie Davis, Ruby Dee, and Odetta, announced it was sponsoring a memorial service at Town Hall the following Friday evening, with proceeds going to the families of the four girls killed in the church and two African American boys shot to death by whites in the mayhem that followed.

The bombing had left many grasping for how to combat the hatred in places like Odetta's hometown. A Harlem barber named James Horton, recently married when he heard the news of the bombing, was quoted in the *Times*: "I told my wife that I would like to dedicate my life to going down there and trying to do something about it. But then I realized that there was nothing I could do." New York Mayor Wagner said Birmingham was "sick and needs to be protected against itself." But he added that reaction to the tragedy "must be purposeful and constructive."[41]

At the packed Town Hall memorial, the chairman of the artists' and writers' group, the black novelist John O. Killens, said the bombing had raised serious doubts about the strategy of nonviolence then prevailing in the civil rights movement. Baldwin caused the biggest stir by accusing whites of collective guilt in the continued plight of Negroes, comparing their inaction in the face of violence and persecution to the complicity of ordinary Germans during the Holocaust. He also denounced Kennedy for a "lack of passion" in civil rights struggles. Odetta and Leon Bibb sang and Ruby Dee asked for an offering, collecting $762 that went to the parents of the six victims to buy gravestones for their children.[42]

Their group soon changed its name to the Association of Artists for Freedom and said it was staying together as "a cultural adjunct, and not in competition with the existing organizations fighting for civil and human rights in our country." The group said its goals were to sponsor arts in black communities and to act as a unifying force for artists concerned about the moral issues of the day, namely civil rights. "In the main, our activities will be neither political nor legislative, but cultural," the group said in a statement.[43]

But its first action was anything if not political: a call for a national Christmas boycott, asking Americans not to shop for presents but instead to give to civil rights organizations. "We had a meeting last week at Odetta's," Killens wrote in a letter to Harry Belafonte explaining the group's work. "Tomorrow we are meeting again at Jimmy Baldwin's, to see where we go from here . . . particularly in terms of how we can conduct this campaign of 'celebrating Christmas differently' this year, going back to the fundamentals of Christ's life, which has nothing to do with Santa Claus or Christmas shopping."[44]

"This year we will give our children the profoundest gift of all; the gift of truth, which is the gift of love," read an open letter from the group that ran in black newspapers, with photos of Baldwin, Davis, and Odetta. "And we will have the duty to tell them that Santa will not come this year because he is in mourning for the children of Birmingham who will get no gifts this year or the next year or the next. And to the children too young to understand we will make gifts and toys with our hands from boxes and cans and string and last year's toys and paste and paint and wood and love."[45]

Boycotts had become an accepted, if risky, tactic in the civil rights struggle to force white leaders to take the concerns of black residents seriously in places like Baton Rouge and Montgomery, though even King had hesitated before agreeing to lead the Montgomery bus boycott that first brought him to prominence. After he signed on, he'd led a local Christmas boycott of Montgomery stores to put added pressure on the city to end segregation on the buses.

But a national Christmas boycott was something else entirely. King broached the idea at a Southern Christian Leadership Conference convention in Richmond, Virginia, and was initially said to endorse it, but later backed away, and none of the national civil rights groups ended up signing on. Roy Wilkins, executive secretary of the NAACP, slammed the tactic, saying it might not be effective from an economic standpoint but would certainly harm children. "It would be unfortunate to further deprive Negro children, already brutalized by segregation, by denying them the annual joy of a Christmas tree and toys," Wilkins told the group in a letter.[46]

Newspapers, including the black press, were divided. Though it said the campaign for black civil rights was laudable, the *New York Times* editorialized that "blotting out the spirit of universal brotherhood and goodwill that is the essence of Christmas would turn what ought to be a day of love into a day of hate." Belafonte, looking back, summed up the conflict a different way. "I think the church is business—do not fuck with the payroll!" he said.[47]

But some families did participate. "We didn't have the tree and all the glitter and all the globs of presents," recalled Guy Davis. "There was a spiritual Christmas going on. We didn't avoid the subject of Christmas but it was put more in a human and humane context . . . realiz[ing] that the world was more than these products that people hustled to buy and to sell and that these things were superficial and the things that really meant something had more to do with our lives."[48]

For Odetta, the boycott might very well have harked back to her own childhood, when her family had been too poor to give her Christmas gifts. But even the fact that the little girls died not far from where she was born didn't make her any more patient with the politics or nitty-gritty work of grassroots activism. She recalled the annoyance of helping the group prepare a public statement for the media. "Ten writers went off into a room with one typewriter and they came out with a statement that felt like each of them said, 'Okay, *you* write a word, then *I'll* write a word,'" Odetta said. "And it had no *focus*. Everybody's ego had to be acknowledged." She'd once tried to join the NAACP, and "it seemed so slow," and now, with the Association of Artists for Freedom, she considered herself done as a joiner. She attended meetings through the end of the year and then moved on. "I decided with that attempt," she said, "that I'm not an organized person."[49]

CHAPTER ELEVEN

THE TIMES THEY ARE A-CHANGIN'

When RCA released Odetta's third record for the label, *It's a Mighty World*, in January 1964, her new producer, Jack Somer, pushed for a single, and Odetta, true to her commitment to the African American struggle, decided to donate her share of the proceeds to civil rights groups. If she couldn't stomach meetings and politics, she would continue to find other ways to help.

In Somer, Odetta at least had a champion in her corner. He was the fair-haired boy at RCA, having started out as an audio engineer before landing in the pop department as a producer and working with people like Lena Horne and his childhood friend, Peter Nero. Odetta would become his favorite. "She was a giant," Somer later gushed, "a wonderful, energetic, sincere, beautiful artist." He added, a bit ruefully, "I did everything I could to serve her and to promote her and to help her."[1]

The LP featured the lineup that would be Odetta's mainstay for the next few years, with Bruce Langhorne on guitar and Raphael "Les" Grinage on bass. Grinage, like his predecessor, Bill Lee, had a jazz background, having performed with Earl Hines, Bill Evans, and Charles Mingus. Like Lee, he brought an improviser's talent to the mix. "I believe that if I miss a note he knows before I do," Odetta once said.[2] When Grinage and Langhorne played with her, the trio warmed up more like a jazz outfit than a folk group, as *Hootenanny* magazine noted:

> Their musical rite is generally initiated by Langhorne, who strums a simple chord progression on the guitar. The bass player joins him and Odetta improvises lyrics—at times happy, or even childlike, and at other times, plaintive or mournful, depending on her mood. Eventually they all sing. They sing about current events, their impending concert, about each other, or about nothing in particular. The process stops as quickly as it begins—and they are ready to perform.[3]

All of Odetta's albums for RCA were recorded at the label's Studio A on East Twenty-Fourth Street, in the wee hours of the morning, as was Odetta's custom. After she'd dipped her toes into contemporary material on her previous record, *It's a Mighty World* largely returned to her comfort zone, focusing mostly on traditional folk. The title track was an exception, though: it was Odetta's first attempt at writing a pop song. The tune itself was a simple, catchy, even danceable vamp, with Odetta strumming a steady rhythm, Langhorne adding bluesy fills behind her, and Grinage supplying the pulse. In keeping with Odetta's usual themes, the song's message was about empowerment:

Take a look at you
You're a mighty soul
You're a mighty soul
And you're part of a mighty world

When the sessions ended at 3 or 4 a.m., the musicians and their producer often headed straight for an all-night Japanese restaurant near Times Square. "Always had the same meal," Somer recalled. "It was steamed sea bass and everybody would pluck the fish off the body with chopsticks, but Les always plucked out the eyes ceremonially. . . . He ate them. He was from somewhere in the South where it was normal everyday procedure. Sometimes it rather spoiled my appetite, but after you've been recording all night, you get hungry."[4]

The album's single had "It's a Mighty World" on the B side. Side A featured Odetta's rousing version of "Got My Mind on Freedom." It had started life as an old spiritual, but during the Freedom Rides, an activist had substituted the word "freedom" for "Jesus" in the lyric: "Woke this morning, with my mind stayed on Jesus." The song had become a favorite in the civil rights movement, whose focus in the early months of 1964 was on securing a vote in Congress for the Civil Rights Act. For Odetta, the song was emblematic of the two concerns that consumed her: freedom for African Americans and personal freedom from the constraints society had placed on her. Odetta had high hopes for the record, Somer said, after deciding to donate the proceeds to the groups then lobbying for passage of the bill. "We released the record as a single, and our wonderful white promotion department . . . never promoted it," he said. "I don't think the NAACP or whoever, maybe it was CORE, maybe it was SNCC, I don't remember. . . . I don't think they made a nickel on it, which I thought was tragic because I thought the song was wonderful."[5]

By the time Odetta went out on a tour of colleges and large theaters in support of the record, the Beatles owned four of the top ten songs on the *Billboard* charts in the weeks following their epoch-making February appearance on *The Ed Sullivan Show*. Reviewers continued to describe Odetta's audiences as "captivated" and moved to "thunderous applause," but some writers made ominous references, intended or not, to the dawn of the rock era. "Any doubts that the folk singers were on the way out . . . were dispelled when Odetta, backed up by a strong show, grossed $1,200 in the Queen Elizabeth [Theatre]," *Box Office* magazine reported after a concert in Vancouver. Two days earlier, Seattle's Moore Theatre remained two-thirds empty for Odetta's concert there.[6]

In May, she took her act on the most extensive foreign tour of her career, six weeks in Scandinavia, England, and Africa. With Langhorne unavailable, Peter Childs, a young Oberlin graduate who had recently been a member of a folk-bluegrass outfit called the Knob Lick Upper 10,000, managed by Al Grossman, agreed to go on the trip as backup guitarist. Grinage came along, and Charlie Rothschild served as road manager.

At thirty-three, Odetta was now a veteran performer with a decade of work behind her, no longer the shy, soft-spoken singer she had been when she started performing. It's on this tour that we get some of our first glimpses of the Odetta that friends and colleagues would remember most: the steely, powerful, charismatic presence who inspired an equal measure of awe and fear in musicians and nonmusicians alike. "Les used to call her 'd'tatris,' short for dictatrix, and she ruled the roost," Childs said. After their Sabena Airlines flight from New York's Kennedy Airport touched down in Brussels on the morning of May 30, the group made its way to the Amigo Hotel in the middle of a thunderstorm. "We were in our hotel room looking out the window at the thunderstorm and the rain splashing down on the cobblestones in Brussels and the lightning was illuminating her face," Childs recalled. "And I don't know how many pictures you've seen of Odetta really smiling happily. But it's like the radiant face of a 16-year-old girl. And that is the primary memory that I will always carry around of Odetta."[7]

In Brussels, Odetta performed for Belgian TV's *Face Au Public*, where her exhilarating finale of "Got My Mind on Freedom," with Grinage singing harmony, brought the crowd to its feet. There was a layover in London to record for ITV—a less jubilant affair, after producers nearly hid Odetta in front of a black background—then the tour moved on to Sweden and Finland for two weeks of twice-daily shows at amusement parks, where she was feted and treated like a star, Rothschild recalled.

They spent the first two weeks of July in Africa, Odetta's second time on the continent. Performing in Tanganyika and Nigeria, Odetta was driven around in a Mercedes and treated like royalty wherever she went. In Lagos, they saw crippled beggars in front of their hotel, Grinage and Childs scored some heavy-duty black ganja, and the whole group partied with some of the military officers who would soon stage a coup to end Nigeria's first brief run at democracy. "Going to Africa with Odetta was an experience," Childs said, "because she was a queen, she was a famous American folk singer . . . she was traditionally built and she was a black sister from America. And they fell all over themselves to get to her. I'm thinking now of all those colonels in the Nigerian army that later ruined Nigeria. But they were fun to party with."[8]

Odetta wanted more than a cursory look this time around. She sought out African artists and out of the way places, trying to get a sense of Africa's essence. During the Lagos trip, she arranged for the group to visit Ede, a traditional tribal town in southwest Nigeria, where the local king, known as the Timi of Ede, was also a master of the "talking drums." Their Mercedes careered through the jungle for several hours before they reached a village with stucco dwellings, where they got out and were met by the Timi's drum corps, half a dozen drummers ranging from a boy of maybe four on up to a thirty-year-old with flaming red eyes.

Their drums, with goatskin heads and leather strings that could be used to raise and lower the instruments' pitch, mimicked the tone of the Yoruba language as they "spoke" about the visitors. "They saw Odetta and they said, 'Here is a woman who is known as a queen among women,'" Childs said. "And they looked at Les who was a portly chap and they said, 'Here is the smiling elephant who shakes the trees as he stalks through the jungle.' And they looked at me and said something about liking the skirts and being unbeatable in a fight."[9]

After sightseeing trips to Egypt and Ethiopia, the group headed home on July 15 on a Pan Am flight from London to Los Angeles, flying over the North Pole. When they arrived at LAX, Childs said, Odetta used the sheer power of her presence to save him from a drug bust.

> I hate to admit to such idiocy, but I had about a pound of pot in my baggage. And it was right there on top, rolled in baggies and stuffed into socks. And she knew I had it. . . . And she was right in line in customs ahead of me. And they were opening every single bag. . . . She went through just ahead of me and then they reached in and opened up my bag. And then Odetta turned and just put something [over] on the customs guy. I don't think she even spoke. She just put something on him, his hand stopped in midair, he closed my suitcase and just passed it through. Now that's the kind of personal presence that I'm talking about.[10]

All in all, it was a much better African sojourn than her first brief encounter two years earlier when she'd felt out of sorts and disappointed that it hadn't felt like home. They returned to the East Coast in time for Odetta and Childs to perform at the Newport Folk Festival at the end of July, and it's probably no coincidence that Odetta wore colorful African robes on stage. With seventy thousand people attending over four days and nights, the festival shattered attendance records and was a huge critical success. "All this happened during a time when many have been saying the folk boom is dead or dying," Robert Shelton noted in the *New York Times*.[11]

Bob Dylan by then had emerged as folk's first among equals, a rock star in the making, and though he still wielded an acoustic guitar and harmonica, his songwriting had already begun to shift from consciousness-raising folk songs like "Masters of War" and "The Times They Are A-Changin'" to more pop-oriented material like "All I Really Wanna Do" and "Mr. Tambourine Man." It was Dylan's Sunday night performance that preceded Odetta's, but given the nation's political mood, she managed to upstage him, at least in the eyes of the critics.

The festival happened in the middle of the Freedom Summer, when young black and white college students descended on Mississippi to help SNCC and CORE register black voters under the watchful and threatening eyes of the Ku Klux Klan and their partners in local sheriff's departments. Almost immediately, two white college students from New York, Michael Schwerner and Andrew Goodman, along with James Chaney, a young black Mississippian, had disappeared and were feared dead. Their bullet-riddled bodies would be discovered a little more than a week after the festival ended.

So although Dylan was the clear audience favorite, it was Odetta's spiritual crescendo, when she brought Peter, Paul and Mary; the Freedom Singers; Pete Seeger; and the Clancy Brothers and Tommy Makem to the stage to sing "Got My Mind on Freedom" and "We Shall Overcome" that summed up the nation's mood. The performers all joined hands as they had the previous year, this time with Odetta out in front of them, her natural hair and African attire adding another layer of intention to the message of freedom for all. "The festival closed in a symbolic finale merging music and social meaning," Shelton wrote in the *Times*. "Odetta led other performers and an audience of 15,000 in two songs of the Negro integration movement.

The social commitment of folk music blended with its esthetic core in a triumphant conclusion. There was a democratizing spirit about this fusion of Negro and white musical forms and about the people who are the conveyor belts of these traditions that was little short of inspirational."[12]

To be sure, although Odetta no longer reigned supreme in folk, she remained a potent force in music. That was evident a month after Newport, when a young Carly Simon, still in college, performed at the Potting Shed in Lenox, Massachusetts, as part of the Simon Sisters, her duo with sister Lucy. Odetta had been Simon's inspiration to begin singing in the first place, and in the gymnasium at Riverdale Country School in the Bronx, Simon had often regaled students with "Bald Headed Woman," even imitating Odetta's hand claps. But when her heroine showed up at the Potting Shed, seated at the front table, it was more than the stage-averse Simon could handle as the duo launched into their first song. "I just fainted. I just lost it and I fainted right onto [Odetta's] table," Simon recalled. "And the next thing I knew I was kind of being brought to back stage with Odetta kind of fanning my face because my sister had had time to tell her this is all because of you, thank you very much Odetta."[13]

Still, one's head would have to have been in the sand not to notice the Beatles, the Dave Clark Five, the Animals, the Rolling Stones, and the Kinks lighting up the US charts that summer and fall, brash British bands inspired by American blues and rock 'n' roll to create a new pop aesthetic for young people to latch onto. Odetta's immediate answer was *Odetta Sings of Many Things* released by RCA in September, and of all her early-period folk albums, it seems the most sea-tossed, as if she—and whoever was managing her career—didn't know how to navigate the waters churning around her. With Langhorne and Grinage backing her, the songs were well played and passionately sung as usual, especially "Wayfarin' Stranger," a traditional folk tune most associated until then with Burl Ives, and "Sea Lion Woman," an old children's song that Nina Simone had reimagined and released that year as the B side of "Mississippi Goddam." But the whole package seemed to add up to less than the sum of its parts, perhaps because it was one of the few Odetta LPs from the period that lacked a strong freedom song to anchor it. If her music was going to evolve, she was going to have to find new ways to inspire her listeners.

Her next spark would flicker from an unlikely source. In the late fall or early winter of 1964–65, Jack Somer was sitting in his second-floor office at RCA when his secretary rang through and said a young man on the phone wanted to play him some music. "Make an appointment for him," Somer told her.[14] A few days later, Paul Simon, twenty-four, walked in with a dub of a song called "Sounds of Silence." He wanted Odetta to record it.

Simon and Garfunkel had included the original acoustic version of "Sounds of Silence" on their debut LP, *Wednesday Morning 3 AM*, which had recently been released to lukewarm reviews. It would be almost a year before their producer at Columbia Records, none other than Tom Wilson, would add electric instruments to the mix without their knowledge and re-release it as a single, making stars of the duo. With that destiny lying in the future, Simon seems to have sought out Odetta to build some prestige as a songwriter.

"Let me think about it," Odetta told Somer, who believed Simon's song was just right for her, but in the end she decided not to record it.[15] However, the episode spurred discussions about what Odetta could record next to advance her career. She suggested an album of songs by Buffy Sainte-Marie, a Canadian-born Cree Indian singer who had just released her first record, which included her antiwar anthem "Universal Soldier."

In the end, they discarded the idea in favor of an LP of songs by another promising young songwriter: Bob Dylan. *Odetta Sings Dylan*, released in March of 1965, would be the first major album of Dylan covers (the little-known Linda Mason had released a forgettable Dylan collection the previous year). The songs, as one would expect, included plenty of Dylan's protest material, such as "The Times They Are A-Changin'," "Masters of War," and "With God on Our Side," but also more introspective tunes like "Don't Think Twice, It's Alright," already practically a nightclub standard among young folk singers. The most remarkable thing about the record is that seven of the songs hadn't yet been released by Dylan, including "Baby I'm in the Mood for You," "Paths of Victory," and "Long Ago, Far Away," all of which Dylan had recorded as demos for the music publisher M. Witmark & Sons a few years earlier—the tapes of which, it seems, Al Grossman had provided to Odetta.

That helps explain the visitor Odetta received during one of the late-night recording sessions in Studio A. "It might have been 1, 2 in the morning, the door to the control room opens up and in walks Bob Dylan," Somer recalled. "And he didn't step in more than 3 or 4 feet, and it was in the middle of a take. She saw him, she stopped playing, she looked through the glass and she said, 'Get your white ass out of here!' And he turned around and left. He wanted to hear what she was doing and she didn't want any part of his being there." Odetta recalled a politer exchange, perhaps one that occurred a bit later outside the control room: "He came by RCA with his entourage. And I said, 'Oh, no. I'm not going to have the writer sit up here telling me I didn't mean it like that.' And he says, 'Well, can I correct some words?'" Working from Dylan's demos, the publisher had incorrectly transcribed some lyrics. After he made the corrections, Odetta recalled, "I said, 'Now ya gotta get out.' And he understood."[16]

Odetta doesn't seem to have been a particular devotee of Dylan's lyrics, requiring lyric sheets even for "Blowin' in the Wind" (released this time under its original title). She didn't try to sound like Dylan or capture the feel of his arrangements. In fact, she seemed to go out of her way to put her own stamp on the material. She took his perky folk ditty "Baby I'm in the Mood for You" and set it to a mid-tempo rock beat that had an almost country flavor. Likewise, on "With God on Our Side," she, Langhorne, and Grinage gave it a propulsive energy that sets it apart from Dylan's more poetic folk minstrel version. And "Masters of War," perhaps the album's most enduring achievement, spotlights the riveting power of Odetta's singing, over a brooding minor key backdrop, taking Dylan's antiwar imagery to an emotional, almost operatic crescendo.

She must have known that her Dylan interpretations would be scrutinized in a way that her renditions of dusty ballads and work songs wouldn't. The session was tense, especially for "Mr. Tambourine Man," often considered the song that set Dylan forth into his most creative period as a songwriter. He wouldn't release it on vinyl until about a week after Odetta's record came out, although he'd been singing it live for the better part of a year. Odetta opted for a nearly eleven-minute-long version—twice as long as Dylan's—a more moody, ephemeral reading of the tune. But three hours and ten takes hadn't satisfied her, and at 3 a.m. Somer decided to douse the lights in the studio and isolate Odetta from the others. "I can do nothing to ease that struggle," Somer recalled. "Odetta is best left alone when a troublesome interpretation is gestating within her; she is deeply jealous of her music, even when it goes badly." He went on:

> Finally, on the 11th take, Odetta arrives at whatever destination she was seeking. "Mmmmmm. . . . " She says into the loudspeaker. It is a sigh of relief, a moan of pleasure, a groan of joy. And three heartbeats later a similar sound comes from the phantom Bruce Langhorne: "Uh-uh. . . . mmmmmm. . . . " From both phantoms comes the soft strum of guitars, followed next by the gutty beat of the bass. And the sighs and groans pick up on the beat. It is an improvisation, a wordless conversation, a celebration of life that grows more vital with each beat. It's a Southern sound, a Black sound, a beautiful sound.[17]

Afterward Somer and the musicians went out for steamed bass and boiled rice and watched the sun come up in the east.

The impact of *Odetta Sings Dylan* was mixed, as were the reviews. "She made Dylan famous," said Wavy Gravy, the counterculture icon and good friend of both Dylan and Odetta. "She made an album of all Dylan songs and it helped to skyrocket the little fella. For sure. . . . She was the Big O." *Variety* echoed this view, calling the LP "a recognition of young singer-composer Bob Dylan as one of the most creative and influential personalities on the folk-pop scene." When Elvis, who had "become fascinated with the work of Odetta" (and Dylan) in the mid-sixties, heard her version of "Tomorrow Is a Long Time," he decided to record it himself.[18]

But not everyone was so impressed. "She is as authoritative as the Delphic oracle in 'The Times They Are A-Changin',' brave and bluesy in 'Walkin' Down the Line'; but she melts the fierceness of 'Masters of War' into a mere lament," *Time* said. That was Robert Shelton's conclusion when Odetta performed the new material at New York's Town Hall, singling out three of the Dylan covers as the weakest moments of the evening. "Two seemed overly syncopated for their content and 'Mr. Tambourine Man,' a most difficult mood piece to project with meaning, became leaden-tempoed and prolix."[19]

Though Odetta insisted that her music had to evolve, some of her early fans were distressed at her new direction. The criticism seems a bit shrill in retrospect, as if they wanted Odetta to remain sealed in amber from her earliest days on the folk scene. Izzy Young blamed Al Grossman for her supposed downfall. "He ruined Odetta," he told the folklorist Richard Reuss that summer. "He tried to make an image of her like the female Belafonte or something—didn't work. And now it's very sad to see her putting out an album of Bob Dylan songs. I mean that is the saddest thing of all."[20]

Once again RCA chose not to release any singles, and the LP never dented the charts. An album of songs by folk music's poet and prophet didn't translate into a hit. "I think she did that [record] in hopes that something would come out of it," Charlie Rothschild said. "But they were very supportive of her, they liked her. It just didn't evolve."[21]

———

When Harry Belafonte asked Odetta to support Martin Luther King's nonviolent campaign in Selma, Alabama, in March of 1965, she heeded the call as usual. Despite the heroic efforts of civil rights workers over several years to register black voters in the South, they remained shamefully disenfranchised. Nowhere was that more evident than in Selma, where whites had used the usual tactics—including literacy tests and physical intimidation—to exclude all but 335 of the city's 15,000 blacks of voting age from the rolls.

With passage of the Civil Rights Act the previous summer, President Lyndon Johnson, in his State of the Union address at the beginning of the year, had announced plans to push for voting rights legislation at about the same time the Southern Christian Leadership Conference and SNCC began a new effort to force the issue in Selma. Sheriff Jim Clark and Alabama State Troopers had no qualms about subjecting civil rights protesters to billy clubs, cattle prods, night-sticks, and even bullets, and when officers shot and killed a young black activist named Jimmie Lee Jackson, it raised both the tensions and the stakes in the Selma campaign.

On March 7—a day that would become known as "Bloody Sun-day"—SNCC's John Lewis had attempted to lead around six hundred marchers from Selma to Montgomery for a protest at the Alabama State Capitol. But when they tried to cross the Edmund Pettus Bridge over the Alabama River, Clark's men and state troopers had viciously attacked them with nightsticks, whips, and tear gas, wounding doz-ens of people and leaving Lewis with a fractured skull.

Two days after Bloody Sunday, King arrived in Selma and led a group of protesters back to the Edmund Pettus Bridge, but after be-ing ordered to turn back, they retreated after a short prayer. Plans were already underway for a repeat of the full march that Lewis had attempted. By then, President Johnson had addressed a joint session of Congress and pushed for a voting rights bill, using language that anyone familiar with the music of the civil rights movement would understand:

> What happened in Selma is part of a far larger movement which reaches into every section and state of America. It is the effort of American Negroes to secure for themselves the full blessings of American life. Their cause must be our cause too. Because it's not just Negroes, but really it's all of us who must overcome the crip-pling legacy of bigotry and injustice. And we shall overcome.

On March 21, a Sunday, the forty-six-mile march from Selma to Montgomery began with thirty-two hundred people at the doors of an African Methodist Episcopal Church, but only three hundred could make the entire trek because of court-ordered limits on cer-tain roads. The *New Yorker* described the initial group as a mix of "local Negroes, Northern clergymen, members of labor unions, dele-gates from state and city governments, entertainers, mothers pushing baby carriages, members of civil rights groups more or less at odds with one another, isolated, shaggy marchers with an air of simple vagrancy, doctors, lawyers, teachers, children, college students," and random civilians.[22]

Over the first two days, the marchers, led by King and protected by US Army soldiers and federalized Alabama National Guardsmen, recrossed the Edmund Pettus Bridge, marched down highways and through swampland, and sang freedom songs, while enduring insults along the way from white onlookers, including children who yelled "Nigger lover!" and "White Nigger!" They also worried over rumors of snipers, a Ku Klux Klan attack, and a segregationist plot to unleash a den of deadly copperheads and cottonmouths at one of their campsites.[23]

By Tuesday evening, the footsore marchers arrived at a farm belonging to black millionaire A. G. Gaston in Burkville, where they would camp for the night. It was there, the *New Yorker* reported, where "Odetta appeared at the campsite, and found all the other marchers, including another singer, Pete Seeger, fast asleep."[24] (Only a few entertainers had made all or part of the march up until that point, including *Bonanza* star Pernell Roberts, journeyman actor Gary Merrill, Seeger, and Len Chandler.)

There's no evidence that Odetta marched the following day, and many years later she confirmed that she had not. But she was among the stars Belafonte had recruited, at King's request, for a celebratory concert Wednesday night, before the final day's march into Montgomery to present Governor Wallace with a list of demands. "I was calling on short notice, and yet the cause was so compelling, the news photos of violence on the Pettus Bridge so fresh, that almost everyone I reached out to agreed to come," Belafonte recalled. "Nina Simone, Joan Baez, Johnny Mathis, Billy Eckstine, Tony Bennett, Odetta, Peter, Paul and Mary, the Chad Mitchell Trio, and more all said yes."[25]

The show was to take place at the last campsite: the athletic field of the City of St. Jude in Montgomery, a forty-acre complex of Roman Catholic institutions for Negroes (including the South's first integrated hospital, plus a school and orphanage). But with the crowd swelling to ten thousand or more, including marchers and supporters who streamed in for the concert, the equipment was hours late in arriving and the ground so muddy that a makeshift stage had to be fashioned on coffins donated by black undertakers in Selma. In the dark, audience members pushed toward the stage, and claustrophobia, panic, and exhaustion set in, delaying the concert. "Overcomed [*sic*] either by the crowd or by the stars, people started fainting . . . in spite of Ossie Davis' constant plea for everyone 'to keep calm,'" *Jet* reported.[26]

The show finally began close to midnight, with a bus behind the stage serving as a makeshift green room. Sammy Davis Jr. sang the National Anthem, Peter, Paul and Mary did "Blowin' in the Wind" and "If I Had a Hammer," Nina Simone snarled out "Mississippi Goddam," and Dick Gregory and Nipsey Russell told jokes. After Shelley Winters addressed the crowd, Belafonte kissed her on the cheek, saying, "If Wallace could have seen that." "When Odetta came back to the bus after performing, the applause from her peers was deafening," according to one report.[27]

In hindsight, it seems almost matter of fact to hear about stars showing up to sing for the marchers in the dead of night, but given the violence that already had occurred during the first Selma march and countless other demonstrations in the South, and the vitriol and hatred coming from white spectators along the way this time around, it was hardly a given that everyone would be protected when they trotted on stage to perform, even with armed troops forming a perimeter around the campsite. "Several more rumors of plots to assassinate Martin were swirling and circulating," Coretta Scott King recalled. "That night, as we stood on the stage, I thought about what sitting ducks we were, out in the open night, with the bright stage lights beaming down on us." Martin Luther King called for "every self-respecting Negro here" to join them in Montgomery for the final demonstration the next day in front of the Capitol.[28]

With the marchers at the campsite, the stars stayed in the Greystone Motel in Montgomery that night, kept awake by shouting segregationists outside. On Thursday morning, March 25, when everyone gathered for the final four-mile march to the city center, a disagreement broke out as to who should go first, the famous names likely to attract the attention of the media or the three hundred marchers who'd braved the entire five-day ordeal. "All you dignitaries got to get behind me," Profit Barlow, a 17-year-old marcher, shouted. "I didn't see any of you fellows in Selma, and I didn't see you on the way to Montgomery. Ain't nobody going to get in front of me but Dr. King." Odetta weighed in. "Man, don't let the morale crumble," she said. "The original three-hundred deserve to be first." Her point of view won the day, with the three hundred leading, followed by King, A. Philip Randolph, and other dignitaries.[29]

During the march in, Odetta briefly linked arms with Rosa Parks, who had been shunted aside at times that morning, unrecognized by some organizers and police. (Asked many years later which songs inspired her the most, Parks said, "Essentially, all the songs Odetta sings.") Odetta said she was marching to pay "an overdue debt." Earlier that month, she'd been defensive when a *New York Times* reporter had asked her why she didn't take part in pickets and demonstrations. "I could run around like a chicken with its head cut off," she said. "But you have to choose. Many times it is felt you're not accomplishing anything unless you get your head knocked."[30]

At a platform erected in front of the Capitol, the entertainers continued singing until all the marchers, now swelled to some thirty thousand, had arrived. "It's a great day, great day, great day," Belafonte told the crowd. "And there's millions on the way!" "'The Star-Spangled Banner' spilled into 'Blowin' in the Wind,' 'Go Tell It on the Mountain,' and 'This Land is Your Land' among patriotic folk songs and spirituals led by singers grouped around the cluster of microphones—Odetta, Leon Bibb, Oscar Brand, Len Chandler in a pith helmet, Joan Baez barefoot in a velvet dress," one of King's biographers wrote. King spoke in front of the Capitol steps where Jefferson Davis had taken the oath as president of the Confederacy. "I know Governor Wallace is waiting for us to leave so that his town can return to normalcy," King told the throngs. He added, "The only normalcy we shall be satisfied with is the normalcy of brotherhood . . . the normalcy of justice . . . the normalcy of peace."[31]

After the rally, participants were warned to get out of Montgomery before dark, as this invading army was clearly in enemy territory. A rush ensued to find rides on chartered buses or with volunteers ferrying marchers out of town in cars and pickup trucks. Harriet Hutchinson (née Cohen), a junior at Newark State College in New Jersey, had come with a group of students and spent the night in the campsite before joining the final march. But after all the speeches, she got separated from her group; she recalled:

> I was wandering around on some street and all of a sudden this very large black woman walks out on the porch and I did a double-take because I knew who it was. And I said, oh my goodness, that's Odetta. And she says, "Honey, you lost?" and I was, yes, I was. I was way lost. So she went inside . . . made a phone call and told me which direction I needed to go to get [transportation]. I was on the last truck out of Montgomery. . . . So basically, Odetta saved my life.[32]

Viola Liuzzo didn't fare so well. Luizzo, thirty-nine, a white mother of five and wife of a Teamsters official from Detroit, had driven to Alabama to volunteer after watching the attack on the Edmund Pettus Bridge. As Liuzzo ferried marchers back to Selma in her green Oldsmobile, Ku Klux Klansmen pulled up beside her car in neighboring Lowndes County and put two bullets in her head, killing her instantly.

More than four decades after Selma, Belafonte recalled that he and Odetta narrowly avoided being in the car with Liuzzo. "We were supposed to have been in her car," he said. "But because she had an urgency, we deferred to her to take the car to go. And when the car did not come back we heard that the Klan had met her on the way and murdered her." When they got the news, Belafonte said, Odetta told him: "You know, Harry, we're gonna have to give some serious consideration to why it was her and not us. What does this tell us we need to do?" Curiously, Belafonte didn't include the story in his memoir, instead recalling that it had been Tony Bennett who had declined a seat in Liuzzo's car for the fateful ride. Whatever the case, it was clear that all those who campaigned for voting rights in Selma did so at some considerable risk. Less than six months later, President Johnson signed the Voting Rights Act into law.[33]

———

It had been nearly six years since Odetta and Danny Gordon had married in Chicago. Odetta had been on the road almost constantly since then, pausing only occasionally to enjoy any kind of domestic life. By April of 1965, their marriage was irrevocably broken. "I knew there were problems," Selma Thaler recalled, but Odetta wasn't one to share much of her private side, even with close friends. "It was not the kind of thing that she would have sat down and told me specifically." Danny filed for divorce in California, citing "extreme cruelty" and "grievous mental suffering." Odetta didn't contest the divorce, which would become final a little more than a year later.[34]

Since the demise of their marriage occurred five years before California popularized the "no fault" divorce, the charges in the complaint must be viewed with more than a little skepticism. In order to obtain even a mutually agreed-upon dissolution, couples had to convince the court that one party had suffered dreadfully at the hands of the other. Aside from bilking Odetta financially, Danny had hardly been the model husband, propositioning Judy Collins less than two years after his wedding, and in a casual manner that suggests it wasn't an isolated incident. Odetta later on made it clear she had given up by then on finding bliss with Danny—and also that her career had to come first. "Anything or anybody who affected my throat has had to get out of my life, O.K.," she said. "Marriage went like that." And she had this advice for young artists, not citing Danny but probably with him at least partly in mind: "Be careful of those who are spotlight-seekers and star-fuckers."[35]

Since Danny had ostensibly been helping manage Odetta, the divorce left her with half a manager in Al Grossman at a time when her career really needed steering. And Grossman now had his hands full, with Dylan's star heading into the stratosphere and an ever-expanding client list including Mimi and Richard Farina, Ian & Sylvia, Gordon Lightfoot, John Lee Hooker, Phil Ochs, and of course, Peter, Paul and Mary.

Odetta had little time to ponder her next move. She headed to the Far East with Langhorne and Grinage in mid-April for a two-month tour, first stopping in Australia, which had been a bit late to embrace the folk boom. Critics were calling the arrival of top US folk artists in Australia that spring and summer, including Odetta, Judy Collins, and Josh White, an "American Folk Music Invasion."[36] They seemed especially eager to hear Odetta, whom they had seen on Harry Belafonte's TV special and heard on their duet single "Hole in the Bucket."

Odetta performed one-night stands in five cities, Brisbane, Sydney, Melbourne, Adelaide, and Perth, and sang on the Australian *Bandstand* TV show, modeled on *American Bandstand*. More of the usual accolades followed her concerts, including her "triumphant" performance in Sydney, where she sang four encores and only failed to impress when she sang Dylan's "Tomorrow Is a Long Time" and "With God on Our Side." In Melbourne, an almost-capacity crowd, mainly of young people, applauded her work songs and blues and "refused to allow Odetta to leave the stage until she had sung at least three encores." "She was a big hit," Charlie Rothschild recalled. "We did five towns. Sellouts. They were decent sized venues. And she was treated as a superstar over there."[37]

If the US was in the midst of racial turmoil, Odetta didn't escape it in Australia, where the aboriginal problem was just starting to come to a head. The country's indigenous people lacked the right to vote, were often refused service in restaurants and hotels, and had little economic opportunity beyond their squalid camps outside of towns. A month before Odetta arrived, a group of Sydney University students, branded the "freedom riders" by the press, had toured aboriginal communities for two weeks to call attention to their plight. When reporters questioned her, Odetta, no longer polite to a fault, weighed in on the controversy with a directness that would be her hallmark as a mature adult. "You have racial prejudice in Australia," she said. "I have seen and heard of some pitiful conditions regarding your aborigines. Things in Australia seem to be running along the same lines as in America."[38]

In May, the tour reached Japan for shows in Tokyo, Osaka, Sapporo, and other cities. At Tokyo's Kōsei Nenkin hall, Odetta overcame the language barrier to get the audience singing and clapping to freedom songs. "The audience was completely caught by the voluminous singing of Odetta," *Billboard* reported. "She sung many folk songs and spirituals, but 'Water Boy' and 'We Shall Overcome' were most impressive. She repeated the latter five times, singing together with the audience."[39] During days off, they toured Hiroshima at Odetta's request and rode a bullet train. Odetta learned a Japanese folk song and Pete Seeger and Alex Comfort's "One Man's Hands" in Japanese to sing in her concerts, winning over her crowds with her effort.

On June 5, she performed at Aichi Cultural Auditorium in Nagoya City. No one singing along in the hall that night better illustrated the spiritual force of Odetta's music than Kenichi Takeda, a skinny nineteen-year-old living in Tokyo who had recently lost his mother to tuberculosis. He was so moved by Odetta that he remained in his seat until every last member of the audience of fifteen hundred had filed politely out of the theater. "It was her voice that immediately penetrated my soul," he recalled. "I remember it rang like bells in a cathedral." Takeda would arrange to meet Odetta on her next trip to Japan, and she became a lifelong friend and his "spiritual mother," he said. Sensing his deep loss, she would later dedicate a version of "Hey Jude" to Takeda from the stage. "She . . . taught me of the greater things that connect us as human beings: the dream of freedom," Takeda said.[40] For Odetta, her Japan visits would soothe her from the daily fractures over race in the United States. "Japan is a second homeland for me because here I can forget racial prejudice and sing truly as an individual human being," she would tell the press in Tokyo a couple of years later.[41]

Back from Asia, she arrived in August at the Newport Folk Festival, where Bob Dylan picked up a black Stratocaster to play an electric set, and his apostasy put a big nail in the coffin of the folk revival. A night earlier, Odetta had performed, "really belting it . . . and the audience loved every minute of it," *Billboard* reported, but more telling was the focus on Dylan by the press and the fans who either loved or hated his new direction. In contrast, on the grounds of the festival, as one reporter noted, "Pete Seeger, Odetta, and even Peter, Paul and Mary, went about virtually unnoticed."[42]

As musical tastes morphed in the US and young fans drifted toward folk rock, there was plenty of excitement for American folk acts overseas, an avenue that Odetta would increasingly turn to. She had the same effect on her foreign audiences that she'd had in front of American crowds when folk music was still new and exciting.

Right after Newport, Odetta returned to Sweden for two weeks of shows, and from there, she, Langhorne, and Grinage flew to Israel. They debuted in Tel Aviv, then moved on to Beersheba, Haifa, and Jerusalem, where they performed at Binyanei Ha'Uma concert hall. According to one account that appeared in the *Jerusalem Post*, hundreds of people stayed behind after Odetta's last encore, "even after the lights were turned on, standing at their seats and clapping frantically." "Israelis have been known for either being very bad or very good audiences," M. Geringer wrote, "but there was never any question from the beginning as to her reception. She captivated us and made the house come down."[43]

She flew back home, clearly energized by her travels. "Let me tell you about the countries we've covered," she enthused to a reporter soon after. "Australia, and Japan. Finland, Sweden, and Denmark. Belgium and England. Israel and Africa. Fantastic! . . . Relationships [overseas] are growing."[44]

On the heels of her ecstatic reception in Israel, Odetta got her first chance to see how her music would play in the place of her birth. She'd been back to Birmingham a couple of times to visit family but never to perform. And she'd sworn off doing shows in places that were segregated. But she made an exception when asked to help raise money for an arts center for impoverished children in Macon County, home to Booker T. Washington's Tuskegee Institute.

Martin Luther King had called Birmingham "the most thoroughly segregated city in the United States"—section 597 of the city code had even made it unlawful "for a Negro and a white person to play together or in company with each other in any game of cards, dice, dominoes or checkers." The city had made progress in the two years since the bombing of the Sixteenth Street Baptist Church, integrating several schools under court order, integrating restaurants and lunch counters, removing "whites only" signs at public water fountains and restrooms, opening some jobs to blacks, and allowing mixed audiences at the Municipal Auditorium where Odetta was scheduled to perform. "We haven't had any miracles here, and we don't expect any," a white minister, the Rev. John C. Turner, had remarked as the city undertook those changes, "but we have made a beginning."[45]

On October 2, shortly after her Eastern Airlines flight touched down at Birmingham International Airport around two in the afternoon, Odetta made her way to the A. C. Gaston Motel. For many years, it had been the only deluxe accommodation open to black visitors in the city and had been used by King and other civil rights leaders as a headquarters during the historic 1963 campaign. Her concert was slated for 8:30 that night. She wasn't about to go wandering around beforehand. "I was lost in that city," she admitted.[46]

Two years earlier, Birmingham voters had elected Albert Boutwell as mayor over Bull Connor, the commissioner of public safety and public symbol of the city's racist regime. Boutwell, a former lieutenant governor, was considered a moderate but had nevertheless defended the city's "habits of tradition" and warned against outside interference in Birmingham's racial struggles. "Anything is better than Connor," a black insurance agent named John Drew, told the *New York Times*. "But the new administration is a complete disappointment to us. It had such a great challenge, but it is a do-nothing administration. The mayor is a weak, sick old man."[47]

Still, Boutwell was trying. The week before Odetta's visit, he'd sent a letter to concert organizers, recognizing "the accomplishments of Odetta Gordon, and the singular contribution she has made and [is] making to the arts and culture of America."[48] But getting an audience for her in Birmingham presented a challenge. For one thing, neither the *Birmingham News* (the largest white-owned newspaper at the time) nor the *Birmingham World* (the longest-running African American–owned paper) advertised or covered the concert. Both white-owned and black-owned Southern papers then often steered clear of race issues for fear of offending advertisers.

The only place to read about Odetta's visit, in fact, was the *Southern Courier*, a paper founded a few months earlier by two Harvard undergraduates—veterans of the Freedom Summer—to cover the events of the civil rights movement in the South that the local press was neglecting. The *Courier* reported that the concert promoter, a veterinarian named Dr. Doris Mitchell, "had run into a stone wall" in Birmingham. "Some people told her that Birmingham was not the place for Odetta to sing, even though this is where she was born," the paper said.[49]

Bill Barclift, a white student at Birmingham-Southern College, told a reporter that Odetta wasn't well known in Birmingham. "Folksinging is a fad in the North that hasn't reached here yet," he said. "All the fads trickle down here eventually, but it is sort of like the Great Lakes—they will get down here some time, but it will take a while because that Mississippi flows slow." A local merchant added,

"Negroes have never heard of her. You've got to remember this is a mining town and most people don't go for cultural stuff." Jesse Lewis, a black advertising executive, predicted fewer than 150 African Americans would attend the show. "This is a show for white people," he said.[50]

The concert, held the same night as the annual Ole Miss–Alabama football game, drew a thousand people in a venue that seats at least five thousand. That probably accounts for the show's late start, with Odetta and promoters hoping for a larger turnout. She finally appeared from behind a velvet curtain wearing a long white gown and opened the show with "If I Had a Hammer," followed by "House of the Rising Sun" and "Joshua Fit de Battle of Jericho." She then dedicated—boldly, given the mostly white Alabama audience—"Ain't No Grave Gonna Hold My Body Down" to the people who died for the civil rights movement, "not excluding Malcolm X," who'd been assassinated earlier in the year.[51]

The applause grew louder after each song. When she introduced her final number, "Got My Mind on Freedom," she beseeched her audience: "Help sing this song. Even if you are not in favor of the civil rights movement, there must be something you want to be free of." The crowd demanded an encore, and she came back out to sing "Ain't Gonna Let Nobody Turn Me 'Round." Then someone shouted "We Shall Overcome!" She obliged, and everyone joined in. She received several standing ovations.[52]

The concert must have been bittersweet for Odetta. Given the size of the crowd, it was hardly a hero's welcome for a returning daughter who'd done so much to promote the cause of black culture, freedom, and pride in America. The lack of interest among working-class blacks in Birmingham was probably more of an indication that they still weren't part of America's cultural mainstream than it was a commentary on her music.

But she'd gotten the crowd going. And after the concert, behind closed doors, probably—unreported even by the *Courier*—she received another dose of recognition: a key to the city that had two years earlier tried to break black spirits with firehouses and attack dogs. It was a gold bangle about three inches long, with "City of Birmingham" highlighted in blue around a gold emblem of city hall. It seems likely that Mayor Boutwell presented it to her. His appointment book for the night of the concert has the notation "Odetta Gordon-8:30 pm Negro singer." She kept the key as one of her prized mementos, although one could certainly understand her muted response when a reporter asked a few weeks later about the trip to Birmingham. "For a big city, that's a little key," Odetta offered. "Don't guess it opens anything."[53]

CHAPTER TWELVE

FREEDOM GETS PERSONAL

S omething was different. The crowds at her concerts noticed it. The reviewers noticed it. Friends noticed it. As the middle 1960s drifted toward the later 1960s, there was a change in Odetta. Maybe it was age. Or experience. Or the demise of a bad marriage. But the woman who had devoted so much to the cause of freedom was herself becoming freer on stage, more comfortable in her own skin as she approached forty. "You had seen this girl perform at least 30 times since 1958, and every time but this one she was uptight, withdrawn, letting her king-sized voice do all the work for her," a *Washington Post* reviewer wrote of a show at the Carter Barron Amphitheater in 1966. "But this night . . . she was loose, almost garrulous, enjoying herself. She was Odetta humanized, and this was something new."[1]

It didn't matter that Odetta got second billing that particular night, with ads trumpeting Peter, Paul and Mary in big type, and a smaller "plus! Odetta" underneath. There she was, conversing with the crowd between songs, strumming her guitar like a rock 'n' roller, and . . . could it be? Yes. Swiveling her hips to the beat. As another reviewer would put it later on: "Today, what she sings, even if the lyrics and the songs' history are redolent of oppressions, is not a protest in the sense it was in the Tin Angel days. Today rather it is a celebration, an affirmation. . . . She glows on stage, she plays guitar with a joy that is rewarding just to observe, and she sings with exultation."[2]

"There's been a change," Odetta explained. "A coming out of the cocoon. Like I've always loved to dance. But I was always self-conscious of size. Then about a year ago, I started going out to disco-theques and just dancing. Not alone in my home, but out in public."[3] One place was the Electric Circus, a "psychedelic disco" and concert venue on St. Mark's Place in Greenwich Village, where Odetta could be seen partying with an orange flower painted on her large hand with the talon-like fingernails.

She began performing more in nightclubs and less in college audi-toriums. And although some of the change could be pegged to the de-clining fortunes of folk music as a draw on campus, Odetta chalked it up to the fact that she was finally "emotionally ready" for the physical intimacy of clubs. "Now I'm not so uptight as I was before and it's not so difficult for me to be close to an audience," she said.[4] Places like the Troubadour in Los Angeles, the Cellar Door in Washington, DC, and, especially, the Village Gate in New York became like second homes.

The Gate, Art D'Lugoff's cavernous cellar club on the corner of Bleecker and Thompson streets, with its huge stage, studio-like acous-tics, and seating for 450, was as close as Odetta ever got to a "singer in residence" gig. Even more attractive than the venue itself, a perfect forum for her earth-shattering vocals, was the way she was treated by the diehard lefty D'Lugoff, a "round, rumpled, bearded man," ac-cording to one music critic, one who was happiest when an ethnically diverse crowd was taking in the jazz and folk music careening off the club's seventeen-foot ceilings. "She was very much at home at the Village Gate," recalled Leonard "Boots" Jaffee, who met Odetta in the middle 1960s and became her unofficial "adopted" son. "She was very much into being a star: 'I want my service. I want my hospitality.' And if she didn't get it she would be very upset. And Art D'Lugoff always made her feel welcome."[5]

Jaffee and Odetta met at a lefty summer camp called the Shaker Village Workshop in Lebanon, New York, where Odetta was per-forming. Jaffee was about fifteen, and they immediately hit it off and started hanging out. "She met my parents and they got along very well," Jaffee said, adding with a laugh, "[a]nd she just started sharing custody."[6] Odetta's marriage had produced no children, so informally adopting the white teenager from Queens seemed to fulfill her mother-ing tendencies, although Odetta wasn't a typical parental figure. When she was in the city, she took Jaffee to concerts and to parties at Maya

Angelou's house and got him harmonica lessons with Paul Butterfield, whose Butterfield Blues Band was now an Al Grossman production.

With her divorce about to be finalized, Odetta longed for another kind of companionship. She returned to Australia for a two-week tour in March of 1966 and promptly found it, or thought she had. Her first show, at Sydney Town Hall, got a lukewarm review in the *Sydney Morning Herald*, the writer praising "Got My Mind on Freedom" but savaging her "Mr. Tambourine Man" and a children's song she'd based on Winnie the Pooh. But she remained upbeat, joking to a reporter that she was working on an entire LP based on the A. A. Milne character, to be called, of course, *Odetta Sings Pooh*. Her good spirits might have been a reflection of what happened while she was in Sydney: she fell in love—rather quickly, as usual—with a twenty-three-year-old white artist named Garry Shead, who was then working for the Australian Broadcasting Corporation in Sydney. Shead's friend, the Australian folk singer Gary Shearston, had invited him to a party at a terrace house in Paddington, promising that other folk singers would be there. "It was very low key, just quiet, a few drinks and things like that, pleasant," recalled Shead, whose figurative paintings now hang in Australian museums and galleries. "I saw this kind of presence in there, by herself. It was kind of low lights. I just had to go over." Thin and soft-spoken, Shead walked up and asked Odetta to dance. "Why did you come over here?" she said, not beating around the bush. "You just looked like a statue, bronzed and looked so beautiful there," he told her.[7]

Shead liked folk music but hadn't heard of Odetta. "I had no idea who she was and was just attracted to her," he said. "There was an empathy straight away. We just started talking. And that's where it all began for me and her." For that brief stay, they became joined at the hip. She told a local reporter she was already "scheming yet another trip [to Australia] as soon as possible." "When she left, we started writing letters and planning kind of our life together in a way," Shead remembered. "I started planning about going to America, how I could get there."[8]

He and Odetta decided they would try to put him on her payroll—although she probably couldn't afford it—and get him a work visa. "Here is a resume and various bits," he wrote to her a short time later.

"I think an assistant film editor job would be the most reliable thing but it may be impossible to get. I hope this helps. All my love, G." Odetta told him to be patient until their roads met again.[9]

From Australia, Odetta had flown to France, once more heeding the call of her friend Harry Belafonte. Martin Luther King was holding a rally in Paris on March 28, promoted as "La Nuit des Droits Civiques" (Civil Rights Night), at the Palais des Sports to raise money for the Southern Christian Leadership Conference (SCLC), and Belafonte asked Odetta and Mahalia Jackson to perform, along with himself and others. With the passage of the Civil Rights Act and Voting Rights Act the previous two years, many white Americans had turned their attention elsewhere, and the SCLC was having trouble getting people to open their wallets. And with deplorable conditions and a lack of economic opportunity still plaguing many black neighborhoods, activists were growing more militant, with the "black power" movement providing an alternative to the SCLC—and eroding some white support for the civil rights agenda. Belafonte suggested they look toward Europe to find more sympathetic ears.

The Johnson administration had made clear its displeasure with King—and his argument that the millions being spent on war in Indochina were more vitally needed to address poverty in the US—by directing the American ambassador in Paris not to attend the rally. But it had been a success nonetheless, raising as much as $50,000. Afterward the performers retreated to the George V Hotel, where they awaited a meal of take-out soul food, as Belafonte recalled:

> We gathered in the suite of actor Peter O'Toole . . . Martin's circle, my French gang, and all the stars who participated or attended, including, on the American side, Mahalia Jackson and Odetta. Food was coming, we assured them, and so it did. Peter O'Toole opened his door to see Martin with a napkin over his forearm, holding a large tray of fried chicken from Jimmy's and plainly imitating a waiter. "Dinner is served," Martin said in that deep baritone of his. As the plates were handed out, he went from star to star, dispensing chicken and pausing ever so briefly to give each a sense of his personal appreciation for their contribution. "You have no idea what it means to our folks back home."[10]

And in Odetta's case, the same went for the many times she'd aided his cause from the Statue of Liberty rally in 1960 to the March on Washington in '63 and Selma in '65. Late in Odetta's life, it would be widely reported that King had once called her "the queen of American folk music," but he doesn't appear to have uttered the phrase publicly. He knew, however, that he could count on her. "Many of us were on call whenever he needed it," Belafonte said. "But his relationship with Odetta was, it really was a family, it's like I ask about the welfare of my children just because they're there and that's my life. In the middle of anything he'd say, 'How's Odetta doing?' [And I'd say,] 'She's doing great,' or 'Not great,' as the case may be."[11]

Still, Odetta never got particularly close to King personally, despite what people assumed. Her early shyness was too much of an impediment. "I was a kid," she would say later, although King was only about two years her senior. "When you're around older people, you don't start spouting off. You sit there and you listen. I was too scared to open my mouth, and even if I had opened my mouth I don't think that I would have been able to contribute anything."[12]

The same could be said of her relationship with Bob Dylan, which remained cordial but not close, despite the obvious debt he owed to her music and the Dylan album she'd recorded to return the favor. Newly divorced that summer and missing Shead a world away, Odetta decided to pay an extended visit to her good friends Selma and Ed Thaler, now living in an old Victorian house on a quiet street in Middletown, New York. "I needed a dose of my Thalers," she recalled. When she arrived, Dylan was there at the behest of Al Grossman, recuperating after his now legendary motorcycle accident, which would precipitate a years-long hibernation from public life. As Selma Thaler recalled of Dylan's accident, "He didn't want to go to the hospital and he didn't really require hospitalization. He just needed to take it easy. And I don't think he was able to play the guitar or that it was inadvisable to. And he took a month off."[13]

With Dylan living on the third floor of the Thalers' home, relaxing, hiding out from the press, and listening to their extensive record collection, Odetta arrived, and they all spent a little time together, with some effort. She was proud of her Dylan album, but he seemed unsure of what to make of it, hearing so many of his tunes in another singer's voice. "He never did say he didn't like the record," Odetta remembered, "but he wondered how people could do the songs so different than how he conceived them." Odetta told him it was impossible for her *not* to have sung them differently. All in all, it wasn't an easy conversation, Thaler recalled. "There was not an easy, slap on the back kind of relationship—we're in the same business, we have the same manager—it wasn't that kind of thing. It wasn't close. . . . Both of them are very difficult to get close to." Odetta would confirm as much later. "I don't know him, really," she said. "I've always said I'm a hermit, and looking at it now, I really am. Really. I think it takes being together to get to know each other, and with him there never has been such a being together. Except maybe once, maybe for an hour or so, after I recorded his songs. But I'm shy of him. And I think he's shy of me."[14]

By summer's end, Odetta had refused to renew her contract with RCA, which had earlier that year released a live album from her Japan tour. Her producer, Jack Somer, was angry but hardly surprised. "I know she left because . . . the company never did justice to her artistry, to her greatness, to her beauty, and to her talent," he said. "Never did." Charlie Rothschild saw the departure as the end of a mutual relationship that didn't pan out. "She didn't give them a hit," he said. "That's what they were looking for. All they could think of was hits."[15]

She quickly signed a two-year, four-record deal with Verve Folkways, a subsidiary of the jazz label Verve formed in conjunction with Moses Asch's Folkways. Verve Folkways was reportedly trying to break into the pop market, with new acts like Laura Nyro and Richie Havens and with more established singers like Odetta and Dave Van Ronk. In an ad in *Billboard*, it alluded to the challenge of trying to maintain relevance for a new generation, saying of the pair that "both are looking for material for future recordings that will delight their legion of old fans and create a host of new ones."[16]

In October, Odetta had a new single out, "Clown Town," a rather pedestrian, orchestra-backed pop song on which she crooned lyrics such as, "Clown town, the world is a clown town, by golly, what a jolly place." On the other side was "Until It's Time for You to Go," an eerily prescient choice, as it was a love song by Buffy Sainte-Marie about a couple who can't stay together because they come from different worlds. "Clown Town," the B side, generated some airplay and was advertised as "a hit" by the "new Odetta" in magazines like *Variety* and *Cashbox*. The *New Amsterdam News* said it was "proving to be the biggest hit recording she has ever made." But despite the hype, "Clown Town" didn't make the charts, and Odetta sounds like a fish out of water singing a lyric she must have found insipid and uninspiring. The approach of backing her with strings and glockenspiel was quickly abandoned.[17]

In early 1967, she began touring and preparing new material with a band that included Les Grinage, along with John Foster on piano and John Seiter on drums. She was far from alone among former folk acts in search of a new direction. "As a commercial product," Leon Bibb had told a reporter, "folk music has been dead about a year." Bibb was discarding folk tunes from his repertoire in favor of Broadway tunes and other fare and performing with a trio. Chad Mitchell, whose Chad Mitchell Trio was one of the most popular folk acts, had quit to become an actor after Dylan went electric at Newport. He was now a cabaret singer, warbling Jacques Brel, Rodgers and Hart, and the Beatles' "Yesterday." "I don't want to be entrapped by the limitations of folk song," he'd said. Even Joan Baez that year would release a record of songs by the Beatles, Paul Simon, Tim Hardin, and Donovan.[18]

The result of Odetta's tinkering was a new LP in May entitled *Odetta* and meant to reintroduce her to the public. There were a couple of blues, spirituals like "Turn Me 'Round" set to a rock beat, the Rodgers and Hart tune "Little Girl Blues" delivered like a moody jazz ballad, and even a Beatles tune, "Strawberry Fields," presented on the album jacket as a "lullaby." It was a musical hodgepodge, seemingly intended to gauge the public's interest in hearing Odetta in a variety of different settings, and thus it had no real center. But the record was full of good moments, especially Odetta's own "Give Me Your Hand," a tuneful pop song with a danceable beat that might have been aimed at Garry Shead.

> *I got my reason to stay*
> *I'll take this road all the way*
> *I got my mind to think*

Even when my heart sinks
I got my feet to go
If you broke down I can tow
Give me your hand

Shead remembered "Give Me Your Hand" as "our song," although he thought it was a Buffy Sainte-Marie tune.[19] That Verve Folkways didn't release it as a single is one of the many missed opportunities of Odetta's career. In fact, her new record company didn't release any singles from *Odetta*, almost guaranteeing that few people outside her old fan base would hear her new repertoire.

Some of those who did hear it thought she was on to something. "It's been obvious for some time that the number of versions of Childe Ballads and the number of work songs, field hollers and other esoteric numbers that the market will tolerate is limited," Ralph Gleason wrote in the *San Francisco Chronicle*. "Yet an artist has to go on, and cannot go on merely repeating and repeating. Odetta's newest album . . . is a giant step towards solving this dilemma." Others were less sure. A reviewer for *Broadside*, a Boston folk music fanzine, praised the blues selections but didn't think her version of John Lennon's psychedelic self-analysis "Strawberry Fields" hit its mark. "On the album cover much is made of that Odetta sings it as a lullaby, but that does not hide the fact that she seems not to know what the song means."[20]

John Seiter, the twenty-three-year-old drummer on the record and the tours that year, promoted as "the new sound of Odetta," wasn't surprised by the reaction. "If you were an Odetta fan, that's not what you were looking for," he said. "I don't know that our act went over so well in the clubs either, what she was trying to do" with the newer material. But Seiter was quick to point out that Odetta remained a star to those who had long been following her music. "She could do anything she wanted to do and they just loved her," Seiter recalled. "And they were all over her after the set, you know, wanting to talk to her, getting her autograph, wanting to take a picture with her, whatever. I mean, she was beloved everywhere we went. . . . She was such a star . . . and we were just the boys in the band." [21]

In June, Odetta landed in Japan for two and a half weeks of concerts, and Shead sold his share in his Sydney apartment, gave most of his belongings to friends, and went to meet her in Tokyo, where they resumed their romance. He watched her concerts from backstage, they took in Kabuki theater, and they visited a Japanese psychic to ask about their future.

At a party one night, Shead proposed to Odetta, and she accepted. They had no idea that a reporter was eavesdropping, and the next day a story went out on wire services that the two were engaged and getting married in a month. (One report erroneously said they'd already married.) They flew back to Sydney together so Odetta could meet his parents and were surprised at the airport by journalists waiting on the tarmac. "I will be staying in Australia for a while and Odetta will be returning to America," Shead told them. "We will share our talents with both countries," Odetta offered. The fact that they barely knew one another became apparent when Shead mentioned he'd just had his twenty-fifth birthday, and a reporter asked Odetta what she'd given him. "I didn't give you anything. I didn't give you a birthday present," she blurted out, embarrassed. [22]

Odetta got a hotel in Sydney because Garry had given up his apartment. "I was really ready to get married to her," he recalled. "She said, 'We will have coffee-colored children.' And I was very happy and I kind of sold everything, I sold my house, left all my things and I was quite really ready to move in with her."[23] Shead, then an experimental filmmaker, decided to make a short film about Odetta, entitled *Give Me Your Hand*. She was filmed singing several songs in a studio and also, at Odetta's request, hanging out with aboriginal children in La Perouse, a "reserve" that kept them isolated from white Australians.

At Gary Shearston's home, the couple did LSD, Odetta's first acid trip. They went for a walk afterward, and still tripping, Shead experienced the feeling that "we were walking at different speeds." Some doubts began to creep in, the biggest of which involved race, as much an issue in Sydney then as in any American city. "In those days, you stood out. I'm a skinny kind of bloke and she was such a very kind of big woman. Walking together I think we attracted a fair bit of attention, so it was really not that comfortable." Odetta's road manager joked that Shead "wouldn't last five minutes in Harlem." Perhaps the trip to meet his parents sealed their fate. "She and my dad got on very well, and my mother. But I think my mom was a bit shocked to see me with a black lady. . . . I think the pressure was just too much on both us, especially me, I suppose. And I kind of left her after that and it's something that's kind of painful and I felt kind of guilt for doing that."[24]

In the end, they were like the couple Odetta sang about in "Until It's Time for You to Go," who couldn't stay together because they came from different worlds. As he related these events half a century later, Shead, who has married several times since, became emotional, remembering a romance that ended while it was in bloom. Back home, Odetta was forced to try to explain to the press what had happened, a level of personal detail she was never comfortable airing. "You might say we got divorced before we got married," she told a reporter, declining to elaborate. Gary Shearston wrote to Odetta that fall and offered his own explanation. "I did have the feeling at home when you were there that things, perhaps, were not going to work out for you and Gary [*sic*]. . . . I could never help but feel that your free-wheeling spirit and intellect had been round many corners Gary had not . . . even thought about."[25]

The end of her engagement must have been particularly distressing to Odetta because it was derailed by race. But she was soon buffeted by her appearance at a Woody Guthrie tribute concert at Carnegie Hall in January of 1968. The concert followed Guthrie's death from Huntington's disease at age fifty-five and featured an impressive list of performers influenced by him, including Bob Dylan (in his first gig since his motorcycle accident), Joan Baez, Pete Seeger, and Richie Havens. If nothing else, it was a reminder that folk music—and musicians like Odetta—were the proud antecedents of rock. "The Woody Guthrie Memorial Show changed my life," Odetta said afterward. "My feet didn't touch the ground the whole day. I've never been there before. I've been happy and excited, but nothing like that."[26]

Later that month, she appeared on a CBS television special on the grand reopening of Ford's Theater in Washington, DC, which had been shuttered since the assassination of Abraham Lincoln. Although the show had a star-studded cast including Harry Belafonte, Andy Williams, Helen Hayes, Peter Fonda, and Julie Harris, critics dismissed most of the songs and dramatic readings as overwrought and sentimental. (Perhaps a nation mired in Vietnam wasn't as receptive to patriotic sentiments as it had been during the folk revival.) Odetta, however, was the big exception, singing a trio of spirituals, including "Go Where I Send Thee," which she announced by schooling her TV audience on the slave origins of the tune. "During those days, there were many people who objected to the system of slavery, including some slaves," she wryly noted. "Perhaps the highlight of all the entertainment was a rhythmic Christmas spiritual by the deep-voiced Odetta, whose singing power and conviction were magnetic," wrote Rick Du Brow, the TV critic for UPI.[27]

Odetta's star turn led to guest spots on Merv Griffin's and Mike Douglas's talk shows and also seemed to buoy Odetta's spirits further. "That Ford's Theater appearance did away with whatever slight I had felt in the past about mass recognition or just getting on television," she said. "It helped clarify things for me—helped me remember my main interest. I was on my way to losing my perspective but now I'm no longer pre-occupied by things that don't really count."[28] One gets the sense, however, that Odetta often was trying to convince herself as much as anyone that she'd put aside her anger at a music business that seemed to wall her off from superstardom.

Despite the uptick in her profile, she remained at a crossroads musically, not having found a successful way to evolve from folk troubadour to something more in line with current tastes. Her voice remained as unmatched as ever, but what to do with it? It was clear by late 1968 that she was getting little help with this dilemma from her manager, Al Grossman. Fed up with what she called his inaction on her behalf, she bitterly severed ties with Grossman, accusing him of racism.

"I got along with him beautifully until I found that what I called his 'racial bias' stopped him from doing anything for me," she recalled, adding, "Now, I consider ourselves friends and business partners, and I go in and talk sensibly to him about it. And nothing would happen. And then I would go in and scream about it. And then nothing happened. And I'd go in and cry a little bit. And nothing would happen. And then I'd have to say, 'It's not going to happen.'"[29]

It's not clear exactly what Odetta meant by accusing Grossman of racism, but several comments over the years provide hints. Odetta pointed out on several occasions that Grossman "built his business on my back and I never benefited from it." She was speaking about the height of her fame when Grossman included his up-and-coming acts as part of package deals that she headlined. "As people were able to get me, he was able to say, 'I want you to take Dylan and Peter, Paul & Mary'; but he never did that with me. As Dylan and Peter, Paul & Mary got up there, he didn't do that with me." That wasn't entirely true. But Odetta also told a story of running into Paul Butterfield in the late 1960s at a Manhattan club and Butterfield complaining that Grossman had told him "he could get him more gigs if he didn't have any black men in his band." (This may have been a rather coldly delivered recognition on Grossman's part that interracial acts were then harder to market.) There have been other suggestions of racism involving Grossman. Les Brown, a co-owner of the Gate of Horn, recalled Grossman paying Big Bill Broonzy $100 for a gig, less than regular union scale of $125, and Grossman telling him, "Because the black musicians have a different union scale, lower scale. . . . It's their fault, not ours."[30]

But others who knew Grossman objected to this characterization. "It's all in her mind," Charlie Rothschild said. "It was not [racism], unless I'm blind. Albert was representing her, Albert was getting her work, I was digging to get her work. She was getting shows, but she never played arenas that Peter, Paul and Mary played. But it wasn't because of racism. Peter, Paul and Mary had a bunch of hits." Frank Hamilton, who was married to a black woman when he worked for Grossman at the Gate of Horn, also didn't view him as a racist. "I was very cognizant of the racism that was taking place even in that urban setting. . . . I never noticed anything with Al. To me it was always business with Al, what was going to make the most money."[31]

As a businessman, Grossman always hunted for new acts that could hit pay dirt. In recent years, he'd signed the hip black singer-songwriter Richie Havens and the young rocker Janis Joplin—who'd started out in Port Arthur, Texas, imitating Odetta. It was the thrill of the chase, along with money and power, that seemed to motivate him. "The problem with Albert was that he became involved in the group's success when we started climbing toward it," Mary Travers recalled of Peter, Paul and Mary's rise. "When we got there, he became bored."[32] Within a few years, in fact, having earned millions from his various management and publishing deals and sapped by the tragic overdose death of Joplin, he would quit the management business in favor of running a recording studio and other business ventures.

If Grossman had decided to exert less energy on Odetta's behalf, it seems likely that he was making a cold business calculation. Odetta had certainly encountered plenty of racism in her life, but in this case what she deemed racism was more than likely simple greed. "Peter, Paul and Mary, even Bob Dylan went with Albert Grossman because he was Odetta's manager," recalled jazzman David Amram, who befriended Odetta. "Once he got them on the boards, selling a lot of records and giving him ten times more clout than he had, he suddenly dumped Odetta unceremoniously and broke her heart." "She based most of her life on soul to soul relationships," Amram added, "and she thought he was a real soul brother in the deepest sense."[33]

She wasn't the only one of Grossman's clients to feel betrayed in the end. Travers accused him of making more money than Peter, Paul or her. Dylan and Grossman would wind up in court over their contract terms, a bitter end to their business arrangement. "Grossman first gained my trust and confidence, and then abused that relationship for his own benefit," Dylan said later.[34]

Some of Odetta's friends wonder what her career might have been like with a manager who truly guided it. "I think one of the reasons Odetta did not become more famous than she was was because her career was never really managed, I don't think," Selma Thaler said. "She would get gigs and then they would invite her again. And I think word of mouth was more what got her the jobs she got."[35]

If Odetta was in search of a career footing as the decade came to a close, her influence on black culture had never been clearer. All over America, African Americans were wearing their hair in Afros, finally embracing the revolution that Odetta had begun almost two decades earlier. "Black pride is mushrooming all over America and with it is the 'Afro look,'" one black newspaper declared. "Now an 'Afro' hair-do is the 'in' look for those who think black. It is not an uncommon sight to see a lady sporting an 'Afro'; in fact, the world acclaimed folk singer Odetta did much to foster the now-popular coiffure." The *Washington Post* said that for many black women, conforming to white standards of beauty was no longer worth the bother of hair straightening. "They are changing to the 'Afro'—as worn by such top Negro entertainers as Odetta and Cicely Tyson," the paper reported. "For many of the women who now wear it, changing to the Afro has been part of today's search for racial self-identification."[36]

The idea that "black is beautiful" became one of the key tenets of the black power movement of the late 1960s. "We have to stop being ashamed of being black!" SNCC leader Stokely Carmichael would roar at his followers. There had been other signposts along the way in the push to boost black self-esteem: Cassius Clay (later Muhammad Ali) boasting "I'm so pretty" after his bouts; Malcolm X extolling his followers not to "mutilate their god-created bodies to try to look 'pretty' by white standards"; James Brown singing "Say It Loud—I'm Black and I'm Proud," cutting off his processed pompadour in favor of an Afro. All owe a debt to Odetta, whose courageous example had wended its way through the culture, from the world of entertainment to the campus commons, the activist enclave, and the uptown hair salon.

The Afros would continue to lengthen in the early 1970s, a symbol of pride—and in some cases of solidarity against the white power structure. Angela Davis, the Birmingham-born activist academic whose bulbous Afro, featured on FBI wanted posters and "Free Angela" pins, would become the iconic image of the hairdo, also traced her follicles back to Odetta.[37] But by that point, who didn't?

CHAPTER THIRTEEN

HIT OR MISS

As the new decade began, Odetta found her career mired in the same place it had been for several years: she had no full-time manager or record deal (her stint with Verve had produced only one album), and she was trying to find a way forward. "She seemed to be not at all in tune with the times," wrote one critic who saw her at the Mariposa Folk Festival in Canada during the summer of 1970. "The folk music she had been doing so powerfully was no longer in demand and her ventures into pop were sadly missing their mark. Like numerous other artists I consider carryovers from the days of folk, she seemed adrift from the mainstream of music and struggling to find a place to plant her feet."[1]

An old friend, Herb Cohen, offered to help. Odetta had known Cohen since the early 1950s in Los Angeles, when he was among the young folkniks who showed up regularly for hootenannies at Butch and Bess Lomax Hawes's home. Back then, Cohen was already thinking about how to monetize folk music. "He decided he was going to pull us all together professionally and have us make money with our songs," Jo Mapes recalled.[2] Cohen's Unicorn Coffeehouse was the first of its kind in the city, and he later opened Cosmo Alley, where Odetta performed a number of times.

According to Robert Carl Cohen (no relation), who had attended Odetta's high school and saw her at Cosmo Alley, Cohen the young impresario already displayed the pugnacious tendencies for which he'd become well known. "She apparently performed gratis across the street from Cosmo Alley, at a jewelry store, which then got a rock through their window," Robert Cohen said. "The word was that Herbie Cohen didn't like her performing free of charge at this jewelry store. He only wanted her to perform at his place." In the rock era, Herb Cohen would become known in musical circles as a litigious, gun-carrying intimidator whose stints with stars such as Frank Zappa, Tom Waits, and Linda Ronstadt all ended in lawsuits. "Something always went wrong at the end," is how Jac Holzman, the founder of Elektra Records, once put it.[3]

Odetta signed with Cohen's Third Story Productions in August of 1970, and he quickly delivered her a multi-album deal with Polydor Records. She began work on *Odetta Sings*, pouring her heart into what would culminate in a fully realized rock album. It featured an all-star group of musicians, including the Muscle Shoals rhythm section that had powered big hits for Aretha Franklin and Wilson Pickett; Carole King on piano; and on backup vocals Merry Clayton, who had recently stamped her ticket to rock immortality by duetting with Mick Jagger on the Rolling Stones's "Gimme Shelter."

For the song list, Odetta mined the best contemporary writers, including Elton John ("Take Me to the Pilot"), Randy Newman ("Mama Told Me Not to Come"), Paul McCartney ("Every Night"), and Jagger and Keith Richards ("No Expectations"). Her muscular vocals may not have had the gravelly soul of Franklin, who by then had almost single-handedly transformed American music with her gritty rhythm and blues, but they seemed well suited to rock, and the Muscle Shoals sound helped Odetta find an edge that had been lacking in her previous efforts at handling contemporary songs.

Odetta even included a pair of new originals. "Movin' It On" was a plea for perseverance in the face of an unjust world, a kind of civil rights anthem for an incremental era when big gains were hard to come by and the tendency to succumb to defeatism had to be fought at every turn. Odetta sang it with contagious exuberance.

Any old way you can make it, baby
Keep on movin' it on
If you can't fly, run
If you can't run, walk

If you can't walk, crawl
Any old way you can make it, baby
Keep on movin' it on

"Hit or Miss," featured on a single with "Take Me to the Pilot," centered around the kind of self-affirmation that Odetta often called upon in her later career. Its catchy drumbeat and funky bass riff seemed geared toward radio play. Given the subsequent popular reception to the album, however, there's a retrospective pathos in the lyrics, or perhaps Odetta was doubting her foray into rock.

Sittin' here all by myself
Tryin' to be everybody else
Can't you see?
I gotta be me
Ain't nobody just like this
I gotta be me
Baby, hit or miss

The album landed by the late fall, and had it been up to the critics, it would have been a smash. They loved it and Odetta's newest incarnation. *Cashbox* called it "spectacular" and concluded, "Now you know why when Odetta sings, people listen!" *Billboard* raved about Odetta's "exceptional talents" and "an equally exceptional album."[4]

Odetta hired a band of long-haired young rock musicians and took her new act on the road, appearing with Elton John at the Troubadour and opening for James Taylor and Neil Diamond. Sometimes she even put down her acoustic guitar and grabbed an electric herself. After her failure to get live audiences to connect with her interpretations of Dylan and the Beatles—not to mention the rejection of her blues material by hard-core folk fans—she clearly had trepidation about how she would be received. And she must have wondered whether the rock generation would embrace her. The previous summer, she'd appeared on the bottom end of a mismatched bill with Led Zeppelin at a New York festival, and, as she tried edifying the crowd with a version of "Home on the Range," she endured "a barrage of boos [that] grew to humiliating proportions" and calls to "Get off the stage!" the *Chicago Tribune* reported. "A lot of people were surprised at the direction of [*Odetta Sings*]," she told *Rolling Stone* when the record came out. "I'm a big woman and I'm black, so you get the stereotype—everyone expects the traditional stuff and there's really not that much traditional stuff in my repertoire. The album isn't really a change. It's all part of a gradual development."[5]

But critical acclaim aside, it became pretty clear that the youth market wasn't buying Odetta as a rock star. At a concert with Diamond at the Greek Theatre in Los Angeles, she was "politely received," *Billboard* said. For an appearance on KCET TV in LA in front of a studio audience, Odetta wore a gold sequined top and white skirt (her head covered by an African scarf), as she sang half a dozen songs with her group. She lit into "Take Me to the Pilot" and other new material, but the applause showed more respect than enthusiasm. And once again, she faced blowback, including from a critic who noted that "she seemed willing to fall in line for the rock audience's approval."[6]

There's little doubt that the album, now long out of print, sold poorly. A later note from one of Odetta's attorneys put her songwriting royalties for the two originals on the LP at less than five hundred dollars. Polydor, trying to recoup losses, in 1972 sued Herb Cohen's firm, Third Story, for going ten thousand dollars over budget (sixty-one thousand dollars today) in producing the record. Cohen, in turn, sued Odetta and the record's producer, John Boylan.[7] Eventually the parties settled out of court, but that was the end of Odetta's run at Polydor and the end of Cohen's brief stint as Odetta's manager.

What went wrong? It's not a case of an artist mishandling material, because Odetta got it mostly right. (If there's any doubt about her abilities in the genre, her electrified version of Woody Guthrie's "Rambling Round Your City," recorded around this time during a Guthrie tribute concert at the Hollywood Bowl and available on several compilations, makes clear that her voice could propel arena rock.) It may have had something to do with Odetta's persona in a business that increasingly relied on image to sell records: a heavy-set black woman with an Afro who often favored African attire just wasn't going to excite the young white teens and twenty-somethings going to rock concerts and buying most of the rock records. She had never cultivated much of a black audience, and a rock album wasn't going to change that equation.

Could it also have been the Aretha Franklin effect? No matter how powerful her voice, Odetta just couldn't match Franklin's soulfulness, which had made the big-boned preacher's daughter a crossover star. As Ralph Gleason had noted in the *San Francisco Chronicle*: "This society is more and more moving toward a rhythmic orientation in its music and the impact of Aretha Franklin on all popular music is, like the Jordan river, deep and wide."[8]

Or did Odetta just not relate to a love song like Paul McCartney's "Every Night" the way she did to the prison and work songs she'd sung to get her hate out? "She tried rock. She tried everything," recalled Odetta's good friend Frederick Warhanek, who'd met her when he was program director at KPFK radio in Los Angeles. "It just wasn't really her. . . . When something doesn't work and you really work at it, it's difficult for an artist to reinvent themselves."[9]

What followed was a long sojourn in the musical desert. Odetta returned to performing folk songs, but the jobs grew scarcer. Odetta had provided regular financial support to her mother, but in the summer of 1972, Flora Felious wrote to Odetta to tell her not to send her any more checks. "Baby you are not working. and dont no where your getting money to send me. now please dont think that I am not thankful. yes I am. But baby how are you paying your Bill. . . . now if you send me eny more money I will send it back." (The checks kept coming.) Charlie Rothschild recalled that Odetta, who had no real savings, was struggling financially in the early 1970s. "For a long time, she lived impoverished here in Manhattan," he said. "And it was sorry to see. She didn't have any money. I don't know whether she was getting aid or assistance or whatever. She was working, doing like shitty jobs and little shitty concerts, just to survive."[10]

A few years earlier, she'd purchased an inexpensive two-bedroom co-op apartment on the eighth floor at 1270 Fifth Avenue, at 108th Street, with views of Central Park. The building was one of the first on Fifth Avenue in Manhattan to accept blacks, longtime residents recalled. Today, the red-brick edifice with the trim green awning cuts a stately figure in a gentrified neighborhood, but back when Odetta arrived, the conditions were poor, according to Peggy Strait, who has lived there for more than half a century. "At that time this was a very undesirable neighborhood," she recalled. "We would have muggers climbing in the windows. Things were so bad that I still have the letter that I wrote to Mayor John Lindsay saying we need to have more protection in this neighborhood."[11]

By the end of 1972, Odetta had another career setback. It looked like the Bessie Smith film that she and Danny had failed to produce was now finally being made, based on a new biography of Smith by Chris Albertson. Albertson had even pushed for Odetta in the lead role, and there were reports that she'd won it, but producers instead chose Roberta Flack, one of the nation's hottest young pop singers. "I wanted Odetta from the beginning because she is close to the spirit of Bessie's music," Albertson said at the time, "but her name wasn't big enough to interest potential backers."[12]

Odetta, who longed to portray Bessie, later called it the most searing disappointment of her career, acknowledging for the first time why she'd sought the role for so long. "Outside of my love for her, maybe I wanted to do it because in doing it, I could also learn, via the acting, her in-charge attitude," she said. "When the deal fell through I went into a blue funk. . . . Never again will I put all my expectations on the line."[13] (The Flack film never materialized, however, and a Bessie Smith bio didn't appear until 2015, when it starred Queen Latifah.)

Odetta tried to stay active as her concert work ebbed, making herself available for benefits, often without pay other than expenses, to support various left-wing causes. If her rage had fueled her singing early on, it continued to stoke her desire to improve the world. "We . . . played so many benefits together," David Amram recalled, "that whenever we played when we were actually paid, it was a banner occasion." Odetta often recoiled at the idea of detailing all of the things she did, as if doing so usurped attention from the causes themselves. But prodded by a reporter, she rattled off a bunch: Vietnam, Laos, police brutality, pollution, the white man's arrogance (the reporter's paraphrase), and "my black children." "You'd better not misquote me on this," Odetta said. "If there's one thing that bothers me it's integration. Integration means black children having to adjust completely to a white child's world. . . . I want the black child to know where he comes from and be able to make a contribution to any situation he is in, black and black, black and white or whatever." And what exactly was she doing to help her black children? "They're not headline getters, sweetie," Odetta said, and that was true enough in most cases, small fund-raisers for school, arts, and church programs.[14]

She got the most ink for singing against the Vietnam War, and while Odetta may not have been Bessie Smith, she had long since shied away from making outright political statements beyond her music. At one early 1970s midnight rally for the kickoff of a "Peace Fast" at All Souls Unitarian Church in Washington, DC, Odetta led young antiwar activists in singing peace songs. "Odetta raised the voice that is like a great cave with firelight leaping on its walls and sang 'This Land Is Your Land,'" the columnist Mary McGrory wrote. Then: "The young people locked arms and rocked back and forth and sang 'We Shall Overcome,' and it was a reminder of the days when demonstrations had worked. . . . Singing and marching had made the difference in the civil rights movement. Nothing seemed likely to move the man in the White House"—Richard Nixon—"to more rapid troop withdrawals." Still, Senator Eugene McCarthy, hero of the left, embraced her and said, "I think I'll recommend Odetta to President Nixon for the Supreme Court as a strict construction-ist from the South." Odetta walked off the stage with both hands raised—one with her fingers in a V for peace, the other in a clenched fist for black power. Her Afro had grown longer.[15]

She embraced her folk repertoire, and even as her popularity waned at home, she remained a good draw overseas and, in most years, spent several months abroad. "Part of what she did was travel out of the country more because folk music was still a thing everywhere else," Boots Jaffee recalled. "And even if it wasn't a thing, American artists were still a thing and so she did that."[16]

There were tours in Israel and Scandinavia and music festivals in Europe. At the Berlin Jazz Festival in 1973, she made such an impres-sion that B. B. King had trouble following her after the crowd gave her a standing ovation, according to a report in *Melody Maker*. "Ap-plause was so great that the King band had difficulty getting back on stage." "Yeah, yeah. We love her too," King told the crowd.[17]

In 1974, Odetta spent more than a month on a tour of the So-viet Union and Eastern Europe, one of the early American cultural emissaries during the era of detente. Voice of America broadcasts had long featured American vernacular music, and Soviet listeners had shown an insatiable desire for it, especially jazz. Young people came out in force to see Odetta at sold-out halls in Moscow, Leningrad, Vilnius, Yerevan, Kislovodsk, Baku, Minsk, and Pyatigorsk in a series arranged privately with the Soviet Ministry of Culture and with the blessing of the US Embassy in Moscow. The same folk music that had become passé back home seemed to enthrall her Soviet crowds, despite the language barrier. "Odetta, an intense American folk singer, has entranced audiences here by belting out a repertory ranging from spirituals to work songs and children's play tunes, backed by nothing more than the driving rhythm of her own guitar," the *New York Times* said. "Between songs, young men or women would often dart up on stage to kiss her and present her bouquets wrapped in cellophane," the *Times* added. "'Odetta,' one young man called out as she was leaving a performance in Yerevan, 'will you ask all your brothers and sisters to come over and sing for us too?'"[18]

An audience of twenty-five hundred brought her back for three curtain calls after a two-hour performance in Rossiya Concert Hall across Red Square from the Kremlin, as a nation that had once welcomed her idol Paul Robeson in the 1930s gave her an equally warm embrace. "I can't believe I'm here," Odetta cried out backstage. "I wanted to come here for a long time," she said. "I was and am interested in the fact that despite our different systems we are human beings. I pick [*sic*] you and you say ouch. It is that area of communication, similarity and oneness I am looking for not only in the Soviet Union but in the United States as well."[19]

She also did concerts behind the Iron Curtain in Yugoslavia and Hungary. A report by the United States Information Agency noted the Soviet press was "highly favorable" about her tour.[20] "Her voice is an instrument of limitless range, rarest depth and purest tone," an editor of the government run *Izvestia* enthused. "Her main virtue consists of her ability to reach the heart and touch our spiritual strings." Most importantly, he concluded:

> Soviet audiences opened their hands not only to applaud the vocal mastery of Odetta. Now, as a historical turn is taking place in the

relationship between the United States and the Soviet Union, a turn from confrontation to partnership, the role of our countries' artists is growing more critical to developing a climate of joint understanding and friendship between two great peoples, from which in large degree hangs the fate of the world.[21]

She'd clearly made an impact. The night of her concert in Minsk, some fans wrote to her in New York. "Odetta!! We are happy to see you in our country, to listen to the wonderful songs of your people. . . . We admire your brilliant talent, your voice. . . . Hope to see you in our city again. Your Soviet friends."[22]

Letters like that one must have heartened her as she continued to try to jump-start her career at home. She worked to burnish her acting résumé, although, like many black actors, she found good parts difficult to come by. In 1974, she appeared in a much-feted TV movie, *The Autobiography of Miss Jane Pittman*, based on the Ernest J. Gaines novel and starring Cicely Tyson as a former slave recounting her hardscrabble life. While the movie broke ground in its unglossy depiction of slavery and won a slew of Emmys, Odetta appeared on camera only briefly—as a slave named Big Laura.

In her serious stage-acting debut, she portrayed a slave yet again the following year in Arthur Miller's *The Crucible* at the Stratford Festival in Ontario. Although excited for the role of Tituba, Odetta couldn't help noting the sameness in the types of parts offered to her. "It's only that people don't think of casting a black person unless the author says so," she said.[23]

Her rave reviews beg the question of why she didn't have more opportunities to act. The drama critic for the *Globe and Mail* said, "[S]he outshone a stage full of Shakespeareans," while the *Montreal Star* pointed out that "Odetta as Tituba was wonderful with her super opulent humanity." "Doing live theater particularly helped me to get away from self-consciousness of the body, which I always had," Odetta said later. "When I made my debut in 'The Crucible' . . . I soon discovered I wouldn't have the guitar to hide behind. And I couldn't even close my eyes anymore!" The lack of a real manager probably forestalled any more sustained entrée into the field.[24]

Musically, she failed to get anything going on a commercial level in the 1970s, and she didn't hide her rage about it. She sang with symphony orchestras in pops concerts around the country, earning the usual good reviews wherever she went, but nothing more. At one point, she cut a tape in Nashville with a young band called the Nashville Huggies, trying to interest the country music establishment, to no avail. "Nothing, zero. Don't call us, we'll call you," was how the *Chicago Tribune* characterized the response. The paper asked Odetta if she was disheartened. "'Disheartened!' booms the rich voice, sending seismic shocks thru Ma Bell's line from New York. 'That's a beautiful understatement. Damn right I'm disheartened— and spitting mad, too. There are a lot of us with talent and experience who can't get record contracts. Seems like companies are interested only in new acts that do freaky things. Those people are strange at best, but talented . . . ?'"[25]

"If I was white and looked like a dog and had the talent that I do have, you'd be hearing more . . . from me," she told another reporter. She claimed, a little disingenuously, that she hadn't caved in to pressure to record a commercial hit or changed musical directions like other rock and folk musicians. "If I did that it would be as if I had been working on my dream house for 23 years and then after getting to where I wanted, I poured kerosene all over it and burned it down."[26]

Once again, she was hardly alone among her contemporaries, although she was quicker to blame racism than most. "The 70s had become a pretty arid musical climate . . . for many of us," Peter Yarrow noted. But Odetta suffered the added indignity that her bedrock influence on popular music was already being diminished. "A lot of people ask me if I went into folk music because of Joan Baez or Bob Dylan," Odetta seethed in one interview. "But I'm the mama and they're the children, and I influenced those singers."[27]

In the summer of 1976, at the John Henry Faulk Festival in West Virginia, Odetta met the blues singer Louisiana Red, and the two fell in love—or at least he did. She seemed to need a little convincing. Born Iverson Minter in Vicksburg, Mississippi, in 1932, Red had had a traumatic childhood, even by the standards of Southern bluesmen.

His mother died of pneumonia when he was a baby and his father was lynched by the Klan when Red was five. He started playing guitar on the streets to earn money at fourteen. By the 1950s, he'd begun recording for various small labels in a country blues style. Despite being an affecting singer and above-average guitarist, he never achieved the kind of fame that Odetta did and had more name recognition in Europe than in the States.

After their initial meeting, Red wrote Odetta an anguished letter, telling her that he missed her and "I sleep with you [*sic*] Photo every night." Soon enough Odetta came around, and by the fall, they were a couple. "We're starting our lives together and now that I'm part of a unit, I think I can come back out here to live again," she told a reporter in San Francisco. For a time they seemed smitten, Odetta introducing Red as her "husband," although they never formally married. A photo of the couple that ran in a Halifax, Canada, newspaper in the summer of 1977, when they appeared in concert together, shows a beaming Red standing behind Odetta with his arms draped around her. She's wearing a headscarf, and her left hand is rested lovingly on his right arm.[28]

Odetta's friends were taken with Red, but they wondered whether the cultured Odetta had much in common with her backwoods companion. "He was such a sweetheart but just a little country," Frederick Warhanek recalled. "Knowing Odetta as I did, I didn't see too much of a future for that." Carrie Thaler had the same foreboding. "They seemed very much in love," she recalled. "Very different worlds. I really liked Red, but you could tell he had no education, had one of the hardest lives I ever heard of, growing up. He was a great guy and they seemed happy together to me, but I didn't spend that much time with them. . . . Someone must have broken somebody's heart."[29]

The relationship—long distance for the most part, unless their musical paths happened to cross or they both had time off together—lasted until about 1978, when it seemed to dim, although Odetta never told her friends why. Red later moved to Europe, where he could count on more regular work, and that's where he lived until his death in 2012.

By the late 1970s and early 1980s, Odetta's appearance began to undergo a change as she entered middle age. She often kept her slightly graying hair hidden under colorful African headwraps, with a small, jeweled bead laced through a few braids of hair adorning the middle of her forehead—what she sometimes called her "third eye." Around her neck, she wore a pendant emblazoned with the words "I Am" to remind herself that no one, even a cold-blooded music executive, has the power to negate a human being. When she performed, she often kept a lighted stick of incense attached to the tuning pegs of her guitar.

Her music changed too. She had jettisoned chain gang songs and work songs like "John Henry" because she said she could no longer summon the hate they required to sing. And while she still had plenty of adoring audiences and earned her share of rave reviews from critics who now identified her as a "living legend," some listeners began to turn on her. Once Odetta's guitar style had been so distinctive and an integral part of how she conveyed emotion in her music, but now she used a rhythmic strum to string together three, four, or more songs at a time, changing only the chords as she moved from, say, "Sail Away, Ladies" to "900 Miles." Vocally, she began adding all manner of slurs, whoops, and filigrees that displayed an impressive control but weren't pleasing to everyone's ear.

A fan named Richard Hart wrote to her in exasperation after attending one of her concerts then.

> Dear Odetta. . . . What happened to that beautiful singing you are so capable of? You have a great voice, why must you make those strange, unbeautiful sounds? Is it so important to be different[?] Is it not enough to sing beautiful folk songs in a normal manner, from beginning to end—instead of singing them in 8 or 10 strung together and complete with screeching, squealing and grating sounds?[30]

Her banter in between songs, often about racism or spirituality, proved to be a double-edged sword in an era noted for its relative political apathy. Her barbs against government inaction on poverty, her calls for social justice, and her pleas that her audience get out and vote inspired some but irritated others, especially when her anger was aroused. "Odetta talks aimlessly and too much," Richard Harrington, music critic for the *Washington Post*, complained. "The time would be better spent keeping her guitar in tune. Failure in that area becomes particularly bothersome in the context of her simplistic chug-a-chug strumming style. After more than two decades, one expects improvement."[31]

John McWhorter, a black writer and linguist, recalled seeing an Odetta show in the early 1980s at New York University, where he was a student. "She rocked the house, the young and mostly white students delighted to be sitting at the feet of a black Earth goddess 'telling it like it is,'" McWhorter remembered. "I thought I had a good time. But later my white roommate rocked me by dismissing the whole thing. His problem with Odetta was her smugness, her obvious expectation that her audience bow to her moral superiority." McWhorter partly questioned whether racism was at work in his friend's critique. "But I also knew that few white performers could have gotten away with the Odetta tone, and that since white eighteen-year-olds could not have played any part in the oppression that Odetta had encountered in her life, it was a bit of an act to require them to accept her saintliness without question."[32]

Some of Odetta's longtime friends suspected that whatever her political message and her desire to edify, she also was struggling emotionally. "When I saw her in the 1980s she seemed disappointed or something like that, and she would almost turn on the audience, sort of kind of lecturing and so on," recalled Lance Greening, who had spent so many nights with Odetta at the Gate of Horn or at the Greenings' Chicago-area home. "I hate to tell tales on people, but she was having a hard time . . . having to do these small shows when she had been doing concerts with tremendous attendance." Roger Deitz, a folk musician who performed with Odetta a lot during this period, mused that journeyman artists like himself couldn't possibly understand what she was going through, doing two or three shows a night at a small club when she'd once sold out Carnegie Hall. "I don't know what it's like when you've been to the mountaintop and then you're now just trying to keep the apartment rent going," he said. "How many people manage to scale the heights to be Tom Paxton or Pete Seeger or Odetta? . . . There are not very many."[33]

It was during this chapter of her life, as her career and personal life foundered, that friends began to realize Odetta's drinking had become a serious problem. She had always been a social drinker. The singer Nancy Griffith recalled Odetta once telling her, "All god's children needs vodka." But now Odetta had trouble stopping. "She did have problems with alcohol, that's definite," Frederick Warhanek said. "I was quite young at the time and I was drinking too much too. And I said both of us got to stop this."[34]

No one can know exactly what demons Odetta wrestled then, because she kept so much of her interior life to herself. But to have been "black and turned away," as her friend Maya Angelou said, then to have savored the warm embrace of adoring crowds and to have felt beloved—in spite of what she'd once been made to believe of her lowly status in the world—and then to have come off the mountaintop to look square at what she'd come to feel was a racist music establishment that was ignoring her talents must have been hard.

"She did use alcohol to medicate her emotional pain, in my view," Selma Thaler recalled. "It had become an issue between us as well. She said, 'Stop tryna' fix me.'"[35] Odetta's drinking caused a rift with Thaler, whose family had been so close to Odetta almost from the beginning of her career and had even lent her thousands of dollars to help her pay back taxes, with the IRS threatening enforcement actions earlier in the decade. But while Odetta swallowed her pride to take the money, she didn't want help with her alcohol problems. The rift lasted several years, but they later resumed their friendship after Carrie Thaler brokered a rapprochement.

Though her struggles were largely hidden from the public and don't seem to have affected Odetta's ability to sing, they did spill over into her work. "We did a folk festival at UCLA [in the early nineties]," recalled Roger McGuinn, the former leader of the Byrds, "and she came out of the dressing room and"—he made a whoosh sound—"big cloud of alcohol." "She was drinking a lot," said McGuinn, who had fallen in love with Odetta's music as a teenager at the Gate of Horn. "She smelled like alcohol every time I saw her. And I saw her several times in different places."[36]

Odetta developed a reputation during this time, fairly or not, as a performer who could be difficult to deal with offstage, oversensitive to any perceived slights or treatment she felt was unbefitting a star, and withering to anyone, even a fan, who interrupted her backstage as she tried to get into the right frame of mind to sing. Her gruffness with promoters and stagehands, particularly those she didn't know well, may have poured forth from the well of resentment she felt at being overlooked in the cultural pantheon. If the establishment wasn't going to let her in the door, then at least she was going to be in control and call the shots at her concerts. Adding to the volatility of these situations was Odetta's preconcert preparation, which required her to shut off the world and get into an almost trancelike state. "I'm two different personalities, one as a performer and one as a civilian," she explained once. "Before a concert, I close everything out—put blinders on—and must be alone. Afterwards I need a few minutes to touch my feet back to earth."[37]

Once shy to a fault, Odetta now had a directness that could be scathing. And she apparently felt no need to explain herself to those impresarios she rubbed wrong; in the end, she had less interest in winning their love than in making sure they knew who was working for whom. Odetta's nonmusical friends rarely saw this side of her, unless they paid an unexpected visit before a concert. For them, she remained a shining light, a mother bear, a tigress of benevolence, whose focus always remained on their well-being. Fellow musicians saw flashes of her fury and tried to make sense of it, although to fully appreciate it maybe you'd have to have been a black female, born under Jim Crow, raised under Jim Crow lite, and had the life and career arc that Odetta had had, with all her triumphs and disenchantments.

David Amram had his own theory about why Odetta was so ornery in the latter part of her career, a trait that earned her the nickname "Odacious" from the trumpeter Clark Terry. "Sometimes when she would get angry or upset, which was for a very good reason . . . and if she wasn't with someone who loved her and cared for her, she had a hard time getting out of that," Amram said. "And people said that's because she used to drink and do this and that. But a lot of people did that. Above and beyond that I think she had a certain built in sense of decency and honor and a purity that she never could abandon. . . . She could never let anything slide."[38]

Most of her fans, of course, wouldn't have suspected any behind-the-scenes turmoil, and that was a tribute to Odetta's professionalism as a performer. On stage, she was a diva, whose presence could still electrify on the best of nights, even as she battled through tough times. "She was still one of the top acts," Roger Deitz said. "I can only see what she was doing [on stage] and . . . if you listen to that voice and the control and what she sang, she certainly wasn't cheating anyone out of the money they spent to go listen to Odetta." Once in the mid-1980s at Godfrey Daniels, a small folk club in Bethlehem, Pennsylvania, Odetta had what organizers remembered as a "breakdown" before the show, sobbing and moaning in the basement green room. No one knew what was going on, but they stood guard to make sure no one bothered her. "And then she would come out and do a dynamite show, regardless," said Dave Fry, the founder of the club.[39]

And there were certainly bright spots even in the hardest of times. In a run stretching from 1983 to 1995, Odetta sang every New Year's Eve at the Cathedral of St. John the Divine on Amsterdam Avenue on the Upper West Side of New York. The church, known for its immense sanctuary and breathtaking stained-glass windows, held an annual "Concert for Peace" to ring in the New Year, with singing, poetry, and spoken prayers for peace by luminaries such as Jason Robards and Leonard Bernstein. After rebuffing an invitation twice, Odetta relented. "She would often shun holiday concerts because she never got any birthday presents as a child (born New Year's Eve) and holidays depressed her," according to a newspaper account. But when Odetta sang "This Little Light of Mine" a cappella from the pulpit and ten thousand people holding lit candles joined in, their voices soaring up to the church's immense vaulted ceilings, it proved transformative. A candlelighting ceremony and Odetta's song became the traditional climax of the program. "The whole season is up for me now," Odetta said. If Odetta's best-known song had been the "Freedom Trilogy" early in her career, "This Little Light" took on the role in her later years. It had been written as a gospel tune and adapted with a civil rights theme in the 1960s, but it also had a simple, universal message of empowerment. With all her ups and downs, Odetta may have sung it as much for her own salvation as for her audience's.[40]

In the same vein, she also began accepting occasional teaching gigs, not necessarily focused on music but on life. A semester-long workshop at Evergreen State College in Washington had the title "Odetta's Philosophy," and hearing her describe it, it seems to have evolved into a kind of group analysis, providing an emotional outlet not only for her students but for herself.

> The only thing I had to bring was a box of Kleenex. We would get into areas of talking and people would start crying; they were able to talk about things they couldn't with their families or their friends or in their classes. We would hold each other and let the tears flow. When they were finished with whatever they were gonna say, (they) would reaffirm themselves by saying, "I am."[41]

During the '80s, Odetta finally found a manager, Len Rosenfeld, who had her best interests at heart. A gentle giant at six feet four, Rosenfeld had repped Josh White, the Clancy Brothers, and other folk acts. He wasn't a high-powered dealmaker by any stretch, but he genuinely cared for Odetta and had a reputation as a manager who put his artists first. "Len was very paternal," recalled Roger Deitz, whom Rosenfeld also managed during that time. "She found someone who was going to care about *her* more than I think he cared about himself and how much money he made."[42] Rosenfeld's selflessness sometimes manifested itself in a tendency to "forget" to cash his own commission checks if he believed his client needed the money more than he did.

Odetta's sister, Jimmie Lee, moved in with her late in the decade, doing secretarial work and helping with bookkeeping and other household management tasks left undone by Odetta, who was a pack rat and so disorganized that she neglected to open the royalty checks that still arrived quarterly. "At this time the Felious fillies were reunited," Jan Ford recalled. "They lived and worked together as a team. Odetta often expressed how good it felt to come home to my mom. They had an unshakeable bond."[43] They helped one another cope with the death of their mother, Flora, in 1988.

Having a constant companion helped ground Odetta, who rarely spoke about her private life but occasionally revealed her difficulties with relationships and her tendency to be a loner. "I'm a gypsy and a hermit," she said in 1986. "I have a lot of children, but none of my own."[44]

She also had to deal with whispers about her sexuality. Odetta's cropped hair as a younger woman, large size, friendships with lesbians, and a singing voice that sounded almost masculine at the low range contributed to the talk from people in the industry and casual observers who assumed that she preferred women. "She was a large woman who had a complex sexual identity," Ash Grove owner Ed Pearl offered. "Odetta was a big woman, strong voice and the short haircut and the whole very forceful personality," Jack Landrón recalled. "She was never very tee-hee womanly so it was almost assumed that she was, I don't think we used the term lesbian, but that kind of lady."[45]

Those rumors have outlived her. (On Answers.com, the question "Was Odetta a lesbian?" is answered by a simple, anonymous "Yes she was.") Her friends, however, insist that Odetta was decidedly heterosexual throughout her life. "She was very, very unlesbian," Frederick Warhanek said. "She did experiment, which was not unusual, but no." "They're judging her by her appearance," posited Carrie Thaler, who had many deep-into-the-night conversations with Odetta. "I would have talked to her about that." And one of her old guitar players who didn't want to go on the record recalled Odetta seducing him during a foreign tour back in the 1960s. "I can guarantee you that she wasn't just purely lesbian," he joked.[46]

Even during the times when she was squirreling herself away at home, Odetta made an exception when it came to going down to the clubs to hear and encourage young singers, maybe even giving singing lessons to the most promising ones. And when she ventured out, it would usually be in style, thanks to a devoted fan from Brooklyn who called himself Stereo Mike. He owned a big black car, and after he got off from his day job, he'd drive into Manhattan to make sure Odetta was treated like a star, David Amram recalled:

> He had a used limo that he would simonize and shine it up. He had one of those chauffeur's caps with a black brim and he'd put on a black suit and he looked like a limo driver. And he would go pick

up Odetta, who would get all dressed up and they would go cruis-
ing down to the Village. . . . Odetta would go, looking like a regal
queen. . . . She used to make these grand entrances and all these
young folk players and singer songwriters would see her coming in
with a limo driver. She enjoyed that so much.[47]

For the genuine star treatment, she could still go overseas. In 1989
Odetta toured Australia again, and her arrival was treated as big news
in the media, with newspaper and radio interviews and performances
on national TV. When she sang in Sydney Town Hall, Garry Shead
went to see her and they reconnected, more than two decades after
their broken engagement. He was married, but clearly they hadn't
lost their affection for one another. "We went out that night and I
went back to her hotel with her," Shead said. "And even though I was
married, we kind of went there together but we didn't do anything,
it was just so lovely. We went to a coffee shop that night in King's
Cross, where she stayed, and it was still the same kind of love we had
for each other."[48]

Toward the end of the decade, there were stirrings of interest in
Odetta's music. A live album, *Movin' It On*, recorded at a concert in
Wisconsin, came out on the independent Rose Quartz label in 1987.
The following year she teamed with her old bass player Bill Lee to
re-record *Christmas Spirituals* (later retitled *Beautiful Star*) for another indie, Alcazar Productions, her first studio release in nearly
twenty years. While the beautifully captured renditions of spirituals
from her 1959 Vanguard LP didn't push many musical boundaries,
they were all the proof needed that Odetta's vocal power and artistry
remained undiminished as she approached sixty—and a further reminder that one of America's great voices had been marginalized for
far too long. "Odetta remains woefully underrecorded after 40 years
in the music business," Bob Darden wrote in *Billboard* in early 1989.
"She only has 20 or so albums to her credit, many of which are currently out of print."[49]

Odetta couldn't help but wonder why the music business had
passed her by for so long. "You definitely got the sense that, you
know, she wanted that recognition again," said Robbie Woliver, one
of the owners of Folk City in Greenwich Village, where Odetta often

held court with up-and-coming musicians and stayed until the lights went out at four in the morning. "She knew that she deserved that recognition and even these new kids that she was watching every day at the club, she knew that they wouldn't be there if it wasn't for her probably."[50]

After a fallow period, folk music had started to gain some traction again thanks to singer-songwriters like Suzanne Vega and Tracy Chapman, both of whom credited Odetta as an inspiration. Odetta had been saying for years, perhaps a bit wistfully, that "another folk boom" was in the offing.[51] Little did she know that it wouldn't be folk music that would rejuvenate her career but another genre that her fans had once rejected for her.

CHAPTER FOURTEEN

BLUES EVERYWHERE I GO

In the early 1990s, Marc Carpentieri was a part-time blues drummer in Huntington, New York, a town of modest homes nestled among blue-blood mansions and Revolutionary War relics on the North Shore of Long Island. Carpentieri's band, Somethin' Blue, played a typical mix of Chicago blues and other related styles, mainly in local bars, its most notable gig having been as an opener for Clarence "Gatemouth" Brown. Carpentieri, then in his late twenties, started MC Records with his wife, Catherine, in their home as a way to distribute cassette recordings of his group, but he soon decided to try his hand at producing other artists. By the latter part of the decade, the fledgling company had built a modest following releasing material from aging Mississippi bluesmen Big Jack Johnson and R. L. Burnside.

Carpentieri was looking for an artist to help take MC Records to a new level of success when, in 1998, he was flipping through a music magazine and came upon a write-up about an Odetta concert. He turned casually to Catherine and said, "Hey, we ought to record Odetta." Carpentieri had first heard Odetta's name in grammar school during a lesson on the March on Washington, and later, as a deejay for WBAU in Hempstead, New York, he occasionally played Odetta's music. He knew her name didn't generate the same kind of recognition that it once had, and the idea of helping revive her career was something that appealed to him. A meeting was arranged to see if he and Odetta would get along, which was hardly guaranteed. "I was kind of scared shitless," Carpentieri recalled of the introduction, which occurred backstage at a small club called Bodles Opera House in Chester, New York, where Odetta was performing. "You know, she could intimidate you with a stare very quickly." But it became clear right away that Carpentieri had passed muster, and Odetta, who had released only one studio recording in the past three decades, decided to give the blues another try.[1]

Ironically, it was Odetta's struggles that may have helped pave the way for her to do this. If one has to suffer to sing the blues, then Odetta had had more than her share of career letdowns, personal setbacks, and emotional lows since her heyday as the Queen of Folk. And the nineties hadn't been especially kind to her either.

To start off the decade, she'd gotten a small role in Spike Lee's jazz film *Mo' Better Blues*, scored by Lee's father, Bill Lee, and the screen time might have brought her renewed visibility. But in what seemed like an increasingly typical disappointment, her scenes had been left on the cutting-room floor. Around 1996, she'd suffered a heart attack, beginning a gradual decline in her health in her sixty-sixth year. In 1997, Len Rosenfeld had become gravely ill, and he died the following year. Fortunately for Odetta, Rosenfeld had asked his friend Doug Yeager if he could take over as Odetta's manager. Earnest, sturdily built, and with a stentorian speaking voice that could almost rival Odetta's singing pipes, Yeager was already managing Josh White Jr. and had worked with Odetta as a concert agent. Yeager would go far above the call to help make Odetta's last decade an artistically productive one.

After Odetta signed with MC Records, she and Carpentieri held auditions for a piano player/band leader, and Odetta rejected the first few, including some well-known and respected ones. "I know what they're going to play before they play it," she complained.[2] Still smarting from the reception of her straight-ahead interpretations of classic blues nearly forty years earlier, Odetta was sure about one thing: she longed for a different sound.

Eventually they settled upon Seth Farber, a keyboard maestro who was equally at home as a rock sideman and Broadway musical director. Farber could effortlessly vamp a blues, stomp out some New Orleans boogie, or add the perfect amount of whimsy to a show tune. His choice turned out to be vital not only to Odetta's new sound but also to the touring act that would follow the record. "She would come over to my place day after day and we would listen, discuss, she would have a list of fifteen or twenty songs from Victoria Spivey, Memphis Minnie, Ethel Waters, various blues singers from the 1920s," Farber recalled. "And she would say, 'What can we do to make this not just a copy of them, make it our own?'" "For me it was like falling in love with a girl in a musical way," he added. "At that time a youngerish white guy and an olderish black woman, if you looked at them on the street you wouldn't see any particular connection, and yet there was this great connection. It was exciting to be entrusted with musically taking care of her."[3]

They assembled a group that included Farber and guitarist Jimmy Vivino from Conan O'Brien's house band and, in late March of 1999 at Tiki Studios in Glen Cove, New Jersey, began laying down tracks from Spivey, Ma Rainey, Sippie Wallace, and, of course, Bessie Smith. But this time Odetta had something new to bring to the table. Her voice, coarsened by age, decades of smoking, and life's hard knocks, now had more of the weathered soul it had lacked when she was thirty years old. She didn't try to recreate the blues shouting that her idols had honed in tent shows and black vaudeville almost a century earlier, and she was no longer trying to be Bessie. She was free at last, and therefore all Odetta, on songs such as "Careless Love," "St. Louis Blues," and "Please Send Me Someone to Love," firmly in control of her contralto but no longer in thrall to her operatic training, adding blue notes and just the right amount of jazz inflection to her vocals to convey emotion.

And yet in other ways, Odetta remained the same as ever, as evinced by songs such as "Unemployment Blues," "Homeless Blues," and "Rich Man Blues." "The world has not improved and there are some steps being taken back," Odetta had said a few years earlier, predicting that she would be trying to raise awareness "until we reach perfection." Now she had a new soapbox. "She was definitely always thinking about the world," Farber said. "Even when we were doing our record, you know, [she would ask] how does this song comment on what's going on in the world, even if it's a blues from 1939. . . . She was kind of a political artist from the beginning and it didn't go away."[4]

The one difficulty with the sessions turned out to be Odetta's deteriorating health. Shortly before the recording began, the sixty-eight-year-old had been hospitalized for an undisclosed ailment, most likely the heart disease that was beginning to take a toll on her. "Sometimes she'd come in like a ball of energy—you just didn't know," Carpentieri recalled. "Even when she came in frail she'd knock it out. You couldn't tell on that record which session she came in and you're practically thinking, *I don't know if she's going to sing a single note*. . . . The performance when the mic comes on is always the same."[5]

When Odetta heard the results of her efforts, it seemed to reenergize her. "We recorded like the first track or two and we go listen to the playback in the booth, you know, great speakers and all that, and she just grabs me and starts dancing with me," Carpentieri said. "And I was like really taken aback. Because I didn't know her that well and she was just so happy, she was so thrilled with that music and how well it turned out." Her friends were ecstatic that after so many years in the cultural wilderness, Odetta had finally found her way out. "I loved those blues albums she did," Frederick Warhanek said. "Her voice had matured a lot and she had a quality to her voice that she never had before. Every time she did an album she was so high from it, and hoping [for recognition]."[6]

As it happened, the recognition that she'd craved for so many years was already coming her way. On September 29, 1999, a week before the album's release, Odetta and eighteen others, including Aretha Franklin, Steven Spielberg, and August Wilson, received the National Medal of the Arts and Humanities from President Bill Clinton at Constitution Hall in Washington, DC. Before the formal ceremony, the president shared a private moment offstage with each artist. According to Doug Yeager, Clinton placed his hand on his heart and told Odetta, "I've loved your music since I was a southern boy in Arkansas. . . . You were a major inspiration to me when I became aware of the civil rights movement."[7]

Later, on stage, Clinton thanked "an extraordinary group of Americans who have strengthened our civilization and whose achievements have enriched our lives." His voice was a bit croaky from illness or fatigue—he'd recently survived an impeachment conviction vote in the

Senate. When it came time to hang the large gold medallion around Odetta's neck, he said:

> For 50 years now Odetta has used her commanding power and amazing grace not just to entertain but to inspire. She has sung for freedom with Dr. King, lifted the pride of millions of children, shaped the careers of young performers like Joan Baez, Bob Dylan and Tracy Chapman. She is the reigning queen of American folk music, reminding us all that songs have the power to change the heart and change the world.[8]

After the ceremony, the Clintons hosted the honorees for dinner and dancing at the White House, and Odetta sat at the president's table. Odetta had mixed feelings at the time about getting the award from Bill Clinton. She'd campaigned for him in 1992, recording "America the Beautiful" and "Michael Row Your Boat Ashore" as part of a group called the Clintones that had included Carly Simon, Judy Collins, Lesley Gore, and others. But she'd come to believe Clinton had fallen short of his promise and had "changed midstream" during a presidency noted, in part, for his support of a tough-on-crime law that swelled the prison population, welfare reform, and the North American Free Trade Agreement. "I thought about that before receiving the medal." she recalled. "And then I thought, this is a medal from the nation, and he just happens to be the president presenting the medal."[9]

In some ways, the award made up for Odetta's feelings of being sidelined by bigger stars, her friend the singer Donal Leace recalled. "I think the Clintons were very special recognition," he said. "To some degree, I think it boils down to that five minutes or three minutes with the cameras going off and all that [at the March on Washington]. I don't think she was broadcasting it, but I don't think she was too terribly happy with the way some people treated her legacy. . . . It sort of validates you."[10]

Odetta had nearly missed out on the whole experience when she'd suffered an accident and lingered close to death just weeks earlier. Coming back from taping an appearance on "World Cafe," a syndicated radio show originating from WXPN in Philadelphia, she tripped on a subway grating on Eighth Avenue outside New York's Penn Station and hit her head, sending her into a coma for several days. With friends and loved ones gathered in her room at Roosevelt Hospital, her organs began shutting down. "Her heart was already weak," Yeager said. "But it was just like it sent the system into shock and she started to have organ failure."[11] But she regained consciousness and stabilized, and a phone call from the White House about her impending award bucked her spirits and helped her make what seemed like a miraculously quick recovery.

And more validation came with the release of *Blues Everywhere I Go* in early October. *DownBeat* called the record "a triumph. . . . She uses her sweeping, dramatic voice to uncover layers of heartache and dramatic content in lyrics that few other singers could get at." The *New York Times* said that "the mother goddess of the folk blues still has plenty of spice in her, as this long overdue turn proves." Although she was ostensibly paying tribute to other blues legends, the *Times* said, "the real tribute belongs to the 70-year-old singer herself, sharing her extensive knowledge of hardship, good loving and the best way to bend the blues."[12]

Not everyone was on board. The *Washington Post* revived an old criticism that seemed off the mark this time around, saying Odetta was still trying to imitate Bessie Smith and her contemporaries. "But Odetta's classically trained alto is too pure, too *precise* to pull off the impersonation," Geoffrey Himes wrote, although he curiously added that the failed knockoffs made the songs more interesting than successful ones would have been.[13]

The largely positive reviews and the burst of PR surrounding the medal from Clinton made it clear that a touring act built around Odetta's blues material was in order. And that was welcome financial relief for Odetta, who didn't have much savings and had had her share of money problems dating back to the 1970s. In the mid-1990s, the IRS had placed a lien on her apartment for back taxes totaling more than $27,000. And by the spring of 1999, she had maxed out her credit cards and was struggling to make the payments.[14]

Now, in addition to clubs like the Tin Angel in Philadelphia and the Knitting Factory in New York, Odetta had the blues festival circuit in the US and Europe to count on. She retired her guitar and became a blues singer, with Farber as her main pianist and traveling companion. "Now she was popular again and work was always offered in," Yeager recalled. "I didn't take everything and I would make sure there were rest days."[15]

The switch to blues gave Odetta a whole new audience, in addition to those 1960s survivors—the crowd she had privately labeled the "folky-poos"—who had once shunned her blues singing and still sometimes longed to hear "John Henry" the way she'd done it on her first record. "She would never have been asked to do the Chicago Blues Festival and things like that that we did, so it expanded her possibilities," Farber said. "She'd show up at a blues festival and there would be some people who would know who she was and some people who wouldn't. But we'd always go over."[16]

In January of 2000 came another honor: a Grammy nomination, the first of Odetta's long career, and it was for blues. When Carpentieri called her to deliver the news, Odetta was speechless. Then she cried. "She has never been nominated for a Grammy award in her 50 years [as a performer]," he told a reporter, "and when I told her she just broke down."[17]

The awards ceremony took place on a rainy February 23 at the Staples Center in Los Angeles. Odetta sat in the audience with friends and family including Jimmie Lee, Jan Ford, and Frederick Warhanek. When the category of traditional blues came up, however, the shiny statuette went to B. B. King, who already had eight Grammys to his credit and would add several more before he was finished. Odetta received the news stoically. "She kept a stiff upper lip," Warhanek said. "Her sister, Jimmie Lee, was in tears, just crying like crazy. And [Odetta] said, 'Just cut it out!' And she made some comment about, you know, he's a brilliant musician and he deserves it too."[18]

Still, her career was in ascendance again. In 2000, she played fifty American cities and toured Europe three times. In 2001, she touched down in seventy cities worldwide. She was once again "captivating" and "enchanting" and soaking up "thunderous applause," according to reviews of her shows, which now centered on piano-based blues, with some bluesified folk mixed in, always with a dollop of political commentary. "Odetta talked of immigrant groups of all colors being taken advantage of on reaching America, and sang 'Got a Little

Light, Let it Shine,'" one critic noted after she performed in Charleston, West Virginia, in this period. "She spoke of AIDS, said 'teen-age pregnancy's been going all through history,' advised 'don't forget those prophylactics' and uncorked 'Careless Love.' As she sang the ancient lament of unwed mother-to-be, she morphed into the physicality, complete with postural back pangs."[19]

She also used her new bully pulpit to try to forge a sense of community in her audiences filled with harried, overworked early-twenty-first-century denizens of whatever city she happened to be visiting that night. That usually meant group singing, 1960s style, and a command to toss off inhibitions and put some feeling into it. "It's the only thing all of you will ever do together," Odetta told the crowd at the end of a rain-swept Ottawa Bluesfest. "Which seemed like a point worth pondering," the local paper noted, "as Odetta left the stage with the audience doing just that. It was a small magical moment."[20]

So much travel for a woman in declining health required that her accompanists do much more than simply back her up musically. Farber—and a few other pianists who filled in when he was unavailable—had to become road managers and learn to deal with Odetta's medical requirements, ingrained routines, and sometimes short fuse.

They took pains to make sure no one interrupted her before and after shows, when she was getting into—or out of—the deep place in her soul that she summoned to perform, although they didn't always succeed. Radoslav Lorković, one of the pianists who accompanied her during her final years, recalled that she could be "angelic" with a nervous teenager who buttonholed her, cutting the tension with, "Welcome, child." But, he said, "somebody would kind of barge in and say, I was at the show in 1972 on March 17, do you remember me? And then the flames would come out. 'How am I supposed to remember?!!' And that person would never be the same again."[21] In the blues documentary *Lightning in a Bottle*, the cameras caught Odetta's fiery temper on full display in her late period as she furiously dressed down a backup band including Dr. John and Levon Helm during a rehearsal for allegedly playing too loud behind the singer Ruth Brown, who seemed happy with her performance. It isn't hard to read the confrontation, given Odetta's history of feeling "drowned out" of the culture.

Mike Koster, who founded the Thirsty Ear festival in Santa Fe, New Mexico, and worked with Odetta a handful of times beginning in 2001, came to expect a bit of offstage unpleasantness but also a transcendent show. "Even though you might be miffed at her or whatever for the way she just treated somebody backstage, she had this tremendous moral authority when she got up there and started singing and telling her stories, of course, which were as powerful as her music and singing," he recalled.[22]

Friends said that, with help, Odetta by then had her problems with alcohol under better control. On stage, she began each concert with a quote from *Return to Love*, a bestselling book by the self-help author and spiritual guru Marianne Williamson. The quote that Odetta recited before she ever sang a note also spoke to her own lifelong search for personal freedom and the validation of her people.

> *Our deepest fear is not that we are inadequate.*
> *Our deepest fear is that we are powerful beyond measure.*
> *It is our light not our darkness that most frightens us.*
> *We ask ourselves, who am I to be brilliant, gorgeous,*
> *talented and fabulous?*
> *Actually, who are you not to be?*
> *You are a child of God.*[23]

She usually followed that up by commanding the crowd to join her on the next song. "We are re-confirming ourselves," she might say. "If your neighbor looks at you like they don't like the key you're singing in, look right back at 'em, bless 'em and continue to sing."

By the end of 2001, Odetta had recorded a second album for MC Records, a tribute to Lead Belly entitled *Lookin for a Home*. Lead Belly's repertoire of work songs and blues allowed Odetta to continue mixing politics and music, with tunes like "Jim Crow Blues" and "Bourgeois Blues," the latter being Lead Belly's lament over the segregation he encountered in restaurants and hotels in Washington, DC, in the late 1930s. While Odetta sounded in even stronger voice than she had the previous year, the release date of *Lookin for a Home*, August 21, put the record in the unfortunate crosshairs of the September

11 attacks, which meant that it got almost no publicity. "I feel that record somehow got lost," Carpentieri said.[24]

In the immediate aftermath of the attacks, entertainers had a difficult time resuming their acts, not wanting to seem oblivious or flip in a time of national mourning. Comedians had the trickiest task: making America laugh, but not too much. When David Letterman returned to the air with his *Late Show* on CBS the week of September 17—the first late-night host to take this fragile step—he sought out guests who would provide a measure of reassurance and evoke a spirit of perseverance. Odetta was on his short list. "They were concerned with, how can we come back on the air," Yeager recalled. "We need someone with presence, spirituality who can give the right presence, the right music and the right solemnity to the occasion."[25]

Odetta appeared as the second musical guest that week. Backed by the Boys Choir of Harlem, she returned briefly to her folk roots and sang a medley of "We Shall Overcome"—altering the lyric to "we shall overcome *today*"—and "This Little Light of Mine," which she delivered with a dignified joy that conveyed exactly the feeling Letterman was hoping to invoke. Her longtime fans tuning in that night would have been struck by two things: she danced on stage, something the old Odetta never would have done, even regaling the audience with what appeared to be a version of Michael Jackson's moonwalk; and she had lost a lot of weight, her health problems having reduced her once large frame to the point where she looked almost svelte in a gray dress and turquoise African cap. During the commercial break, she brought the house down with "Amazing Grace."

Despite the lack of publicity, *Lookin for a Home* earned two W. C. Handy blues award nominations, and in 2002, Odetta performed another seventy dates worldwide. The following year, Jimmie Lee died, and the loss of her closest companion sent Odetta into a tailspin. "After my mom's death, auntie fell into a great depression," Jan Ford recalled.[26] Odetta stopped eating, and her weight dipped even further. But she continued to perform.

Although it devastated her, Jimmie Lee's passing had one unforeseen consequence that brought Odetta much joy during her last half decade of life: she formed a familial bond with the New York–based filmmaker Michelle Esrick, who had met Odetta several years earlier and saw now that she was hurting and offered to help. The two women grew so tight that Odetta began referring to Esrick as her daughter, and Esrick to this day calls Odetta "my mother," although she has two biological parents whom she loves. "She took care of me just as much as I took care of her; emotionally, spiritually, we had each other's back," Esrick said. If someone raised an eyebrow when Odetta introduced Esrick, a Jew from Florida, as her kin, Odetta had an answer for that too: "What, you've never heard of adoption?"[27] Like Boots Jaffee and Kenichi Takeda, Esrick gave Odetta the gift of motherhood. In return, Odetta made them all feel special and cared for, helping them get in touch with their "I Am." Despite her self-designated hermit status, Odetta had practically run a side business over the years doling out maternal advice and hard-earned wisdom to her faithful friends and "adopted" children.

As Odetta's health declined, Esrick in particular would be there, along with Doug Yeager, making sure she got the care she needed to keep singing through a series of health crises. In July of 2005, Odetta tripped on cobblestones near her home on Fifth Avenue and broke her hip. She spent weeks at Mt. Sinai Hospital and several months recuperating at the New Jewish Home on West 106th Street. With her healthcare bills piling up, she had no real nest egg to draw upon, and canceling months' worth of gigs was something she could ill afford to do. Friends tried to help out financially. Elizabeth Elliott, a friend from Colorado, bought a piece of art from her. "She wouldn't take money from me and so I said, 'Odetta, if you don't really love that piece of art, I would really love to buy it.' And she said, 'Well, what do you think it's worth?' and I said, 'Oh, I wouldn't take any less than a thousand dollars for it.' The piece of art was nothing. It's a print. I couldn't tell you who it's by. It's a woman clown with a tear rolling down its cheek."[28]

The Jazz Foundation, which helps elderly musicians make ends meet, also stepped in, paying the mortgage and maintenance on Odetta's apartment and getting her a private room at the nursing home so that she could begin to sing and rehearse. When she felt well enough to perform again, the foundation continued to assist her, with gigs at foundation events. "We had to say, 'Odetta, I've got a gig coming up for you, and it's just enough, the same exact amount as the mortgage,'" recalled Wendy Oxenhorn, the foundation's executive director.[29]

By the end of September, Odetta had recovered enough to travel to London and sing "Tomorrow Is a Long Time" and "Mr. Tambourine Man" at a Bob Dylan tribute concert at the Barbican. Her new piano-based renditions went over well. "The best performance of the night came from the veteran gospel and blues singer Odetta, whom Dylan massively admired," the *Guardian* reported.[30]

As the year drew to a close, MC released what would be Odetta's final album, *Gonna Let It Shine*, a live record of spirituals recorded at Fordham University in New York with the Holmes Brothers, a soul-blues group from her hometown of Birmingham. She continued to tour, walking with a cane at first and later using a wheelchair to get around, but soldiering on, even opting for dental implants to finally close up the gap in her front teeth that had long bothered her. "She was so powerful in her presence, I never even noticed the wheelchair," Radoslav Lorković recalled. "In a way, it made her more queenly."[31]

In January of 2007, during a grueling West Coast tour, Odetta's health gave out as a crowd waited to hear her perform at the Throckmorton Theatre in Mill Valley, California. Friends came to her side as she lay in bed in her hotel room, including Wavy Gravy, Ramblin' Jack Elliott, Frederick Warhanek, and Carrie Thaler. Odetta refused to see a doctor, until Gravy threatened her with a "sit in." "Everybody said, 'Wavy Gravy, we can't get her out of bed to go see the doctor.' I said well let me take a crack at it," he recalled. "I says, 'Odetta, you're gonna go up and see the doctor or I'm gonna lay down on the floor and sing "We Shall Overcome."' She got up and went to see the doctor."[32]

Doctors diagnosed her with severe pulmonary fibrosis, a scarring of the lungs, and said that her heart was so severely diseased that it was functioning at only 11 percent of capacity. They delivered the verdict that she should never perform again and would need to be on oxygen. But Odetta refused to fade away, refused to give up her place in the spotlight after so long in the shadows. When her cardiologist wouldn't sign papers allowing her to travel with an oxygen tank, Esrick found her another doctor. "She said, 'Michelle, I have to perform. I can't just lay on the bed and wait to die,'" Esrick recalled. "She said, 'I wanna die on stage.'"[33]

She recovered enough from the crisis in Mill Valley—or summoned the will—to do sixty concerts around the world in 2008, singing from a wheelchair, relying on oxygen before and after every show. For every out-of-town gig, Yeager had to arrange for an oxygen tank to travel on a flight with her, which took two days of paperwork and red tape amid the post-9/11 airport security apparatus. Yeager also found volunteers in every city who helped care for Odetta around the clock, made sure she ate, helped her dress, and gave her oxygen when she wasn't performing. "She'd be short of breath but she'd be able to sing and she wouldn't have the oxygen on the stage," Seth Farber said. "That was the one hour that was the best hour of her day."[34]

The next year was filled with poignant moments. In March, she made a surprise appearance at her own tribute concert outside Washington, DC, sponsored by the World Folk Music Association and featuring Janis Ian, Oscar Brand, Josh White Jr., Tom Paxton, and Ronnie Gilbert of the Weavers. At the end of the show, the performers were supposed to sing "This Little Light of Mine" as a serenade to Odetta, who had made the trip, against her doctor's wishes, from New York in an SUV alongside her oxygen tank, and was seated in a private box. But instead, Odetta insisted that she be wheeled out onto the stage and sang it herself. "And of course Odetta sang very strongly," White recalled. "It was Odetta in a wheelchair, you closed your eyes and you wouldn't know she was in it."[35]

In May she was back in Santa Fe for a festival celebrating women, where organizer Mike Koster, who had dealt with Odetta's feistiness so many times, barely recognized her. "It was weird for me to see Odetta so weakened, oxygen tube in her nose, skinny and stooped, little of the old fight left in her bones, singing about death with a diminished voice but with great emotional force," he recalled.[36]

The next month, she flew to Italy with Radoslav Lorković to appear at Musicultura, an annual festival held in a stunning outdoor amphitheater framed by neoclassical columns in Macerata. Odetta was slated to sing only a few songs, but she was so frail that organizers had to bring her in for five days so that she could get a full day's rest after her flight and another after her rehearsal. Her performance, before a sold-out crowd of twenty-five hundred and broadcast on Italian TV, didn't disappoint, and fans had no clue that she was getting oxygen in her dressing room. "That weakness, that frailty gave her performance even more intensity," said Vania Santi, who arranged the show. "I always thought she lived for the music for that feeling of communicating with people, inspiring people through the music."[37]

By the time she sang at the Hardly Strictly Bluegrass Festival in San Francisco's Golden Gate Park on October 4, returning to the city where it had all begun for her fifty-five years earlier, "she was dying really," recalled Dave Keyes, who accompanied her on piano for an hour-long set. "When she was on stage, she summoned all the strength that she had."[38] In the middle of performing "House of the Rising Sun," Odetta dramatically inserted death-oriented lines a cappella from the old English ballad "One Morning in May," which she had recorded nearly half a century earlier, as the audience and a number of stars, including Elvis Costello, Emmylou Harris, and T Bone Burnett looked on, astonished.

> *When I was a young girl I used to seek pleasure,*
> *When I was a young girl I used to drink ale;*
> *Out of the alehouse and into the jailhouse,*
> *My body is ruined, they left me here to die.*

Costello later brought his young son to get a photo with Odetta, telling Keyes, "This is royalty and I want to tell my son when he grows up that you met royalty."[39]

Her last concerts were two sold-out performances later that month at a Toronto nightclub called Hugh's Room, and her condition worsened dramatically. On Saturday, November 8, with her kidneys failing, Odetta checked into the emergency room at Lenox Hill Hospital on New York's Upper East Side, and by the next evening she was listed in critical condition in room 719 of the intensive care unit. Doctors at first said she might not survive another day, but they put her on dialysis, and she hung on. Less than a week earlier, Barack Obama had been elected president, a once-unthinkable milestone in the long struggle for equality by African Americans, a struggle in which Odetta had played a key role. Yeager taped a three-foot-tall poster of Obama on the wall of her room, and the yearning to perform at the inauguration kept her fighting for life. "Odetta believes she is going to sing at Obama's inauguration, and I believe that is the reason she is still alive," Yeager posted to her fans.[40]

Letters of support and flowers poured into the hospital from all over. At times it seemed as if Odetta might pull through yet again. She gained back enough strength to tell friends that Obama's election was the culmination of her life's work. "She lit up the hospital," Wavy Gravy told *Rolling Stone*. "She was just joyful."[41]

On Thanksgiving she shared a message with fans from her hospital bed. "The world is trembling under the weight of many problems," she wrote but urged people to give thanks for friends and community. In the end, her heart, kidneys, and lungs were too damaged. "The last two things she said to me, she grabbed my hand and she said, 'Doug, I'm just trying to hang on for the inauguration,'" Yeager recalled. "Then she kind of went out and she came back up and she said, 'You gotta get the costumes all ready for me.' Those were the last words I heard her say."[42]

Odetta died at 5:12 p.m. on December 2, 2008, of organ failure and heart disease. Her body was cremated, and friends and family, including Jan Ford, Michelle Esrick, Boots Jaffee, Yeager, and Josh White Jr., took turns on a frigid and windy day throwing her ashes into the Harlem Meer, the large artificial lake on the northwest corner of Central Park that Odetta had often gazed upon from her apartment window. She didn't get to sing at Obama's inauguration seven weeks later, but many of Odetta's friends felt sure that her spirit was there on January 20, 2009, probably singing "This Little Light of Mine" as the nation's first black president took the oath of office.

"WHO WILL BE
THE ODETTA OF NOW?"

On the night of February 24, 2009, thousands of people packed Riverside Church in New York's Morningside Heights neighborhood, filling the pews and balconies and spilling over into the aisles to spend the next four hours eulogizing, memorializing, and celebrating Odetta. In many ways, it was a testament to the sheer number of lives she touched—from the innumerable musicians she inspired to the myriad causes she supported and raised money for to the untold numbers of people who absorbed her stirring example of racial pride—in a long career that may not have gone entirely according to plan but left a lasting mark nonetheless. "Odetta did not need a percussionist to find a beat for her music," the Reverend Brad Braxton told the gathering of white and black mourners. "The syncopation in her song was the human heartbeat in all of us that pounds away with a hope for a brighter world."[1]

There were moving tributes and remembrances from Pete Seeger, Joan Baez, Maya Angelou, Peter Yarrow, Ramblin' Jack Elliott, Oscar Brand, David Amram, Josh White Jr., and Maria Muldaur, among many others. Most of them offered a variation on Muldaur's testimony: "I heard the voice of Odetta and it changed my life."[2] Weeks shy of ninety, Seeger led everyone in a sing-along of "Take This Hammer," the song Odetta had shouted like a storm in Topanga Canyon half a century earlier. Wavy Gravy, who had done so many benefits with Odetta, read a haiku he'd written for the occasion.

Odetta sang out
Her mighty song "Oh, Freedom"
Now she's free at last

Harry Belafonte recalled "the hundreds of times I have had to call upon her for many moments in the civil rights movement" before declaring, "Odetta gave me the motor, the engine, the vision, about how to use the moment that was cast upon me."[3]

There was plenty of joy, an abundance of camaraderie among a roomful of strangers, and much music. A group including Steve Earle, Peter Yarrow, Josh White Jr., and Tom Chapin sang "This Land Is Your Land," the song Odetta hoped would become the new national anthem. Sweet Honey in the Rock intoned "God's Gonna Cut You Down," a gospel folk song that Odetta used to sing a cappella to bring down the house at Carnegie Hall. In a touching finale, all the musicians who were there, along with friends and family and nearly everyone in the church, joined in to sing "This Little Light of Mine," Odetta's ode to the civil rights cause and to the universal urge to feel free.

Despite the outpouring, the public seemed pretty quick to forget what a vital force Odetta had been in the America of the 1950s and 1960s. A decade after her death, John Seiter, her former drummer, said that when he starts whipping out the names of people he performed with back then, "some people have never heard of her. And you just go, *what?*" Odetta's friend Selma Thaler has had those moments too. "You know, I've seen on PBS they have historical folk music programs or whatever," Thaler said. "She's never in them. It bothers the hell out of me."[4]

Still, there has been recognition of the imprint Odetta left on the world. In 2011, *Time* named the top one hundred "most extraordinary English-language popular recordings" since the magazine's founding in 1923. Odetta's "Take This Hammer," from *Odetta at the Gate of Horn*, was one of ten songs chosen from the 1950s, alongside "Jailhouse Rock," "Tutti Frutti," and "I've Got You Under My Skin." In 2014, the Alvin Ailey Dance Company created the touring ballet *Odetta*, in which the dancers interpreted her songs and some of her spoken monologues about race. That same year, the movie *Selma* was released, and it was Odetta's version of Bob Dylan's "Masters of War" that played during the climactic scene when marchers were beaten down trying to cross the Edmund Pettus Bridge.

New York City, where she lived most of her life, installed a plaque honoring Odetta at her 1270 Fifth Avenue co-op. In a small ceremony featuring music and several speeches, her neighbor Peggy Strait noted that Odetta had been active in the building to the very end, joining a fight to preserve a clause in the building's tenancy agreement that allowed apartments to be transferred to heirs without the board's review. "She stood for the rights of people," Strait said. "She fought locally for the same things she fought for out in the world."[5]

Odetta's influence on a new musical generation continues. In 2015, the singer and multi-instrumentalist Rhiannon Giddens channeled Odetta in a new version of "Water Boy" on her solo debut. More recently, when Miley Cyrus performed Dylan's "Baby I'm in the Mood for You" on *The Tonight Show*, it was Odetta's arrangement that she adapted.

Perhaps Odetta would have been most gratified to hear that her own song "Hit or Miss" had taken on a second life, appearing (with unintended irony) in a Southern Comfort commercial and on a single by Tom Jones—recognition for the songwriting abilities that she undersold and probably underused.

In 2016, the National Museum of African American History and Culture opened in Washington, DC, and Odetta was featured in an exhibit alongside Lead Belly and Josh White, including one of the few images of her performing during the March on Washington and one of her Africanesque robes.

Her friends will always wonder about unexploited opportunities and unfortunate decisions that sidelined Odetta for so many years. "Nobody managed her," Selma Thaler observed. "Nobody told her what to wear. Nobody advised. She was on her own. And she was a classic. You know classics sort of fade in and out. It's hurtful to me; it really is, because I think she was so extraordinary."[6]

But then again, they remind themselves, her lifelong quest to uplift African Americans and engage the human spirit did leave behind an important legacy. "I think an argument could be made that she never found her niche," her former guitarist Peter Childs said. "But Lord, look what she did in the process of looking for it. The core of the whole 1960s thing was spiritual. It had to do with feeling the common humanity of the human race, feeling that the whole human race was a bunch of bodies moving. . . . I really believe that the real effect that she had, the real contribution, is impossible to put into words."[7]

Harry Belafonte reached a similar conclusion. "The power of what she brought and contributed cannot be measured just in terms of how many people showed up at the concert," he said. "That's a numerical judgment. But I think the people who heard her became deeply committed to a force and something that she brought to the table that was so artful."[8]

At her memorial, Belafonte mused about who might be the next Odetta to come along to help fight the next fight and bring to light the next injustice, in words that seem more relevant today than ever before. "Who did she inspire? Who will be the Odetta of now? Who will have her courage to stand up in the face of so much and relentlessly impose art and goodness and conscience on the needs of her time. Who will fill that space?"[9]

ACKNOWLEDGMENTS

When a biographer sets out on his long journey, he's faced with the seemingly insurmountable task of documenting a human being's existence from cradle to grave. Fortunately for posterity, Odetta had many friends and musical comrades-in-arms, despite her oft-repeated claim to be a "hermit," and my heartfelt thanks belongs to those who agreed to share their memories and insights, which formed the connective tissue of this story.

For starters, Odetta's niece, Jan Ford, provided vital information about Odetta's early years. Also indispensable were the talented filmmaker Michelle Esrick and Leonard "Boots" Jaffee, whom Odetta considered her "adopted" daughter and son; and Odetta's final manager, Doug Yeager, who guided her career so lovingly in her final decade.

Much appreciation for everyone who agreed to speak with me about Odetta—in person, on the phone, or over email, Skype, or Messenger. Your stories were invaluable: David Amram, Joan Baez, Harry Belafonte, Marcia Berman, Mitch Blank, Peter Boone, Jesse Cahn, Mark Carpentieri, Lynn Gold Chaiken, Peter Childs, Robert Carl Cohen, Judy Collins, Julian Coryell, Barbara Dane, Guy Davis, Robert De Cormier, Roger Deitz, Elizabeth Elliott, Michelle Esrick, Billy Faier, Seth Farber, Sondra Farganis, Rachel Faro, Jan Ford, Jeffrey Buckner Ford, Dave Fry, Ed Germain, Sara Germain, Dean Gitter, Wavy Gravy, Lance Greening, Frank Hamilton, Rutha Mae Harris, Harriet Hutchinson, Leonard "Boots" Jaffee, Dave Keyes, Mike Koster, Jack Landrón, Bruce Langhorne, Donal Leace, Hillary Mapes Levine, Radoslav Lorković, Jo Mapes, Roger McGuinn, Larry Mohr, Milt Okun, Pauline Oliveros, Barry Olivier, Wendy Oxenhorn,

Ed Pearl, Art Podell, Liz Queler, Rosaly Roffman, Jahanara Romney, Charlie Rothschild, Vania Santi, Leda Schubert, John Sebastian, John Seiter, Garry Shead, Carly Simon, Jack Somer, Vivienne Stenson, Peggy Strait, Shel Talmy, Kenichi Takeda, Lesley Greening Taufer, Terri Thal, Carrie Thaler, Selma Thaler, Happy Traum, Frederick Warhanek, Josh White Jr., John Winn, Robbie Woliver, Peter Yarrow, Doug Yeager, and Izzy Young.

I couldn't have done this book without the assistance of librarians and archivists around the country, who copied material and provided other crucial research help. Thanks especially to Todd Harvey of the American Folklife Center at the Library of Congress; Steven Weiss and Aaron Smithers of the Louis Round Wilson Library, University of North Carolina at Chapel Hill, home of the Southern Folklife Collection; Rebecca Toov of the University of Minnesota Archives; Kathy Shoemaker of the Stuart A. Rose Manuscript, Archives, & Rare Book Library, Emory University; Paul H. Thomas of the Hoover Institution Library, Stanford University; Jim Baggett of the Birmingham Public Library; Anne Causey of the Albert & Shirley Small Special Collections Library, University of Virginia; Kate Blalack of the Woody Guthrie Center; and Joe Lauro and Mark Heidemann of Historic Films.

Thanks also to those who shared material from their personal collections, including Ronald Cohen, for interview transcripts and concert flyers; the Dylanologist extraordinaire Mitch Blank, for concert footage, live recordings, and access to Izzy Young's notebooks; Thelma Blitz, for her recording of Odetta's memorial at Riverside Church; Selma and Carrie Thaler, along with Carrie's husband, Howard Gale Ford, for their trove of beautiful Odetta photographs; Marcia Berman, for her tape of a Southern California hootenanny from 1955; Garry and Roseanne Shead, for articles about Odetta's visits to Australia; and Sara Germain, for local research and information from her datebooks spanning several decades.

I want also to extend my gratitude to the Schomburg Center for Research in Black Culture in Harlem—a division of the New York Public Library—which houses Odetta's personal papers. The many librarians there, including Steven G. Fullwood, a former associate curator, were always ready to help with my many queries over the years.

Ronald Cohen and Josh Bookin both read the draft manuscript and provided very valuable comments and suggestions.

I'm grateful to research assistants who helped me gain access to material in various corners: Adam Schutzman, who transcribed an important radio interview; Tim and Sid Moran, and also Steve Lorenz, for some terrific research at the Library of Congress; and Zac Bauman, for a most bountiful dive into a faraway database. For much-needed digital imaging assistance, a tip of the cap to Rommel Alama. And for foreign translations of newspaper clippings, many thanks to Veronica Majerol, Alessandra Potenza, and Rex Bowman, the latter of whom is also one of my journalistic mentors.

Speaking of mentors, I'm grateful to Elijah Wald for his continual wisdom and help in navigating the rigors of publishing.

Thanks to everyone at Beacon Press, including Gayatri Patnaik, Susan Lumenello, Melissa Nasson, Marcy Barnes, Olivia Bauer; Jane Gebhart, who expertly copyedited the manuscript; and especially my editor, Rakia Clark, whose enthusiasm for the project was contagious and whose incisive comments and questions made this a better book.

And, finally, to Wendy, Sam, and Hannah for their unerring support and for always reminding me of the things that are most important in life.

SELECTED DISCOGRAPHY

Odetta's recorded output of more than twenty-five albums over a half century—which includes a gap of nearly two decades in the 1970s and '80s when she released no new material—is remarkably consistent overall. She never made a bad record, but a number stand out. Her two LPs released originally on the Tradition label, *Odetta Sings Ballads and Blues* from 1956 and *Odetta at the Gate of Horn* the following year, are among the masterpieces of the folk revival and capture her at her raw and powerful best. When you listen, you'll get a visceral sense of what her shouted chain gang songs, work songs, and spirituals would have meant to Americans at the dawn of the civil rights era.

Her Vanguard catalog isn't far behind, especially *My Eyes Have Seen*, which includes the classics "Bald Headed Woman" and "Water Boy," and *Odetta at Carnegie Hall*, which provides an excellent window into the early live shows that captivated audiences around the nation. Her first folk record for RCA, 1963's *Odetta Sings Folk Songs*, was the most commercially successful release of her career, with the addition of Bruce Langhorne as her lead guitarist giving her music a new drive and swing.

If you can find her out-of-print Polydor LP from 1970, *Odetta Sings*—it was never released on CD, but can be had on vinyl on eBay—you'll be rewarded by hearing Odetta's only rock album, which includes two originals, "Hit or Miss" and "Movin' It On"—and you might even start to wonder, what if . . . ?

Of her later career albums, several are well worth buying. The independent release *Beautiful Star* from 1988 comprises new renditions of the spirituals she originally recorded for Vanguard nearly thirty years earlier (for the classic *Odetta Sings Christmas Spirituals*) and reunites her with her 1950s bass player, Bill Lee. Odetta's first two albums for MC Records, *Blues Everywhere I Go* in 1999 and *Lookin For a Home* in 2001, show her successfully making the transition to piano-based blues—a switch that made her once again a popular performer on the festival circuit after a lengthy dry spell.

For those who want to dig a little deeper, honorable mentions go to *The Tin Angel* (originally titled *Odetta & Larry*), which documents her seminal 1954 performances at San Francisco's Tin Angel club with banjoist Larry Mohr, and *Odetta Sings the Ballad for Americans* from 1960, on which she passionately assumes the singing-narrator role of the patriotic cantata, originally made famous by Paul Robeson. In more than sixty years since its release, Odetta's version has lost neither its power nor its relevance.

In the absence of a career-defining retrospective compilation—which is sorely lacking—these individual performances all testify to Odetta's enduring talent and her unmistakable artistry.

SELECTED BIBLIOGRAPHY

BOOKS AND ARTICLES

Aarons, Leroy F. "Odetta Comes Out of Her Cocoon." *Washington Post,* September 5, 1966.

Adler, Renata. "Letter from Selma." *New Yorker,* April 10, 1965.

Angell, Stephen Ward. *Bishop Henry McNeal Turner and African-American Religion in the South.* Knoxville: University of Tennessee Press, 1992.

Angelou, Maya. *Heart of a Woman.* New York: Random House, 2009.

———. *I Know Why the Caged Bird Sings.* New York: Random House, 1997.

Baez, Joan. *And a Voice to Sing With.* New York: Simon and Schuster, 1987.

Baldwin, James. "A Negro Assays the Negro Mood." *New York Times Magazine,* March 12, 1961.

Barnett, LaShonda Katrice. *I Got Thunder: Black Women Songwriters on Their Craft.* New York: Thunder's Mouth Press, 2007.

Belafonte, Harry. *My Song.* New York: Vintage Books, 2011.

Branch, Taylor. *At Canaan's Edge: America in the King Years, 1965–68.* New York: Simon and Schuster, 2006.

Brinkley, Douglas. *Rosa Parks: A Life.* New York: Viking, 2000.

Byrd, Ayana D., and Lori L. Tharps. *Hair Story: Untangling the Roots of Black Hair in America.* New York: St. Martin's Press, 2001.

Carpenter, Bil. "Sweet Home Alabama." *Goldmine,* February 28, 1997.

Carson, Clayborne, senior editor. *The Papers of Martin Luther King Jr., Vol. 5.* Berkeley: University of California Press, 2005.

Clancy, Liam. *The Mountain of the Women: Memoirs of an Irish Troubadour.* New York: Doubleday, 2002.

Cohen, Ronald D. *Rainbow Quest: The Folk Music Revival and American Society, 1940–1970.* Amherst: University of Massachusetts Press, 2002.

Collins, Judy. *Singing Lessons: A Memoir of Love, Loss, Hope, and Healing.* New York: Pocket Books, 1998.

———. *Sweet Judy Blue Eyes: My Life in Music.* Waterville, ME: Thorndike Press, 2011.

Du Bois, W. E. B. *The Souls of Black Folk.* Mineola, NY: Dover Publications, 1994 [orig. copyright 1903].

Dunaway, David King. *How Can I Keep from Singing? The Ballad of Pete Seeger*. New York: Villard Books, 2008.

Dylan, Bob. *Chronicles*. New York: Simon and Schuster, 2004.

Ford, Tanisha. *Liberated Threads: Black Women, Style, and the Global Politics of Soul*. Chapel Hill: University of North Carolina Press, 2015.

Garrow, David J. *Bearing the Cross: Martin Luther King Jr. and the Southern Christian Leadership Conference*. New York: Harper Collins, 1986.

Gates, Henry Louis, Jr. *The Henry Louis Gates Jr. Reader*. New York: Basic Civitas Books, 2012.

Gavin, James. *Intimate Nights: The Golden Age of New York Cabaret*. New York: Back Stage Books, 2006.

Gibson, Bob, and Carole Bender. *Bob Gibson: I Come for to Sing*. Gretna, LA: Pelican Publishing, 2001.

Grams, Martin, Jr., and Les Rayburn. *The Have Gun—Will Travel Companion*. Churchville, MD: OTR Publishing, 2000.

Greenberg, Mark. "Power and Beauty: The Legend of Odetta." *Sing Out!* 36, no. 2, August–September–October 1991.

Hajdu, David. *Positively 4th Street*. New York: Picador, 2001.

Halprin, Sara. *Seema's Show: A Life on the Left*. Albuquerque: University of New Mexico Press, 2005.

Ian, Janis. *Society's Child*. New York: Jeremy P. Tarcher/Penguin, 2008.

King, Coretta Scott. *My Life, My Love, My Legacy*. New York: Henry Holt, 2017.

LaMonte, Edward Shannon. *Politics and Welfare in Birmingham, 1900–1975*. Tuscaloosa: University of Alabama Press, 1995.

MacDonald, J. Fred. *Blacks and White TV: African Americans in Television Since 1948* (originally *Blacks and White TV: Afro-Americans in Television Since 1948*). Chicago: Nelson-Hall, 1983.

Makeba, Miriam. *Makeba: My Story*. New York: New American Library, 1987.

McKeon, Belinda. "Odetta's Musical Odyssey Not Finished Yet." *Irish Times*, June 24, 2006.

Meyerson, Harold, and Ernie Harburg. *Who Put the Rainbow in The Wizard of Oz?* Ann Arbor: University of Michigan Press, 1993.

Morris, Bob. "No More New Year-Birthday Blues." *New York Times*, December 31, 1995.

National Association for the Advancement of Colored People. *Anti-Negro Propaganda in School Textbooks*, 1939. Pamphlet.

O'Connor, Rory. "Albert Grossman's Ghost." *Musician*, June 1, 1987.

Okun, Milt, and Richard Sparks. *Along the Cherry Lane*. Beverly Hills, CA: Classical Music Today, 2011.

Packer, George. *Blood of the Liberals*. New York: Farrar, Straus and Giroux, 2000.

Petrus, Stephen, and Ronald D. Cohen. *Folk City: New York and the American Folk Music Revival*. Oxford, UK: Oxford University Press, 2015.

Raymond, Emilie. *Stars for Freedom: Hollywood, Black Celebrities, and the Civil Rights Movement*. Seattle: University of Washington Press, 2015.

Richardson, Tony. *Long Distance Runner: A Memoir.* New York: William Morrow, 1993.

Rothel, David. *Richard Boone: A Knight Without Armor in a Savage Land.* Madison, NC: Empire Publishing, 2000.

Schilling, Jerry, with Chuck Crisafulli. *Me and a Guy Named Elvis: My Lifelong Friendship with Elvis Presley.* New York: Gotham Books, 2006.

Seeger, Pete. *The Incompleat Folksinger.* New York: Simon and Schuster, 1972.

Slick, Grace. *Somebody to Love? A Rock-and-Roll Memoir.* New York: Warner Books, 1998.

Smith, R. J. *The Great Black Way: L.A. in the 1940s and the Lost African American Renaissance.* New York: Public Affairs, 2006.

Sounes, Howard. *Down the Highway: The Life of Bob Dylan.* New York: Grove Press, 2001.

Southworth, Gertrude Van Duyn, and John Van Duyn Southworth. *American History.* Syracuse, NY: Iroquois Publishing Company, 1933.

Spencer, Kathleen L. *Art and Politics in Have Gun—Will Travel: The 1950s Television Western as Ethical Drama.* Jefferson, NC: McFarland & Company, 2014.

Spitz, Bob. *Dylan: A Biography.* New York: McGraw-Hill, 1989.

Szwed, John. *Alan Lomax: The Man Who Recorded the World.* New York: Viking Penguin, 2010.

Van Matre, Lynn. "Odetta's Friend Jo: 'Got the Joy Back.'" *Chicago Tribune,* June 14, 1974.

Van Ronk, Dave, with Elijah Wald. *The Mayor of MacDougal Street: A Memoir.* Cambridge, MA: Da Capo Press, 2005.

Wald, Elijah. *Dylan Goes Electric! Newport, Seeger, Dylan, and the Night That Split the Sixties.* New York: Dey Street, 2015.

———. *Josh White: Society Blues.* New York: Routledge, 2000.

Wein, George. *Myself Among Others: A Life in Music.* Cambridge, MA: Da Capo Press, 2003.

Williamson, Marianne. *A Return to Love.* New York: Harper Perennial, 1993.

Works Progress Administration. *Los Angeles in the 1930s: The WPA Guide to the City of Angels.* Berkeley: University of California Press, 2011.

ARCHIVAL RESOURCES
Archives
American Folklife Center, Library of Congress (AFC)

Schomburg Center for Research in Black Culture, New York Public Library (SCRBC)

Southern Folklife Collection, University of North Carolina, Chapel Hill (SFC)

Media
Bill Grauer Productions, Inc. v. Odetta Felious, Supreme Court of the State of New York, filed April 24, 1959, retrieved from microfiche.

Dinner with the President, Columbia Broadcasting System, January 31, 1963, Paley Center for Media.
Inaugural Evening at Ford's Theatre. Columbia Broadcasting System, January 30, 1968, Paley Center for Media.

Interviews
Jo Mapes interview by Ronald D. Cohen, July 23, 1993. Ronald D. Cohen Collection, SFC.
Odetta interview by Camille O. Cosby for the National Visionary Leadership Project, 2007. AFC, Library of Congress.
Odetta interview by Celestine Ware at WBAI-FM, New York, April 14, 1971. Pacifica Radio Archives.
Odetta interview by Hartford Smith Jr. for *Seeds of Discontent*, WDET, Wayne State University, 1968. American Archive of Public Broadcasting.
Odetta interview by Peggy Bulger, November 3, 2003. AFC. Accessed at https://www.loc.gov/today/cyberlc/feature_wdesc.php?rec=4735.
Odetta interview by Ronald D. Cohen, August 6, 1992. Ronald D. Cohen Collection, SFC.
Odetta interview in Los Angeles, September 1958. Don Hill and David Mangurian Collection, AFC.
Odetta interviews by Shawn Wilson for thehistorymakers.org, March 17, 2006, December 6, 2006.
Odetta interviews by Studs Terkel on WFMT, Chicago, October 31, 1956, September 4, 1957. Library of Congress, Division of Recorded Sound.
Odetta memorial recording, February 24, 2009, Riverside Church, New York City. Collection of Thelma Blitz.
Odetta Papers, SCRBC.
Israel G. Young interview by Richard Reuss, July 8, 1965. Mitch Blank collection.

NOTES

PROLOGUE: A VOICE LIKE THUNDER

1. Seeger, *Incompleat Folksinger*, 312–13.
2. Carly Simon, author interview, May 21, 2018.
3. *Saturday Review*, quoted in Cohen, *Rainbow Quest*, 68; "Music: Good Night, Irene," *Time*, August 14, 1950, accessed at http://content.time .com/time/subscriber/article/0,33009,858914,00.html.
4. Louis R. Guzzo, "Odetta Is Profound Folk-Singer," *Seattle Times*, April 25, 1964, n.p.
5. Harry Belafonte, author interviews, May 12, 2017, May 15, 2018.

CHAPTER ONE: FROM BIRMINGHAM TO LOS ANGELES

1. Selma Thaler, author interviews, August 13, 2016, May 8, 2017. Odetta related the story to Thaler decades later.
2. Odetta, National Visionary Leadership interview.
3. Odetta, WBAI interview.
4. National Visionary Leadership interview.
5. National Visionary Leadership interview.
6. Selma Thaler interviews; Odetta, autobiographical sketch, circa early 1960s, Odetta Papers.
7. Odetta, Bulger interview; Odetta, Wilson interviews.
8. LaMonte, *Politics and Welfare*, 69; Packer, *Blood of the Liberals*, 110.
9. "Says the Ku Klux Klan," *Chicago Defender*, January 14, 1933, 14.
10. Sonia Sanchez, interviewed by Camille O. Cosby for the National Visionary Leadership Project, 2005, AFC.
11. Works Progress Administration, *Los Angeles in the 1930s*, 4.
12. W. E. B. Du Bois, "I Go A-Talking," *Crisis* 6, no. 3 (July 1913): 131; W. E. B. Du Bois, "Colored California," *Crisis* 6, no. 4 (August 1913): 193–94.
13. Odetta, Cohen interview; Odetta, National Visionary Leadership interview.
14. Odetta, Cohen interview.
15. Odetta, Cohen interview.
16. *Anti-Negro Propaganda*, 7, 12.

17. Southworth and Southworth, *American History*, iii.
18. Southworth and Southworth, *American History*, 167–68.
19. Southworth and Southworth, *American History*, 211–12.
20. Ben S. Page, transcript of undated interview with Odetta, Odetta Papers.
21. Greenberg, "Power and Beauty," 2–6.
22. Greenberg, "Power and Beauty," 2–6.
23. Morris, "No More New Year-Birthday Blues," 35.
24. Hill and Mangurian Collection interview.
25. "Immediate Evacuation of Japanese Demanded," *Los Angeles Times*, February 25, 1942, 1.
26. Odetta, National Visionary Leadership interview.
27. Transcript of Odetta interview by Billy Taylor for *CBS Sunday Morning*, 1987, Billy Taylor Papers, Library of Congress.
28. Frank Hamilton, author interview, November 11, 2015.
29. Smith, *The Great Black Way*, 45; Odetta interview by David Dye on WXPN radio, Philadelphia, January 19, 2004, accessed at http://www.npr.org/templates/story/story.php?storyId=97800151.
30. Aarons, "Odetta Comes Out of Her Cocoon," A4; Joan Barthel, "Odetta Speaks Through Her Songs," *New York Times*, March 7, 1965, X11.
31. Odetta interview by Sean Patrick Farrell for the Last Word video series, *New York Times*, 2007, accessed at http://www.nytimes.com/video/arts/music/1194832844841/last-word-odetta.html?playlistId=1194811622353.
32. Jo Mapes, author interviews, January 8, 2017, January 22, 2017, July 10, 2017.
33. Jo Mapes, Cohen interview; Jo Mapes interviews; Van Matre, "Odetta's Friend Jo: 'Got the Joy Back,'" Section 2, 3.
34. Jo Mapes interviews.
35. Jo Mapes, unpublished autobiography manuscript, Ronald D. Cohen Collection, SFC; Jo Mapes interviews.
36. Jo Mapes interviews.
37. Jo Mapes, Cohen interview.
38. Jo Mapes interviews; Lynn Gold Chaiken, author interview, May 24, 2016.
39. Jo Mapes interviews.
40. Odetta interview on National Public Radio, December 30, 2005, accessed at http://www.npr.org/templates/story/story.php?storyId=5074594.

CHAPTER TWO: STRAIGHTENED MY BACK, KINKED MY HAIR

1. *Turnabout—The Story of the Yale Puppeteers*, Shire Films, 1992.
2. Odetta, National Visionary Leadership interview.
3. Robert Carl Cohen, author interview, August 27, 2017.
4. "Joy of Singing Unites Choral Groups of City," *Los Angeles Times*, February 20, 1949, A2.
5. Odetta, Cohen interview.

6. Jo Mapes autobiography.

7. Odetta, National Visionary Leadership interview.

8. Meyerson and Harburg, *Who Put the Rainbow in The Wizard of Oz?*, 222.

9. Meyerson and Harburg, *Who Put the Rainbow in The Wizard of Oz?*, 239.

10. "Children's Show Wins," *Los Angeles Times*, December 2, 1950, A7; Frank Hamilton interview.

11. Dunaway, *How Can I Keep from Singing?*, 169.

12. Odetta, Cohen interview; Van Matre, "Odetta's Friend Jo," Section 2, 3.

13. Jo Mapes interviews.

14. Mark Greenberg, "Power and Beauty," 2–6.

15. Odetta, Hill and Mangurian Collection interview.

16. "Odetta Presented in Concert," *Ottawa Campus*, October 15, 1965, 4.

17. Marcia Berman, author interview, December 13, 2015.

18. James Baldwin, "Letter from a Region of My Mind," *New Yorker*, November 17, 1962, 65.

19. Odetta, National Public Radio interview.

20. Frank Hamilton interview.

21. Frank Hamilton interview.

22. Halprin, *Seema's Show*, 168–69.

23. "Robeson Suggest U.S. Test Marxism," *New York Times*, October 8, 1946, 13.

24. Odetta, National Visionary Leadership interview.

25. Dorothy Woods, "Highlights of Tulare," *Los Angeles Sentinel*, May 12, 1949, C8.

26. Odetta, Cohen interview.

27. Odetta, Cohen interview; Odetta, National Visionary Leadership interview.

28. Odetta, Wilson interviews.

29. Byrd and Tharps, *Hair Story*, 22.

30. Leroy Vaughn, "Celebrating Our Heritage: The Life of Marcus Garvey," *Los Angeles Sentinel*, February 4, 2000, A4; Carter G. Woodson, "Treatment of Negro Due to His Psychology," *New Journal and Guide*, December 16, 1933, 3.

31. *Los Angeles Sentinel*, January 18, 1951, B2–B3.

32. Baldwin, "A Negro Assays the Negro Mood," 103.

33. Jan Ford, author interview, July 13, 2018.

34. Cathy Yarbrough, "Singer Shuns 'Top 40' Success," *Atlanta Constitution*, March 16, 1973, 8B.

35. Odetta, Ware interview; Jo Mapes interviews.

36. Odetta, 1986 National Public Radio interview, excerpted on *Democracy Now*, December 30, 2008, accessed at http://www.democracynow.org/2008/12/30/dr_bernice_johnson_reagon_remembers_musical; Odetta, Ware interview.

37. Jan Ford interview.

CHAPTER THREE: THE TOAST OF NEW YORK

1. Pete Seeger, interviewed by National Public Radio, December 3, 2008.
2. "Hardyman Tells of New China's Might," *Daily People's World*, January 12, 1953, 6; House Committee on Un-American Activities testimony, May 23, 1956. Odetta's name comes up during the questioning of John Adams Kingsbury, who was reported to have given a speech at the event at which Odetta sang.
3. Odetta, Wilson interviews; "Robeson to Sing Again in Los Angeles," *Daily People's World*, June 17, 1953, 7; Susan Kelly, "Odetta," *Guy & Pipp Gillette Newsletter*, no. 18, February 1980, 1–2.
4. Gretchen Pierce, "Legendary Odetta Found Halifax Audience a Dream," *Mail-Star*, February 23, 1976, n.p.
5. Odetta, Cohen interview.
6. George F. Hoover, "By George!," *Los Angeles Collegian*, April 9, 1954, 2.
7. Pauline Oliveros, author interview, February 17, 2016.
8. Jo Mapes interviews.
9. R. H. Hagan, "The Lively Arts: Odetta Felious Rings Louder Than Engines," *San Francisco Chronicle*, August 28, 1953, 18.
10. Odetta, Cohen interview.
11. Odetta interview by Caroline Horn, November 1999, accessed at http://www.carolinehorn.com/writing_folksandangels.html.
12. "Night Club-Vaud Reviews," *Billboard*, September 19, 1953, 41.
13. Walter Winchell, ". . . Of New York: Broadway Confidinchell," *Washington Post*, September 17, 1953, 45; Robert W. Dana, "Tin Angel to Blue Angel for Singer," *New York World Telegram and Sun*, September 21, 1953, 15.
14. Quoted in Belafonte, *My Song*, 111.
15. Harry Belafonte interviews.
16. Odetta memorial recording.
17. Belafonte, *My Song*, 120.
18. Doug Yeager, author interviews, July 13, 2016, July 22, 2016, March 18, 2018.
19. Jo Mapes, Cohen interview; Ed Pearl, author interview, February 23, 2016.
20. Barbara Dane, author interviews, August 27, 2015, August 31, 2015.
21. Odetta, Last Word interview.
22. Jo Mapes autobiography.
23. Aarons, "Odetta Comes Out of Her Cocoon," A4.
24. David Rosenthal, "Odetta Sings Folk Songs Yet; Now It's for New Generation," Associated Press, appearing in the *Blade*, June 23, 1978, P-2.
25. *Odetta at Town Hall*, Vanguard Records, 1963.
26. Gavin, *Intimate Nights*, 99.
27. Odetta memorial recording.
28. Odetta memorial recording.
29. Carpenter, "Sweet Home Alabama," 68.

CHAPTER FOUR: GETTING POLITICAL

1. Dean Gitter, author interviews, July 6, 2015, July 22, 2016, and July 19, 2017.
2. Dean Gitter interviews.
3. Contract between Odetta Felious and Tom Wilson, March 1, 1956, Bill Grauer Productions, Inc. v. Odetta Felious case file; Dean Gitter interviews.
4. Dean Gitter interviews.
5. Dean Gitter deposition in Bill Grauer Productions, Inc. v. Odetta Felious.
6. Dean Gitter to Odetta, October 5, 1956, entered into evidence in Bill Grauer Productions, Inc. v. Odetta Felious.
7. Gitter to Odetta, October 5, 1956; Dean Gitter interviews.
8. Gibson and Bender, *Bob Gibson*, 33; Frank Hamilton interview.
9. Odetta, National Visionary Leadership interview.
10. "Night Club Reviews—Gate of Horn, Chi," *Variety*, November 14, 1956, 69.
11. Odetta, Terkel interviews.
12. Barnett, *I Got Thunder*, 179.
13. Dean Gitter to Odetta, November 13, 1956, entered into evidence in Bill Grauer Productions, Inc. v. Odetta Felious.
14. Chestyn Everett, "Random Reviews," *Los Angeles Tribune*, November 20, 1959, 20.
15. Robert Bagar, *New York Journal-American*, circa 1957, cited in press release, Odetta Papers.
16. Wald, *Josh White*, 266.
17. Contract between Odetta Felious and Dean Gitter, December 10, 1956, Bill Grauer Productions, Inc. v. Odetta Felious case file.

CHAPTER FIVE: THE FUSE IS LIT

1. Petrus and Cohen, *Folk City*, 155.
2. Odetta memorial recording; Brand remembered the year as 1947, but he was referring to the 1957 concert.
3. Selma Thaler interviews.
4. Selma Thaler interviews; Carrie Thaler, author interview, January 4, 2017.
5. Clancy, *The Mountain of the Women*, 199.
6. Angelou, *Heart of a Woman*, 91.
7. McKeon, "Odetta's Musical Odyssey," C7.
8. Dean Gitter interviews.
9. Van Ronk, with Wald, *The Mayor of MacDougal Street*, 55.
10. Van Ronk, with Wald, *The Mayor of MacDougal Street*, 55; Terri Thal, author interview, November 12, 2016; Slick, *Somebody to Love?*, 57.
11. Dean Gitter interviews.
12. Dean Gitter interviews.
13. Dean Gitter interviews.

14. Contract between Dean Gitter and Albert Grossman, September 20, 1957, Bill Grauer Productions, Inc. v. Odetta Felious case file; Dean Gitter interviews.
15. O'Connor, "Albert Grossman's Ghost," 29.
16. Charlie Rothschild, author interviews, May 3, 2016, July 11, 2017; Sounes, *Down the Highway*, 103.
17. *Odetta at the Gate of Horn*, Tradition Records, 1957.
18. Robert Shelton, "Popular American Folk Songs on LP," *New York Times*, January 26, 1958, 10X.
19. Odetta, Hill and Mangurian Collection interview.
20. June Starr, "A Panegyric Upon Odetta," *Oberlin Review*, November 19, 1957, 2, 4.
21. Lesley Greening Taufer, author interview, March 21, 2016.
22. Lance Greening, author interview, April 8, 2016; Lesley Greening Taufer interview.
23. "TV Cites Tan Contributions," *Afro-American*, May 3, 1958, 8.
24. Odetta to Samuel Freifeld, August 5, 1958, Odetta Papers.
25. Odetta, Hill and Mangurian Collection interview.
26. Odetta, Hill and Mangurian Collection interview.

CHAPTER SIX: TV SENSATION

1. John D. Morris, "50 Groups Demand Broad Rights Bill," *New York Times*, April 9, 1959, 22.
2. Odetta, National Visionary Leadership interview.
3. J. S. H., "Odetta in Debut as Folk Singer," *New York Herald Tribune*, April 25, 1959, 6.
4. Bill Grauer Productions, Inc. v. Odetta Felious case file.
5. Selma Thaler interviews; Lesley Greening Taufer interview.
6. Josh White Jr., author interview, January 25, 2016; Peter Yarrow, author interview, July 6, 2016.
7. Lesley Greening Taufer interview.
8. Sidney Fields, "A Voice That More Than Sings," *New York Mirror*, December 18, 1960, n.p.; Izzy Young, "Frets and Frails," *Sing Out!* 9, no. 1 (Summer 1959): 26.
9. George Wein, Tumblr post, accessed at http://newportfolkfest.tumblr.com/post/102451108878/odetta-newport-folk-festival-1959-wein; Wein recalled Odetta's Storyville gig as 1958.
10. Will Leonard, "Folk Song Famine Over—Gate's Open and Swinging," *Chicago Tribune*, June 21, 1959, J11; James Reed, "Odetta, 77, Transcendent Voice Fused Heritage, Hopes into Civil Rights Movement," *Boston Globe*, December 4, 2008, B8.
11. Joan Baez, author interview, March 16, 2017.
12. Baez, *And a Voice to Sing With*, 195–96.
13. Baez, *And a Voice to Sing With*.
14. "Folk Festival Really 'Steaming Up'—Bigger Than Expected, Say Officials," *Newport Daily News*, July 10, 1959, 1; Robert Shelton, "Folk Joins Jazz at Newport," *New York Times*, July 19, 1959, Section II, 7.

15. Robert Shelton, "Folk Music Festival," *Nation*, August 1, 1959, 59.
16. Odetta press release, early 1960s, Odetta Papers, SCRBC.
17. *Little Sandy Review* 9, circa 1961, 9.
18. Odetta memorial recording; Baez's tribute was delivered on video; Joan Baez interview.
19. Wein, *Myself Among Others*, 315; "Joan Baez Talks About the Lovers, Cads and Music in Her Life," *Chicago Tribune*, June 21, 1987, L6.
20. Shelton, "Folk Joins Jazz at Newport," Section II, 7.
21. Harry Belafonte, liner notes to *My Eyes Have Seen*, Vanguard Records, 1959.
22. Wally George, "Court of Records," *Los Angeles Times*, August 30, 1959, J35.
23. Bill Oliver, "LA's Ash Grove Shelters Folk Music Beehive," *Sing Out!* 9, no. 3 (Winter 1959–1960): 36–37.
24. Ed Pearl interview.
25. Lynn Gold Chaiken interview; Michael Davenport, "Live & Legit," *Canyon Crier*, October 1, 1959, 8; "Odetta Captivates Audience, Makes You Glad to Be Alive," *New Mexican*, September 29, 1959, 2.
26. Joy Tunstall, "Odetta Impressive in Detroit Song Debut," *Pittsburgh Courier*, June 7, 1960, n.p.
27. Belafonte, *My Song*, 209.
28. Odetta memorial recording.
29. Raymond, *Stars for Freedom*, 35.
30. Kay Gardella, "Specs Aren't Special Says Star Belafonte," *Sunday News*, December 6, 1959, 13.
31. Robert De Cormier, author interview, June 19, 2016.
32. Robert De Cormier interview.
33. Harry Belafonte interviews.
34. "Television Reviews—Tonight with Belafonte," *Variety*, December 16, 1959, 27; Fred Danzig, "'Night with Belafonte' Wins Praise of TV Fans," United Press International, appearing in *Chicago Defender*, December 14, 1959, 17.
35. L. I. Brockenbury, "Brock's Vox," *Los Angeles Sentinel*, December 17, 1959, A6.
36. Jack Landrón (aka Jackie Washington), author interview, March 5, 2016.
37. Carlie Collins Tartakov, "Odetta," article written for International Women's Week, University of Massachusetts, March 28, 1980, Odetta Papers.
38. Ian, *Society's Child*, 11–12.
39. Selma Thaler interviews; Charlie Rothschild interviews.
40. Marion Purcelli, "Success Comes in a Plain Envelope," *Chicago Daily Tribune*, January 31, 1960, S5.

CHAPTER SEVEN: THAT LOVELY ODETTA . . . PLAYING A MURDERESS

1. Harry Belafonte to Odetta, December 16, 1959, Odetta Papers.
2. Belafonte to Odetta.
3. Makeba, *Makeba: My Story*, 86.

4. Purcelli, "Success Comes in a Plain Envelope," S5.

5. Jay Milner, "The Folk Music Craze," *New York Herald Tribune*, February 11, 1960, 20; "It's Folksy . . . It's Delightful, It's a Craze," *Newsweek*, June 6, 1960, 112–13.

6. Robert Shelton, "Modest Proposal for Disk Jockeys," *New York Times*, March 6, 1960, X20.

7. Jeffrey Buckner Ford, author interview, August 3, 2017.

8. Jeffrey Buckner Ford interview.

9. Ernie Ford, *The Ford Show*, NBC, March 10, 1960.

10. Jeffrey Buckner Ford interview.

11. Percy Shain, "Pat Was Not So Pat, But Ernie Had It, Man," *Daily Boston Globe*, March 11, 1960, 10.

12. J. M., "Singer Odelta's [sic] Fans Given Proof of Artistry," *Detroit Free Press*, March 19, 1960, n.p.

13. Selma Thaler interviews.

14. Tony Gieske, "Accent on Jazz," *Washington Post*, April 24, 1960, 139; Leda Schubert, personal communication with author, October 5, 2018.

15. "Heed Their Voices," *New York Times*, March 29, 1960, 25.

16. Steve W. Duncan, "Stars, Students Note Civil Rights Day," *Afro-American*, May 28, 1960, 8.

17. Duncan, "Stars, Students Note Civil Rights Day."

18. "Statue of Liberty," *New Yorker*, May 28, 1960, 26–27.

19. "Statue of Liberty," *New Yorker*.

20. "New Negro Is Key in Struggle," *New Amsterdam News*, May 21, 1960, 1.

21. Odetta, National Visionary Leadership interview.

22. Fields, "A Voice That More Than Sings," n.p.; Hedda Hopper, "Looking at Hollywood," *Chicago Daily Tribune*, June 1, 1960, B1.

23. Gene D. Phillips, "Faulkner and the Film: Two Versions of 'Sanctuary,'" *Literature/Film Quarterly* 1, no. 3 (July 1, 1973): 263; Richardson, *The Long Distance Runner*, 146.

24. Mike Connolly, "Rambling Reporter," *Hollywood Reporter*, August 18, 1960, 2; Mike Connolly, "Rambling Reporter," *Hollywood Reporter*, n.d.

25. Quoted in Raymond, *Stars for Freedom*, 35–36.

26. A. S. (Doc) Young, "The Big Beat," *Los Angeles Sentinel*, November 17, 1960, A14; Odetta, National Visionary Leadership interview.

27. "Cinema: Southern Discomfort," *Time*, February 24, 1961, accessed at http://content.time.com/time/magazine/article/0,9171,828790,00.html; *New Republic*, March 6, 1961, n.p.; Glenn Douglas, "Odetta Enroute [sic] to New Film Laurels," *Chicago Defender*, April 13, 1961, 23.

28. Odetta memorial recording.

29. Peter Yarrow interview.

30. Carpenter, "Sweet Home Alabama," 68.

31. Baez, *And a Voice to Sing With*, 58.

32. Belafonte, *My Song*, 207.

33. Ed Pearl interview.

34. Jerome Aumente, "Odetta: She Never Stops Changing, for If She Did, Folk Music Would Stop for Her," *Detroit News Pictorial Magazine*, June 19, 1966, 44.

35. Dorothy Kilgallen, "Catholic Chaplain Enjoys Television Jazz Programs," *Tonawanda News*, June 28, 1962, 12.

36. Angell, *Bishop Henry McNeal Turner*, 261.

37. Greenberg, "Power and Beauty," 2–6.

CHAPTER EIGHT: ENTER BOB DYLAN

1. Bob Dylan, *Playboy* interview, March 1978, accessed at http://www.interferenza.com/bcs/interw/play78.htm.

2. Dylan, *Chronicles*, 237.

3. Spitz, *Dylan: A Biography*, 82–83.

4. Jahanara Romney (née Bonnie Jean Boettcher, aka Bonnie Beecher), author interview, October 18, 2017.

5. Robert Shelton, "Odetta Is Heard in a Song Program," *New York Times*, March 6, 1961, 28; program from Town Hall concert, March 4, 1961, Odetta Papers.

6. Carrie Thaler interview.

7. Guy Davis, author interview, July 23, 2016.

8. Jo Mapes interviews.

9. Vivienne Muhling (née Stenson), author interview, August 9, 2016.

10. For background on the western genre, I'm indebted to Spencer, *Art and Politics in Have Gun—Will Travel*.

11. MacDonald, *Blacks and White TV*.

12. Peter Boone, author interview, April 25, 2016.

13. All quotations from *Have Gun—Will Travel*, CBS, November 3, 1961.

14. Grams Jr. and Rayburn, *The Have Gun—Will Travel Companion*, 390.

15. Richard Boone, "'Have Gun' Starting Sixth Season," United Press International, appearing in *Middletown Times-Herald*, August 31, 1962, n.p.

16. Darcy Demille, "Data 'N Chatter," *Afro-American*, October 5, 1963, 11.

17. Baldwin, "A Negro Assays the Negro Mood," 103–4.

18. Andrea Benton Rushing, "Hair-Raising," *Feminist Studies* 2, no. 2 (Summer 1988): 333.

19. Bob Queen, "Wash and Dry, Without Curls or Grease: Are Women Changing Hair Style to 'Au Naturel' African Way?," *New Pittsburgh Courier*, September 2, 1961, 2.

20. Roloff, "Folk Singer Odetta Moving to Career Peak," 8; Dorothy Kilgallen, "Voice of Broadway," *Anderson Daily Bulletin*, May 25, 1961, 4.

21. J. R. Goddard, "Folk Music: Lesser Odetta," *Village Voice*, June 1, 1961, 17.

22. Ralph J. Gleason (unsigned), "Monterey Jazz Festival in a Brilliant Finale," *San Francisco Chronicle*, September 26, 1961, 36.

23. Lesley Greening Taufer interview.

24. Odetta, Cohen interview.

25. William McPherson, "She Sings in Key of Love," *Washington Post*, August 3, 1961, C17; Collins George, "A Quiet Beauty," *Detroit Free Press*, March 11, 1961, n.p.

26. Max Jones, "Odetta, the Beautiful Folk Singer, Says—" *Melody Maker*, December 16, 1961, 18; Aarons, "Odetta Comes Out of Her Cocoon," A4.

27. Morris Kaplan, "U.S. Negro Artists Go to Africa to Join in Cultural Exchange," *New York Times*, December 14, 1961, 54.

28. "Africa Is No Cultural Desert," *Lima News*, July 21, 1962, 3; "Odetta Had Me in Tears," *Daily Times*, December 22, 1961, 5.

29. "Odetta Had Me in Tears," *Daily Times*.

30. "Caught in the Act," *DownBeat*, August 17, 1961, 47; Joan Barthel, "Odetta Speaks Through Her Songs," *New York Times*, March 7, 1965, X11.

CHAPTER NINE: IN THE HEART OF JIM CROW

1. John Winn, author interview, May 18, 2016.

2. John Winn interview.

3. Judy Collins, author interview, September 21, 2017.

4. Judy Collins interview; Collins, *Singing Lessons*, 102.

5. Odetta Gordon and Daniel Gordon, joint federal tax return, 1962, Odetta Papers; Charlie Rothschild interviews.

6. Tony Wilson, "Odetta—'Call Me a Singer of Folk Songs,'" *Melody Maker*, August 10, 1968, 14.

7. Garrow, *Bearing the Cross*, 181.

8. "Dateline U.S.A.," *Melody Maker*, April 21, 1962, 8.

9. Josh White Jr. interview.

10. Odetta-Hartford Smith Jr. interview; "Officials at UT Disturbed by Report Dr. King Invited," *Dallas Morning News*, October 20, 1962.

11. Bill Hampton, "Songs from Their Hearts," *Daily Texan*, January 12, 1962, 6.

12. Odetta-Hartford Smith Jr. interview.

13. Odetta-Hartford Smith Jr. interview.

14. Jack Landrón interview.

15. Rutha Mae Harris, author interview, March 12, 2016.

16. Shirley Blood, "Odetta Loves Folk Music: 'It Draws People Together,'" *Cedar Rapids Gazette*, October 8, 1964, 14.

17. Andrew Rosenthal, "Odetta," *New York Times*, December 4, 2008, A42.

18. Bernice Johnson Reagon, recollections of Odetta, accessed at http://www.bernicejohnsonreagon.com/odetta.shtml.

19. Doris Lockerman, "Odetta Was Born with a Voice Like a Weapon—Switches It from Blunt Cudgel to Thistledown," *Atlanta Constitution*, March 1, 1962, 26.

20. Reagon, recollections.

21. Bernice Johnson Reagon interview on *Democracy Now*, December 30, 2008, accessed at http://www.democracynow.org/2008/12/30/dr_bernice _johnson_reagon_remembers_musical.

22. Stuart Culpepper, "Odetta's Artistry Thrills Atlantans," *Atlanta Constitution*, March 5, 1962, 3.
23. Bob Scott, "Court of Records," *Los Angeles Times*, July 22, 1962, A27; John S. Wilson, "Odetta and the Blues," *DownBeat* 29, no. 5 (September 27, 1962): 37.
24. "Folk Singing: Sybil with Guitar," *Time*, November 23, 1962, accessed at http://content.time.com/time/subscriber/article/0,33009,829501,00 .html; Frank Hamilton interview.
25. Richard B. Hadlock, "Sometimes I Feel Like Cryin'," *DownBeat* 29, no. 30 (December 6, 1962): 34.
26. E. Kyle Minor, "Music; Odetta, Still Singing the Blues," *New York Times*, July 9, 2000, accessed at http://www.nytimes.com/2000/07/09 /nyregion/music-odetta-still-singing-the-blues.html.
27. "Odetta at Town Hall," *Little Sandy Review* 23, circa 1962, 5.
28. Alfred G. Aronowitz and Marshall Blonsky, "Three's Company: Peter, Paul and Mary," *Saturday Evening Post*, May 30, 1964, 30.
29. Charlie Rothschild interviews; O'Connor, "Albert Grossman's Ghost," 30; Sandra Shevey, "Mary Travers Has Her Say After 10 Years as Silent Partner," *Hartford Courant*, January 2, 1972, 7D.

CHAPTER TEN: MARCH MUSIC
1. Eric Winter, "TV Trip for New York Folknik," *Melody Maker*, January 19, 1963, 12; "Il Tranquillo, 'Studio Uno,'" *La Stampa*, January 13, 1963, 4.
2. Adrian Mitchell, "Voice of Many Triumphs," *Daily Mail*, January 11, 1963, n.p.
3. Shel Talmy, email to author, May 19, 2017.
4. "Folk TV Concert to Salute JFK," *Billboard*, January 19, 1963, 18.
5. Nat Hentoff, "That Old McCarthy Hoot," *Village Voice*, March 14, 1963, 5–6.
6. MacDonald, *Blacks and White TV*.
7. Lynn Gold Chaiken interview.
8. *Dinner with the President*; all quotations from the show are from this source.
9. Lynn Gold Chaiken interview.
10. Lynn Gold Chaiken interview.
11. Judy Collins interview; Collins, *Sweet Judy Blue Eyes*, 197.
12. Percy Shain, "Glowing Tribute to Liberty Ideal," *Boston Globe*, February 1, 1963, 28; Rick Du Brow, "'Dinner with the President' Provided Acute Indigestion," United Press International, appearing in *Bristol Courier and Levittown Times*, February 1, 1963, 16.
13. Robert Shelton, "Style in Transition Marks Odetta Show," *New York Times*, April 6, 1963, 9.
14. Happy Traum, author interview, July 18, 2017.
15. Jack Keenan, "The Men Behind Belafonte and Odetta," *Hootenanny*, November 1964, 44; "Odetta Links Folk Song, History," newspaper clipping, circa 1965, Odetta Papers.

16. Odetta, recorded live at the Hollywood Bowl, Los Angeles, August 2, 1963, accessed at http://pastdaily.com/wp-content/uploads/2013/12 /Folk-Night-Hollywood-Bowl-Aug.-2-1963-Part-1.mp3.

17. Mimi Clar, "Folk Singers Hailed by Packed Bowl," *Los Angeles Times*, August 4, 1963, H4; Peter Yarrow interview.

18. Leroy F. Aarons, "A Treat Served Up at Carter Barron," *Washington Post*, August 28, 1963, C5.

19. "Washington March Is On," United Press International, appearing in *Desert Sun*, August 28, 1963, 1.

20. For the quote and the analysis of SNCC dress styles, I'm indebted to Ford, *Liberated Threads*, 78.

21. "Nation: Beginning of a Dream," *Time*, September 6, 1963, accessed at http://content.time.com/time/magazine/article/0,9171,870446,00.html.

22. ABC radio report, August 28, 1963, NAACP Papers, accessed on Pro-Quest History Vault.

23. Lula Patterson, "It Was No High Dress Affair, Reports Our Lula," *Afro-American*, September 7, 1963, 8; "The March," *New Yorker*, September 7, 1963, 30.

24. Mrs. Robert Hemphill, "Parole Area Highlights," *Evening Capital*, September 1, 1963, 12; Patterson, "It Was No High Dress Affair," 8; E. W. Kenworthy, "200,000 March for Civil Rights in Orderly Washington Rally; President Sees Gain for Negro," *New York Times*, August 29, 1963, 1, 15.

25. French radio report on the March on Washington, August 28, 1963, accessed at http://www.ina.fr/audio/PHD94020134/marche-contre-le -racisme-a-washington-audio.html.

26. Sue Kronk, "Stars to Put Ban on Segregated Spots," *Lawrence Daily Journal-World*, August 29, 1963, 5; French radio report.

27. French radio report; *Pittsburgh Post-Gazette*, September 7, 1963, 13.

28. Bruce Langhorne, author interview, July 3, 2015.

29. Kronk, "Stars to Put Ban on Segregated Spots," 5.

30. "Washington March Is On," United Press International, appearing in *Desert Sun*, August 28, 1963, 1.

31. "Odetta on Parade," *Winnipeg Free Press*, February 22, 1964, 16; Odetta memorial recording.

32. Odetta, WXPN radio interview.

33. Hajdu, *Positively 4th Street*, 183; A. W. Godfrey, "Civil Rights and the Spirit of '63," *Newsday*, August 28, 1981, 62.

34. Harry Belafonte interviews.

35. *Billboard*, January 19, 1963, 18.

36. "Newport Folk Festival," *Boston Globe*, July 14, 1963, 63.

37. Joan Baez interview; Carpenter, "Sweet Home Alabama," 68.

38. Jack Somer, author interview, August 30, 2016.

39. Charlie Rothschild interviews.

40. "Six Dead in Church Bombing," United Press International, appearing in *Washington Post*, September 16, 1963, accessed at https://www .washingtonpost.com/wp-srv/national/longterm/churches/archives1.htm;

Fred Powledge, "Alabama Bombing Protested Here," *New York Times*, September 17, 1963, 26.

41. Alabama Bombing Protested Here," *New York Times*.
42. M. S. Handler, "Negro Passivity Is Held Outdated," *New York Times*, September 21, 1963, 8.
43. "Cultural Group Is Born Out of Major American Tragedy," *New Journal and Guide*, November 30, 1963, 18.
44. John O. Killens to Harry Belafonte, October 1, 1963, John Oliver Killens Papers, Stuart A. Rose Manuscript, Archives & Rare Book Library, Emory University.
45. M. Chafin, "Negro Leadership Split on Christmas Boycott," *Chicago Defender*, November 9, 1963, 1.
46. Along the N.A.A.C.P. Battlefront," *Crisis* 70, no. 9 (November 1963): 555–56.
47. "Strike Against Santa Claus," unsigned editorial, *New York Times*, September 28, 1963, 18; Harry Belafonte interviews.
48. Guy Davis interview.
49. Nigel Williamson, "Miss Odetta," *Folk Roots* 20, no. 11 (1999): 47; Don Armstrong, "Odetta—Citizen of the World," *Crisis* 9, no. 6 (June/July 1983): 51.

CHAPTER ELEVEN: THE TIMES THEY ARE A-CHANGIN'

1. Jack Somer interview.
2. Charles Thurston, "Odetta and Her Guitar: That Respectful Feeling," *Detroit Free Press*, May 17, 1966, 26.
3. Jack Keenan, "The Men Behind Belafonte and Odetta," *Hootenanny*, November 1964, 44.
4. Jack Somer interview.
5. Jack Somer interview.
6. Joe Botsford, "Odetta Does It Again; Excites 1,000 Fans," *Milwaukee Sentinel*, January 20, 1964, n.p.; Mark Bricklin, "Folk Singer Odetta Thrills Young Folks at Temple U. 'Soul' Concert," *Philadelphia Tribune*, October 10, 1964, 11; "Vancouver," *Box Office* 85, no. 3 (May 11, 1964): K-4.
7. Peter Childs, author interviews, April 9, 2016, October 2, 2016.
8. Peter Childs interviews.
9. Peter Childs interviews.
10. Peter Childs interviews.
11. Robert Shelton, "Symbolic Finale," *New York Times*, August 2, 1964, section ii, 9.
12. Shelton, "Symbolic Finale."
13. Carly Simon interview.
14. Jack Somer interview.
15. Jack Somer interview.
16. Jack Somer interview; Odetta, National Visionary Leadership interview.
17. Jack Somer, "A Little Tambourine Music," *Stereo Review*, April 1974, 72.

18. Wavy Gravy (née Hugh Romney), author interview, October 18, 2017; Schilling, with Crisafulli, *Me and a Guy Named Elvis*, 141; "Record Reviews," *Variety*, March 24, 1965, 70.

19. "On Broadway," *Time*, April 2, 1965; Robert Shelton, "Odetta Returns for Folk Song Recital," *New York Times*, March 15, 1965, 38.

20. Young, Reuss interview.

21. Charlie Rothschild interviews.

22. Adler, "Letter from Selma," 121.

23. Adler, "Letter from Selma," 124.

24. Adler, "Letter from Selma," 148.

25. Belafonte, *My Song*, 302.

26. Report on the Selma march, *Jet*, April 8, 1965, 60, 62.

27. Ross Ragen, "Voting Rights Marchers Reach Alabama Capitol," Associated Press, appearing in *Wichita Falls Times*, March 25, 1965, 8A; Gertrude Wilson, "How the Stars Fared at Montgomery Rally," *New Amsterdam News*, April 3, 1965, 2.

28. King, *My Life, My Love, My Legacy*, 133; Donald Janson, "Stars Give Show for Rights March," *New York Times*, March 25, 1965, 27.

29. Branch, *At Canaan's Edge*, 160; Adler, "Letter from Selma," 152–53.

30. Douglas Brinkley, "Indebted to Odetta," *Gambit Weekly*, April 27, 2004, accessed at https://www.bestofneworleans.com/gambit/indebted -to-odetta/Content?oid=1242760; Frank Hunt, "30,000 Roar as King Declares 'Freedom' War," *Afro-American*, April 3, 1965, 1; Barthell, "Odetta Speaks Through Her Songs," X11.

31. CBS News archival footage of Selma to Montgomery march, March 25, 1965, accessed at http://www.cbs46.com/story/28565970/watch-newly -discovered-video-of-selma-to-montgomery-march; Branch, *At Canaan's Edge*, 163; Hunt, "30,000 Roar," 1.

32. Harriet Hutchinson, author interview, June 18, 2016.

33. Odetta memorial recording.

34. Selma Thaler interviews; Leo Vincent Daniel Gordon v. Odetta F. Gordon, Superior Court of the State of California, filed April 9, 1965.

35. Odetta, *CBS Sunday Morning* interview; Odetta, Caroline Horn interview.

36. Craig McGregor, "Odetta at the Town Hall," *Sydney Morning Herald*, April 24, 1965, 11.

37. Dale Plummer, "Odetta Sings as She Feels," *Sydney Morning Herald*, April 25, 1965, 77; "One (Wo)Man Show," *Variety*, May 5, 1965, 54; Charlie Rothschild interviews.

38. Mary Portolesi, "Adelaide to Hear Odetta," *News*, April 27, 1965, n.p.

39. J. Fukunishi, "Music Capitals of the World: Tokyo," *Billboard*, June 5, 1965, 28.

40. Kenichi Takeda, written remembrance provided to author; Kenichi Takeda, author interview, July 18, 2019.

41. *Nikkan Sports* clipping, May 20, 1967, n.p.

42. Joe Town and Eddie Papa, "Caught at the Newport Folk Festival," *Billboard*, August 7, 1965, 6; cited in Wald, *Dylan Goes Electric!*, 243–44.

43. Letter to the editor, *Jerusalem Post*, September 13, 1965, 3.
44. Pam Johnson, "From Classical to Coffee House, Odetta Gets Better," *Miami News*, October 31, 1965, n.p.
45. John Herbers, "Birmingham's Progress Is Slow in Race Relations," *New York Times*, March 18, 1964, 25.
46. Johnson, "From Classical to Coffee House, Odetta Gets Better."
47. Herbers, "Birmingham's Progress Is Slow in Race Relations," 25.
48. Albert Boutwell to Doris J. Mitchell, September 28, 1965, Albert Burton Boutwell Papers, Birmingham Public Library.
49. Clay Musselman, "Concert Tickets Hard to Sell," *Southern Courier*, October 3–4, 1965, 1.
50. Musselman, "Concert Tickets Hard to Sell."
51. Ernestine Taylor, "Odetta Sings in Birmingham," *Southern Courier*, October 9–10, 1965, 2.
52. Taylor, "Odetta Sings in Birmingham."
53. Albert Burton Boutwell Daily Appointment Books, 1965, Birmingham Public Library; Johnson, "From Classical to Coffee House, Odetta Gets Better."

CHAPTER TWELVE: FREEDOM GETS PERSONAL
1. Aarons, "Odetta Comes Out of Her Cocoon," A4.
2. Ralph J. Gleason, "The New Odetta—Better Than Ever," *San Francisco Chronicle*, November 10, 1969, 52.
3. Aarons, "Odetta Comes Out of Her Cocoon," A4.
4. Arthur Zeldin, "Odetta of the Cathedral Voice . . . A Force in a Featherweight Field," *Toronto Daily Star*, October 5, 1966, 42.
5. John S. Wilson, "A Nightclub Made for Sound," *New York Times*, September 25, 1966, 10M; Leonard "Boots" Jaffee, author interview, May 20, 2016.
6. Leonard "Boots" Jaffee interview.
7. Garry Shead, author interview, June 18, 2016.
8. Garry Shead interview; "Odetta Again," *Age*, March 14, 1966, 7.
9. Garry Shead to Odetta, circa August 1966, Odetta Papers.
10. Belafonte, *My Song*, 310.
11. Harry Belafonte interviews.
12. McKeon, "Odetta's Musical Odyssey Not Finished Yet," C7.
13. Sounes, *Down the Highway*, 219–20; Selma Thaler interviews.
14. Odetta, Wilson interviews; Selma Thaler interviews; McKeon, "Odetta's Musical Odyssey Not Finished Yet, C7.
15. Jack Somer interview; Charlie Rothschild interviews.
16. Verve Folkways ad, *Billboard*, January 21, 1967.
17. Verve Folkways ad, *Variety*, October 26, 1966, 52; "Odetta Waxes 'Clown Town,' a Pop Tune," *New Amsterdam News*, October 8, 1966, 9.
18. John Pagones, "On the Town," *Washington Post*, April 24, 1966, G6; Robert Shelton, "Chad Mitchell Expands as a Cabaret Performer," *New York Times*, July 1, 1966, 39.
19. Garry Shead interview.

20. Ralph J. Gleason, "Odetta's Dilemma—And 'Cream' From London," *San Francisco Chronicle*, September 3, 1967, 35; Ralph Earle, "Odetta," *Broadside*, undated clip, circa 1967, 28.
21. John Seiter, author interview, April 16, 2016.
22. Untitled news clipping, Garry Shead collection.
23. Garry Shead interview.
24. Garry Shead interview.
25. "Didn't Marry Young White Australian, Says Odetta," *Jet*, September 14, 1967, p. 53; Gary Shearston to Odetta, November 30, 1967, Odetta Papers.
26. Pat Hanna, "New Look for Talented Odetta," *Rocky Mountain News*, February 23, 1968, 75.
27. *Inaugural Evening at Ford's Theater*; Rick Du Brow, "Dignity Key to Format at Reopening of Ford's Theater," United Press International, appearing in *Bucks County Courier Times*, January 31, 1968, 22.
28. Hanna, "New Look for Talented Odetta," 75.
29. Odetta, Cohen interview.
30. Barnett, *I Got Thunder*, 186; Carpenter, "Sweet Home Alabama," 68; Odetta, Cohen interview; Cohen, *Rainbow Quest*, 114.
31. Charlie Rothschild interviews; Frank Hamilton interview.
32. Shevey, "Mary Travers Has Her Say After 10 Years as Silent Partner," 7D.
33. David Amram, author interview, August 29, 2015.
34. Sounes, *Down the Highway*, 116.
35. Selma Thaler interviews.
36. Roland Forte, "'Black Is Beautiful,'" *Call and Post*, February 17, 1968, 6A; Joy Elliott, "The Afro," *Washington Post*, August 18, 1968, G13.
37. Cathy Horyn, "Go with the 'Fro," *Washington Post*, March 15, 1994, E1.

CHAPTER THIRTEEN: HIT OR MISS

1. Stephen Sorensen, "Odetta's Life and Times," *Boston After Dark*, June 8, 1971, 17.
2. Jo Mapes, Cohen interview.
3. Robert Carl Cohen interview; Stephen Miller, "Herb Cohen 1932–2010; Manager of Stars, Big Fan of Lawsuits," *Wall Street Journal*, March 26, 2010, accessed at https://www.wsj.com/articles/SB1000142405274 8703409804575144051974708636.
4. *Cashbox*, November 28, 1970, 28; "Diamond, Big Brother, Farquhar, Hand, Derek & Dominoes, Odetta, Buckley, Avalon, Exuma Top LPs," *Billboard*, November 18, 1970, 68.
5. J. Marks, "Odetta Sails on the Winds of Change from Folk Music to Today's Rock and Roll," *Chicago Tribune*, May 16, 1971, E1; quoted in "Odetta Sings on Fifth 'Boboquivari' Program," *Herald*, August 30, 1971, TV-4.
6. Eliot Tiegel, "Talent in Action: Neil Diamond, Odetta," *Billboard*, September 4, 1971, 20; Richard Cromelin, "Folksinger Odetta Does an About-Face," *Los Angeles Times*, January 16, 1975, H11.

7. Polydor, Inc. v. Third Story Productions, Inc., Superior Court of the State of California, No. C 15976.

8. Ralph J. Gleason, "Judy and Joanie: End of the Trail?," *San Francisco Chronicle*, March 2, 1969, 27.

9. Frederick Warhanek, author interviews, December 18, 2016, January 16, 2017, March 12, 2018.

10. Flora Felious to Odetta Gordon, August 27, 1972, Odetta Papers; Charlie Rothschild interviews.

11. Peggy Strait, author interview, July 22, 2017.

12. Hollie I. West, "Role as Bessie Smith," *Washington Post*, December 16, 1972, B7.

13. Jacqueline Trescott, "Up From the '60s, Odetta Finds a Song," *Washington Post*, January 16, 1980, D7.

14. David Amram, "For Odetta," accessed at http://www.insomniacathon .org/rrIDAFO01.html; Marilynn Preston, "Magical Odetta Sings of 'Us' and 'Now' in America, *Chicago Today*, March 22, 1970, 10.

15. Mary McGrory, "Peace-Fasters' Song," *New York Post*, April 14, 1970, 30; Sally Quinn, "Fasting to Affirm Life," *Washington Post*, April 13, 1970, B1.

16. Leonard "Boots" Jaffee interview.

17. Steve Lake, "Bizarre Berlin," *Melody Maker*, November 10, 1973, 62.

18. Christopher S. Wren, "Odetta Rhythms Warm Soviet Listeners," *New York Times*, June 23, 1974, 42.

19. Michael McGuire, "Russia Souled Out by Odetta," *Chicago Tribune*, May 27, 1974, B6.

20. US Information Agency, 42nd Semiannual Report, covering January 1–June 30, 1974.

21. Melor Sturua, "When Odetta Sings," *Izvestia*, June 21, 1974, n.p.

22. Soviet fans to Odetta, June 8, 1974, Odetta Papers.

23. Audrey M. Ashley, "A New Career for Odetta," *Ottawa Citizen*, August 9, 1975, 59.

24. Herbert Whittaker, "Odetta a Dominating Force in Neptune's Gamma Rays," *Globe and Mail*, July 21, 1977, 14; *Montreal Star*, quoted in press release by Kazuko Hillyer International, Odetta Papers; Susan Wilson, "Odetta: Still Saying It with Music," *Boston Globe*, January 24, 1985, 10.

25. Les Bridges, "Odetta: A Concert-Hall Voice in a Coffeehouse," *Chicago Tribune*, May 25, 1973, B1.

26. Cathy Yarbrough, "Singer Shuns 'Top 40' Success," *Atlanta Constitution*, March 16, 1973, 8B.

27. Les Ledbetter, "Odetta Hopes for Rediscovery in Shift to Rock Style," *New York Times*, May 9, 1973, 40.

28. Louisiana Red to Odetta, 1976, Odetta Papers; Blake Green, "Odetta—Time for Coming Home," *San Francisco Chronicle*, October 12, 1976, 22.

29. Frederick Warhanek interviews; Carrie Thaler interview.

30. Richard Hart to Odetta, February 6, 1978, Odetta Papers.

31. Richard Harrington, "Old Times with Odetta at the Childe Harold," *Washington Post*, September 15, 1978, B8.
32. John McWhorter, "Saint Maya," *New Republic*, May 28, 2014, accessed at https://newrepublic.com/article/117924/saint-maya-angelou -product-blissfully-bygone-america.
33. Lance Greening interview; Roger Deitz, author interview, January 6, 2008.
34. Odetta memorial recording; Frederick Warhanek interviews.
35. Selma Thaler interviews.
36. Roger McGuinn, author interview, May 1, 2017.
37. Vicki Sanders, "Odetta: A Singer with a Soaring Spirit," *Berkshire Sampler*, June 30, 1974, 17.
38. David Amram interview.
39. Roger Deitz interview; Dave Fry, author interview, March 10, 2018.
40. Morris, "No More New Year-Birthday Blues," 35.
41. Armstrong, "Odetta—Citizen of the World," 51.
42. Roger Deitz interview.
43. Odetta memorial recording.
44. Lynn Van Matre, "Queen of the Folkies Wears Her Crown Lightly," *Chicago Tribune*, December 5, 1986, D3.
45. Ed Pearl interview; Jack Landrón interview.
46. Frederick Warhanek interviews; Carrie Thaler interview.
47. David Amram interview.
48. Garry Shead interview.
49. Bob Darden, "Gospel Lectern," *Billboard*, February 25, 1989, 69.
50. Robbie Woliver, author interview, May 14, 2018.
51. "Words of the Week," *Jet*, July 4, 1983, 40.

CHAPTER FOURTEEN: BLUES EVERYWHERE I GO

1. Mark Carpentieri, author interview, February 20, 2017.
2. Mark Carpentieri interview.
3. Seth Farber, author interview, November 2, 2015.
4. Letta Tayler, "Getting Personal with Baez, Odetta," *Newsday*, March 22, 1996; Seth Farber interview.
5. Mark Carpentieri interview.
6. Mark Carpentieri interview; Frederick Warhanek interviews.
7. Doug Yeager, Odetta biographical sketch.
8. *Weekly Compilation of Presidential Documents* 35, no. 39 (October 4, 1999): 1847–1853.
9. Tom Nelligan, "Odetta: An American Voice," *Dirty Linen*, April 2000, 51.
10. Donal Leace, author interview, July 18, 2016.
11. Doug Yeager interviews.
12. Hadley Frank-John, "Odetta: Blues Everywhere I Go," *DownBeat* 67, no. 3 (March 2000): 72; Ann Powers, "The Pop Life: Favorite CD's You Nearly Missed," *New York Times*, January 13, 2000, E5.

13. Geoffrey Himes, "Odetta: 'Blues Everywhere I Go,'" *Washington Post*, February 18, 2000, 17.
14. Notice of Federal Tax Lien on 1270 Fifth Ave, Apt. 8R, filed April 15, 1994; Chase Manhattan Bank USA v. Odetta F. Gordon, filed April 14, 1999, New York County Civil Court.
15. Doug Yeager interviews.
16. Seth Farber interview.
17. Isaac Guzman, "Odetta's Dreamer," *Newsday*, February 18, 2000.
18. Frederick Warhanek interviews.
19. Pat Hendricks, "Folk Blues Icon Odetta Enchanting," *Charleston Gazette*, October 30, 2000, 2C.
20. Chris Cobb, "Die-Hard Fans Undeterred by Wet, Grey Day: Gospel Choirs Lift Rain-Soaked Spirits," *Ottawa Citizen*, July 10, 2000, A10.
21. Radoslav Lorković, author interview, January 16, 2016.
22. Mike Koster, author interview, May 12, 2017.
23. Williamson, *A Return to Love*, 190.
24. Mark Carpentieri interview.
25. Doug Yeager interviews.
26. Odetta memorial recording.
27. Michelle Esrick, author interview, December 15, 2018.
28. Elizabeth Elliott, author interview, April 25, 2016.
29. Odetta memorial recording.
30. Robin Denselow, "Talking Bob Dylan Blues," *Guardian*, September 28, 2005, accessed at https://www.theguardian.com/music/2005/sep/28/popandrock.bobdylan.
31. Radoslav Lorković interview.
32. Odetta memorial recording.
33. Michelle Esrick interview.
34. Seth Farber interview.
35. Josh White Jr. interview.
36. Michael Koster, "Odetta's Music Backdrop for Civil Rights Era," *Santa Fe New Mexican*, December 13, 2008, B5.
37. Vania Santi, author interview, May 22, 2018.
38. Dave Keyes, author interview, February 21, 2018.
39. Dave Keyes interview.
40. Statement on Odetta's health by Doug Yeager, in Sean Michaels, "Odetta Survives Kidney Failure," *The Guardian*, accessed at https://www.theguardian.com/music/2008/dec/01/folksinger-odetta-kidney-failure.
41. "Tributes: Honoring Artists Who Died This Year," *Rolling Stone*, December 25, 2008–January 8, 2009, 38, 42.
42. David Hinckley, "Odetta Left Message of Hope," *New York Daily News*, December 4, 2008, 29; Doug Yeager interviews.

EPILOGUE: "WHO WILL BE THE ODETTA OF NOW?"

1. Odetta memorial recording.
2. Odetta memorial recording.

3. Odetta memorial recording.
4. John Seiter interview; Selma Thaler interviews.
5. Jeff Mays, "Home of Harlem Folk Singer Odetta Marked with Plaque," DNA Info.com, July 18, 2012, accessed at https://www.dnainfo.com/new-york/20120718/east-harlem/home-of-harlem-folk-singer-odetta-marked-with-plaque.
6. Selma Thaler interviews.
7. Peter Childs interviews.
8. Harry Belafonte interviews.
9. Odetta memorial recording.

IMAGE CREDITS

10. Courtesy of Turnabout Theatre Archive, Los Angeles Public Library.
11. © 43 North Broadway, LLC.
12. Courtesy of Ralph Rinzler Folklife Archives, Smithsonian Institution. Photo by Robert C. Malone.
13. Courtesy of Ralph Rinzler Folklife Archives, Smithsonian Institution. Photo by Robert C. Malone.
14. Courtesy of Dutch National Archives. Photo by Jac. de Nijs.
15. Photo by Al Fenn/The LIFE Picture Collection/Getty Images.
16. Courtesy of Dutch National Archives. Photo by Jac. de Nijs.
17. Courtesy of National Archives and Records Administration. Photo by Rowland Scherman.
18. Courtesy of the Thaler Family Collection. Photo by Edward Thaler.
19. © Sony Music.
20. Courtesy of Alabama Dept. of Archives and History. Photo by Jim Peppler.
21. Courtesy of Kenichi Takeda.
22. Courtesy of Kenichi Takeda.
23. © Peter Cunningham.
24. Courtesy of the Thaler Family Collection. Photo by Edward Thaler.
25. Official White House photo.
26. © Econosmith.com.
27. © Musicultura.

INDEX